Wasáse

Wasáse

INDIGENOUS PATHWAYS
OF ACTION AND FREEDOM

Taiaiake Alfred

University of Toronto Press

Previously published by Broadview Press 2005 © Taiaiake Alfred

Library and Archives Canada Cataloguing in Publication

Alfred, Taiaiake
        Wasàse : indigenous pathways of action and freedom / Taiaiake Alfred.

Includes bibliographical references and index.

ISBN 978-1-55111-637-2

        1. Native peoples—Social life and customs. 2. Native peoples—Intellectual life.
3. Native peoples—Ethnic identity. 4. Native peoples—Cultural assimilation. I. Title.

E98.S7A43 2005   305.897   C2005-902850-5

We welcome comments and suggestions regarding any aspect of our publications—
please feel free to contact us at news@utphighereducation.com or visit our Internet site
at www.utppublishing.com.

North America
5201 Dufferin Street
North York, Ontario, Canada
M3H 5T8

2250 Military Road
Tonawanda, New York, USA, 14150

ORDERS PHONE: 1-800-565-9523
ORDERS FAX: 1-800-221-9985
ORDERS E-MAIL: utpbooks@utpress.utoronto.ca

UK, Ireland, and continental Europe
NBN International
Estover Road, Plymouth, PL6 7PY, UK
ORDERS PHONE: 44 (0) 1752 202301
ORDERS FAX: 44 (0) 1752 202333
ORDERS E-MAIL: enquiries@nbninternational.com

The University of Toronto Press acknowledges the financial support for its publishing
activities of the Government of Canada through the Canada Book Fund.

Edited by Betsy Struthers.
Cover & Interior Design by Liz Broes.

This book is dedicated to the memory of my grandmother, Florence Karoniaiénhne Montour Alfred, who was the heart of our family, and in memory of my wife's mother, Annette Mary Joseph, and my friend Roy Beauvais, who were both proud warriors and beloved in their struggles.

contents

foreword

by Leroy Little Bear

As a Native American who has been involved in the academy for many years attempting to educate from a Native American perspective, I take this opportunity to write a foreword for this challenging and thought-provoking book as a blessing and a chance to add thoughts from previous writings that pass on culture, philosophy, and revitalization.

Prior to the arrival of Europeans on the North American continent, Native Americans were organized into nations with group life-ways that resulted in philosophies, customs, values, beliefs, and governance systems arising from Native American paradigms. These paradigms consist of and include ideas that there is constant flux/motion, that all of creation consists of energy waves, that everything is animate, that everything is imbued with spirit, that all of creation is interrelated, that reality requires renewal, and that space is a major referent. Gary Witherspoon observes, "The assumption that underlies this dualistic aspect of all being and existence is that the world is in motion, that things are constantly undergoing processes of transformation, deformation, and restoration, and that the essence of life and being is movement."[1] As regards interrelationships, the Task Force on the Criminal Justice System and Its Impact on the Indian and Métis Peoples of Alberta states:

> The wholistic view leads to an implicit assumption that everything is inter-related. Inter-relatedness leads to an implicit idea of equality among all creation. Equality is brought about by the

implicit belief that everything—humans, animals, plants, and inorganic matter—has a spirit. Anthropomorphic matters are not important because metamorphosis readily occurs. The common denominator is the spirit.[2]

The Native American paradigm incorporates the idea of renewal. There is a tacit assumption that, in the cosmic flux, there exists a particular combination of energy waves that allows for our continuing existence. If this particular combination of energy waves dissolves, the particular reality we are in will disappear into the flux. A consequence of the idea of renewal is a large number of renewal ceremonies in Native American life-ways. It may be said that Native American history is not a temporal history but a history contained in stories that are told and re-told, in songs that are sung and re-sung, in ceremonies that are performed and re-performed through the seasonal rounds. All of the above aims at harmony and balance.

Space is a very important referent in the minds of Native Americans. Certain events, patterns, cycles, and happenings occur at certain places. From a human point of view, patterns, cycles, and happenings are readily observable from the land—for example, animal migrations, cycles of plant life, seasons, and so on. The cosmos is also observable and its patterns detected from particular spatial locations. According to Joseph Campbell, "People claim the land, by creating sacred sites, by mythologizing the animals and the plants—they invest the land with sacred powers. It becomes like a temple, a place for meditation."[3] In accordance with this theory, Native Americans have many sacred sites and stories about sacred sites all over North America.

Given the opportunity, a culture attempts to mold its members into ideal personalities. The ideal personality in Native American cultures is a person who shows kindness to all, who puts the group ahead of individual wants and desires, who is a generalist, who is steeped in spiritual and ritual knowledge—a person who goes about daily life and approaches "all his or her relations" in a sea of friendship, easygoing-ness, humour, and good feelings. She or he is a person who attempts to suppress inner feelings, anger, and disagreement with the group. She or he is a person who is expected to display bravery, hardiness, and strength against enemies and outsiders. She or he is a person who is adaptable and takes the world as it comes without complaint. That is the way it used to be! That is the way it should be!

The arrival of Europeans on this continent changed all that. They are the interference. They are a people, we have come to discover, with no collective ethos. In other words, they have no common spirit and beliefs that hold them together. What is common to them is a very strong belief in individuality and the pursuit of individual material gain. The British people who were the main colonizers of this continent are acultural in an indigenous sense because the history of Britain is one of successive takeovers by foreigners. The effect of these successive takeovers is to erase any semblance of indigeneity to the land from which they came. A lack of culture results in unrestrained freedom, which is best explained by the Calvinist school of thought. Calvin himself explained: "When that light of divine providence has once shone upon a godly man, he is then relieved and set free not only from the extreme anxiety and fear that were pressing before him, but from every care."[4] In other words, cultural prescription and circumscription do not enter their minds. Expedience is the operative mode.

If a culture is a mechanism for socialization with a built-in reward system for those that subscribe to it, what happens when one culture is imposed on another? In the words of Clyde Kluckhohn, "The young escape the control of their elders, not to accept white controls but to revel in newly found patterns of unrestraint."[5] The hope on the part of the European colonizers that their way of life is going to be "gobbled up" by North American Indians never came to be. Their simplistic approach of assimilation resulted not in acceptance of their ways but in cultural pollution. The result is what this writer calls "cultural blanks." A person who is a "cultural blank" is a person with no cultural code or set of norms to guide his or her behaviour. The only norm is expedience.

Wasáse is a book that speaks to the imperceptible way that European thought has polluted the minds of Native Americans resulting in cultural blanks. It speaks to reflection: reflection on the pollution. It speaks to revitalization: revitalization of the "Warrior's Way" which is the only way Native Americans will be able to find their way out of the colonizer's quagmire and embody, once again, "all my relations."

NOTES

1 Gary Witherspoon, *Language and Art in the Navajo Universe* (Ann Arbor, MI: University of Michigan Press, 1977) 48.

2 The Task Force on the Criminal Justice System and Its Impact on the Indian and Métis Peoples of Alberta, *Justice on Trial, Report of the Task Force*, Vol. I (Edmonton, AB: Queen's Printer, 1991) 9–1.

3 Joseph Campbell with Bill Moyers, *The Power of Myth* (New York, N Y: Doubleday, 1988) 92–93.

4 Felix Gilbert *et al.*, *The Norton History of Modern Europe* (New York, NY: W.W. Norton and Co., 1970).

5 Clyde Kluckhohn, "The Philosophy of the Navaho Indians," *Ideological Differences and World Order*, ed. F.S.C. Northrop (New Haven, CT: Yale University Press, 1949) 382.

acknowledgements

We gather together and see that the cycle of life continues. As human beings, we have been given the responsibility to live in balance and harmony with each other and with all of creation. So now, we bring our minds together as one as we give greetings and thanks to each other as People.

Now our minds are one.

We are thankful for our mother, the earth, for she gives us all that we need for life. She sustains and supports us as our feet move upon her. We are joyful in knowing that she continues to care for us as she has from the beginning of time. To our Mother, we send greetings and thanks.

Now our minds are one.

We give thanks to the waters for quenching our thirst and providing us with strength. Water is life, and we are thankful for its purity. We know its power in many forms—waterfalls and rain, mists and streams, rivers and oceans. With one mind, we send greetings and thanks to the spirit of the Water.

Now our minds are one.

We turn our minds to all of the fish of the world. They cleanse and purify the waters of life, and they offer themselves to us as food. So we turn now to the Fish and send our greetings and thanks.

Now our minds are one.

Now we turn our minds to the many kinds of life-sustaining plant life in the fields and forests. The earth is covered with plants growing and working many wonders. With our minds gathered together, we give thanks and look forward to seeing Plant Life continue in all its diversity for many generations to come.

Now our minds are one.

With one mind, we turn to offer special thanks to all of the food plants. Since the beginning of time, the grains, vegetables, beans, and berries have helped people survive. We honour all of the Food Plants together as one and send them greetings and thanks.

Now our minds are one.

Now we turn to the medicines of the natural world. From the beginning, they have taken away our sickness. We are grateful they are always waiting to heal us. And we are happy there are special people among us who hold knowledge of the healing plants. With one mind, we send greetings and thanks to the Medicines and to the Medicine Keepers.

Now our minds are one.

We gather our minds together to send greetings and thanks to all the animal life in the world. We honour their wisdom and their strength. Animals have many lessons to teach us human beings, and they offer themselves to us as sustenance. We coexist with them where we live and in the forests and mountains. We are glad that the Animals are still here, and we hope that it will always be so.

Now our minds are one.

We now turn our thoughts to the trees. The earth has many families of beautiful trees, each with their own instructions and duties. Some trees provide us with shelter and shade, others with fruit and the other useful things we need to survive. Trees are symbols of peace, strength, and a reverence for life for peoples all over the world. With one mind, we greet and give thanks to the Trees.

Now our minds are one.

We put our minds together as one and thank all the birds who fly about in the sky. Their beautiful songs each day remind us to enjoy and appreciate life. To all the Birds—from the smallest to the largest—we send our joyful greetings and thanks.

Now our minds are one.

We are thankful for the powers we know as the Four Winds. We hear their voices in the moving air as they refresh us and purify the air we breathe. From the Four Directions they bring the change of seasons and messages. The Four Winds give us strength. With one mind, we send our greetings and thanks to the Four Winds.

Now our minds are one.

Now we turn to the west and our grandfathers, the thunder beings. With their voices lightning and thunder, they bring the water that renews all life. We bring our minds together as one to send greetings and thanks to our grandfathers, the Thunderers.

Now our minds are one.

We now send greetings and thanks to our eldest brother, the sun. Each and every day he travels the sky from the east to the west, bringing with him the light of a new day. He is the source of all fires and of all life. With one mind, we send greetings and thanks to our brother, the Sun.

Now our minds are one.

We now put our minds together and give thanks to our oldest grand-mother, the moon, who lights the night sky and governs the movement of the ocean tides. Her strength and wisdom are inside and around all women. By her changing face we mark the changing seasons, and it is the moon who watches over the arrival of children here on earth. With one mind, we send greetings and thanks to our grandmother, the Moon.

Now our minds are one.

We give thanks to the stars who are spread across the sky like bright sparks. We see them in the night, helping the moon to light the darkness and bringing dew to the fields and gardens. When we travel at night, they guide our way. With our minds gathered together as one, we send greetings and thanks to all of the Stars.

Now our minds are one.

We gather our minds to greet and thank all the enlightened teachers who have come to inspire and help the people throughout the ages. When we forget the Original Teachings and how to live in harmony, they remind us of the way we were instructed to live as people. With one mind, we send greetings and thanks to these caring Teachers.

Now our minds are one.

Now we turn our thoughts to the Creator and to the life-force of the universe. We send greetings and thanks for all the gifts of creation. Everything we need to live a good life is here in our natural world. For all of the love that is still around us, we gather our minds together as one and send our choicest words of greetings and thanks for the power of love, life, and of creation.

Now our minds are one.

We have now arrived at the place where we end our words. In thanking and acknowledging all of the things we have named, we did not intend to leave anything out. If something was forgotten, we leave it to each of you to send such greetings as we have spoken, and to offer gratitude in your own way.

Onen enska neiokwanikonra. Now our minds are one.[1]

Many people helped me to write this book.

Thanks first and foremost to my love Rose, who believes in me, and to the true warriors of all nations and ages who in sharing their thoughts and teachings have shown me the way and have made this book what it is. I honour these women and men for their courage, tenacity, generosity, and wisdom.

I will always hold close to my heart the names of the friends, students, and colleagues who helped me complete this journey of understanding. I am sincerely grateful to those people who took the time to read early versions of my work and who provided me with validation, guidance, and deeper insight, especially Stephanie Irlbacher-Fox at Cambridge University and Glen Coulthard at the University of Toronto, who gave so much of their time and energy to reading the manuscript even while in the midst of their own important work. I acknowledge the guidance of Michael Doxtater and Alfred Keye from Six Nations; Billy Two Rivers, Kanahsohon Deer, Tiorahkwathe Gilbert, Tommy Teyowisonte Deer, and Marie Deer in Kahnawake; and Jake Swamp and Nonni and Teddy Peters at Akwesasne for helping me fully understand and to translate words, concepts and phrases from my language into English. Thanks, too, to the people who helped me in many and varied ways with the work I needed to do on this book and on myself, and who have given me inspiration through their own struggles and successes: my colleagues Jim Tully, Jeff Corntassel, and Arthur Kroker; my Indian Sister, Archana Ojha; Jewel Peters, Deanna Therriault, Tanya Kappo, Darlene Okamaysim, Bonnie Whitlow, Nick Claxton, Shauna McRanor, Janice Knighton, Jacinda Mack, Lana Lowe, Cliff Atleo, Jr., Brad Young, Noenoe Silva, Kahente Horn, Rita Dhamoon, Lisa Strelein, Bruce and Marion Cumming, Janet "JRoe" Rogers and Fran Powless; Susanne Thiessen, Sheila Watts, Mary-Anne Daniels, the very smart and well-organized women whose dedicated work running the Indigenous Governance Programs at the University of Victoria enables my freedom to travel and to write; my gracious and hard-working literary agent Kathryn Mulders; and my editor at Broadview Press, Betsy Struthers, for her creative engagement with my ideas and artful critique of my words. Lastly, for his immensely generous and kind heart and for showing me what being a tough guy is all about, thanks to my wife's father, Ansgar Lenser, Sr.

I will close this thanksgiving with a word to my parents, my sister, my niece Nikki and nephews Aidan-John, Cole, and Drake that the success I have achieved stands on the solid foundation of love they, my family, give me.

I am grateful to all of you for any good that comes from the words I have written. *Niawenkowa akwekon.*

NOTES

1 The Rotinoshonni Thanksgiving Address is my adaptation of a version in the Haudenosaunee Environmental Task Force's "Greetings to the Natural World," published in *Haudenosaunee Environmental Restoration: An Indigenous Strategy for Human Sustainability* (Cambridge, England: Indigenous Development International, 1995).

first words

It is time for our people to live again. This book is a journey on the path made for us by those who have found a way to live as *Onkwehonwe*, original people. The journey is a living commitment to meaningful change in our lives and to transforming society by recreating our existences, regenerating our cultures, and surging against the forces that keep us bound to our colonial past. It is the path of struggle laid out by those who have come before us; now it is our turn, we who choose to turn away from the legacies of colonialism and take on the challenge of creating a new reality for ourselves and for our people.

The journey and this warrior's path is a kind of *Wasáse*, a ceremony of unity, strength, and commitment to action. Wasáse is an ancient Rotinoshonni war ritual, the Thunder Dance. The new warrior's path, the spirit of Wasáse, this Onkwehonwe attitude, this courageous way of being in the world—all come together to form a new politics in which many identities and strategies for making change are fused together in a movement to challenge white society's control over Onkwehonwe and our lands. Wasáse, as I am speaking of it here, is symbolic of the social and cultural force alive among Onkwehonwe dedicated to altering the balance of political and economic power to recreate some social and physical space for freedom to re-emerge. Wasáse is an ethical and political vision, the real demonstration of our resolve to survive as Onkwehonwe and to do what we must to force the Settlers to acknowledge our existence and the integrity of our connection to the land.

There are many differences among the peoples that are indigenous to this land, yet the challenge facing all Onkwehonwe is the same: regaining freedom and becoming self-sufficient by confronting the disconnection and fear at the core of our existences under colonial dominion. We are separated from the sources of our goodness and power: from each other, our cultures, and our lands. These connections must be restored. Governmental power is founded on fear, which is used to control and manipulate us in many ways; so, the strategy must be to confront fear and display the courage to act against and defeat the state's power.

The first question that arises when this idea is applied in a practical way to the situations facing Onkwehonwe in real life is this: How can we regenerate ourselves culturally and achieve freedom and political independence when the legacies of disconnection, dependency, and dispossession have such a strong hold on us? Undeniably, we face a difficult situation. The political and social institutions that govern us have been shaped and organized to serve white power and they conform to the interests of the states founded on that objective. These state and Settler-serving institutions are useless to the cause of our survival, and if we are to free ourselves from the grip of colonialism, we must reconfigure our politics and replace all of the strategies, institutions, and leaders in place today. The transformation will begin inside each one of us as personal change, but decolonization will become a reality only when we collectively both commit to a movement based on an *ethical* and *political* vision and consciously reject the colonial postures of weak submission, victimry, and raging violence. It is a political vision and solution that will be capable of altering power relations and rearranging the forces that shape our lives. Politics is the force that channels social, cultural, and economic powers and makes them imminent in our lives. Abstaining from politics is like turning your back on a beast when it is angry and intent on ripping your guts out.

It is the kind of politics we practise that makes the crucial distinction between the possibility of a regenerative struggle and what we are doing now. Conventional and acceptable approaches to making change are leading us nowhere. Submission and cooperation, which define politics as practised by the current generation of Onkwehonwe politicians, are, I contend, morally, culturally, and politically indefensible and should be dismissed scornfully by any right-thinking person and certainly by any Onkwehonwe who still has dignity. There is little attention paid in this book to the conventional aspects of the politics of pity, such as self-government processes, land claims agreements, and aboriginal rights court cases, because building on what we have achieved up until now in our efforts to decolonize society is insufficient and truly unacceptable as the end-state of a challenge to colonialism. The job is far from finished. It is impossible to predict what constraints and opportunities will emerge, but it is clear that we have not pushed hard enough yet to be satisfied with the state's enticements. Fundamentally different relationships between Onkwehonwe and Settlers will emerge not from negotiations in state-sponsored and government-regulated processes, but only after successful Onkwehonwe resurgences against white society's entrenched privileges and the unreformed structure of the colonial state.

As Onkwehonwe committed to the reclamation of our dignity and strength, there are, theoretically, two viable approaches to engaging the colonial power that is thoroughly embedded in the state and in societal structures: armed resistance and non-violent contention. Each has a heritage among our peoples and is a potential formula for making change, for engaging with the adversary without deference to emotional attachments to colonial symbols or to the compromised logic of colonial approaches. They are both philosophically defensible, but are they both equally valid approaches to making change, given the realities of our situations and our goals? We need a confident position on the question as to what is the right strategy. Both armed resistance and non-violent contention are unique disciplines that require commitments that rule out overlapping allegiances between the two approaches. They are diverging and distinctive ways of making change, and the choice between the two paths is the most important decision the next generation of Onkwehonwe will collectively make.

This is the political formula of the strategy of armed resistance: facing a situation of untenable politics, Onkwehonwe could conceivably move toward practising a punishing kind of aggression, a raging resistance invoking hostile and irredentist negative political visions seeking to engender and escalate the conflict so as to eventually demoralize the Settler society and defeat the colonial state. Contrast this with the strategic vision of non-violent contention: Onkwehonwe face the untenable politics and unacceptable conditions in their communities and confront the situation with determined yet restrained action, coherent and creative contention supplemented with a positive political vision based on re-establishing respect for the original covenants and ancient treaties that reflect the founding principles of the Onkwehonwe-Settler relationship. This would be a movement sure to engender conflict, but it would be conflict for a positive purpose and with the hope of recreating the conditions of coexistence. Rather

21

than enter the arena of armed resistance, we would choose to perform rites of resurgence.

These forms of resurgence have already begun. There are people in all communities who understand that a true decolonization movement can emerge only when we shift our politics from articulating grievances to pursuing an organized and political battle for the cause of our freedom. These new warriors understand the need to refuse any further disconnection from their heritage and the need to reconnect with the spiritual bases of their existences as Onkwehonwe. Following their example and building on the foundation of their struggles, we have the potential to initiate a more coordinated and widespread action, to reorganize communities to take advantage of gains and opportunities as they occur in political, economic, social, and cultural spheres and spaces created by the movement. There is a solid theory of change in this concept of an indigenous peoples' movement. The theory of change is the lived experience of the people we will encounter in this book. Their lives are a dynamic of power generated by creative energy flowing from their heritage through their courageous and unwavering determination to recreate themselves and act together to meet the challenges of their day.

A common and immediate concern for anyone defending the truth of their heritage is the imperative to repel the thrust of the modern state's assault against our peoples. The Settlers continue to erase our existences from the cultural, social, and political landscape of our homelands. Onkwehonwe are awakening to the need to move from the materialist orientation of our politics and social reality toward a restored spiritual foundation, channelling that spiritual strength and the unity it creates into a power that can affect political and economic relations. A true revolution is spiritual at its core; every single one of the world's materialist revolutions has failed to produce conditions of life that are markedly different from those which it opposed. Whatever the specific means or rationale, violent, legalist, and economic revolutions have never been successful in producing peaceful coexistence between peoples; in fact, they always reproduce the exact set of power relations they seek to change, rearranging only the outward face of power.

One problem of indigenous politics is that there is no consistency of means and ends in the way we are struggling to empower ourselves. Approaches to making change that advocate reforming the colonial legal system or state policy or that seek empowerment through the accumulation of financial resources may seem to hold promise, but they are opposed to basic and shared Onkwehonwe values in either the means they would use to advance the struggle or in the ends they would achieve. Legalist, economic, and, for that matter, violent insurgent approaches are all simply mimicking foreign logics, each in a different way. How you fight determines who you will become when the battle is over, and there is always means-ends consistency at the end of the game. For Onkwehonwe, the implication of a legalist approach is entrenchment in the state system as citizens with rights defined by the constitution of the colonial state, which is the defeat of the idea of an independent Onkwehonwe existence. The implication of the economic development approach is integration into the consumer culture of mainstream capitalist society, which is the defeat of the possibility of ways of life associated with Onkwehonwe cultures. And, of course, violence begets violence. The implication of an approach to making change using armed force to attack institutions and the structure of power is an ensuing culture of violence that is, in its very existence, the negation of the ideal of peaceful coexistence at the heart of Onkwehonwe philosophies.

Despite the visible and public victories in court cases and casino profits, neither of these strategies generates the transformative experience that recreates people like spiritual-cultural resurgences can do. The truly revolutionary goal is to transform disconnection and fear into connection and to transcend colonial culture and institutions. Onkwehonwe have been successful on personal and collective levels by rejecting extremism on both ends of the spectrum between the reformist urgings of tame legalists and the unfocused rage of armed insurgents.

Consider the futility of our present politics and the perversity of what I will call "aboriginalism," the ideology and identity of assimilation, in which Onkwehonwe are manipulated by colonial myths into a submissive position and are told that by emulating white people they can gain acceptance and possibly even fulfillment within mainstream society. Many Onkwehonwe today embrace the label of "aboriginal," but this identity is a legal and social construction of the state, and it is disciplined by racialized violence and economic oppression to serve an agenda of silent surrender. The acceptance of being aboriginal is as powerful an assault on Onkwehonwe existences as any force of arms brought upon us by the Settler society. The integrationist and unchallenging aboriginal vision is designed to lead us to oblivion, as individual successes in assimilating to the mainstream are celebrated, and our survival is redefined strictly in the terms of capitalist dogma and practical-minded individualist consumerism and complacency.

Within the frame of politics and social life, Onkwehonwe who accept the label and identity of an aboriginal are bound up in a logic that is becoming increasingly evident, even to them, as one of outright assimilation—the abandonment of any meaningful notion of being indigenous.

Outright assaults and insidious undermining have brought us to the situation we face today, when the destruction of our peoples is nearly complete. Yet resurgence and regeneration constitute a way to power-surge against the empire with integrity. The new warriors who are working to ensure the survival of their people are not distracted by the effort to pass off as "action" any analysis of the self-evident fact of the defeat of our nations. They don't imagine that our cause needs further justification in law or in the public mind. They know that assertion and action are the urgencies; all the rest is a smokescreen clouding this clear vision.

The experience of resurgence and regeneration in Onkwehonwe communities thus far proves that change cannot be made from within the colonial structure. Institutions and ideas that are the creation of the colonial relationship are not capable of ensuring our survival; this has been amply proven as well by the absolute failure of institutional and legalist strategies to protect our lands and our rights, as well as in their failure to motivate younger generations of Onkwehonwe to action. In the face of the strong renewed push by the state for the legal and political assimilation of our peoples, as well as a rising tide of consumerist materialism making its way into our communities, the last remaining remnants of distinctive Onkwehonwe values and culture are being wiped out. The situation is urgent and calls for even more intensive and profound resurgences on even more levels, certainly not moderation. Many people are paralyzed by fear or idled by complacency and will sit passively and watch destruction consume our people. But the words in this book are for those of us who prefer a dangerous dignity to safe self-preservation.

People have always faced these challenges. None of what I am saying is new, either to people's experience in the world or to political philosophy. What is emerging in our communities is a renewed respect for indigenous knowledge and Onkwehonwe ways of thinking. This book hopes to document and glorify this renewal, in which Onkwehonwe are linked in spirit and strategy with other indigenous peoples confronting empire throughout the world. When we look into the heart of our own communities, we can relate to the struggles of peoples in Africa or Asia and appreciate the North African scholar Albert Memmi's thoughts on how, in the language of his day, colonized peoples respond to oppression: "One can be reconciled to every situation, and the colonized can wait a long time to live. But, regardless of how soon or how violently the colonized rejects his situation, he will one day begin to overthrow his unliveable existence with the whole force of his oppressed personality."[1] The question facing us is this one: For us today, here in this land, how will the overthrow of our unliveable existence come about?

Memmi was prescient in his observations on the reaction of people labouring under colonial oppression. Eventually, our people too will move to revolt against being defined by the Settlers as "aboriginal" and against the dispossession of our lands and heritage, and we will track our oppression to its source, which is the basic structure of the colonial state and society. Memmi also wrote, "revolt is the only way out of the colonial situation, and the colonized realizes it sooner or later. His condition is absolute and cries for an absolute solution; a break and not a compromise."[2] Settlers and tamed _____ in purportedly stable and peaceful countries like Canada, _____ s, and New Zealand may reject those words, but _____ vil is so well disguised and deeply denied in these _____ sistent colonialism has become mundane and inter- _____ ife, and its effects subsumed within our cultures _____ ly in the smug placidity of middle- and upper-class _____ ications of Memmi's utterance are surely frighten- _____ e have to break? Break up, break apart, break me…? _____ experience and mentality, of course. All of the world's big pro_____ ty very small and local problems. They are brought into force as realities only in the choices made every day and in many ways by people who are enticed by certain incentives and disciplined by their fears. So, confronting huge forces like colonialism is a personal and, in some ways, a mundane process. This is not to say it is easy, but looking at it this way does give proper focus to the effort of decolonizing.

The colonizers stand on guard for their ill-gotten privileges using highly advanced techniques, mainly co-optation, division, and, when required, physical repression. The weak people in the power equation help the colonizers too, with their self-doubts, laziness, and unfortunate insistence on their own disorganization!

Challenging all of this means even redefining the terminology of our existence. Take the word, "colonization," which is actually a way of seeing and explaining what has happened to us. We cannot allow that word to be the story of our lives, because it is a narrative that in its use privileges the colonizer's power and inherently limits our freedom, logically and mentally imposing a perpetual colonized victim way of life and view on the world. Onkwehonwe are faced not with the same adversary their ancestors confronted, but with a colonization that has recently morphed into a kind of post-modern imperialism that is more difficult to target than the previous and more obvious impositions of force and control over the structures of government within their communities. Memmi's "break" must itself be redefined.

The challenge is to reframe revolt. Classically, the phases of revolt are thought of along a continuum moving from the self-assertion of an independent identity, to seeking moderate reforms of the system, to protesting and openly rejecting authority, and then to revolutionary action to destroy the state and replace it with another order of power. Thinking along these lines, it is ironic that our own politicians find themselves being unwitting conservatives. Twenty years ago they were positioned at the cutting edge of change—Red Power, political and cultural revivalism, court challenges for rights, land claims, etc. But now that those same people are in positions of leadership, they are resisting attempts to move the challenge to the next stage. Our politicians find themselves cooperating with their (former) enemies and adversaries to preserve the non-threatening, very limited resolutions they have worked with the colonial powers to create and define as end objectives. They have accommodated themselves to colonialism, not defeated it. And they have forgotten that the ancestral movement always sought total freedom from domination and a complete revolt against empire, not halfway compromises and weak surrenders to watered-down injustices.

I have heard it said, prophetically, in my own community that "the people will rise up again when the chiefs' heads are rolling on the ground." While it is clear that guerrilla and terrorist strategies are futile—certainly so from within the centre of industrial capitalist countries—the spirit of the ancestors who went to war against the invaders is compelling and honourable. I refuse to pass moral judgement against those oppressed people who act against imperial power using arms to advance their cause; their acts of resistance are only the moral equivalents to the heinous and legalized capitalist crimes that are destroying people's lives and the land. And where people meet state violence with arms to defend themselves and their lands in necessary acts of self-preservation, they are of course justified in doing so. But, because I hold a strong commitment to struggles for freedom, I do not believe that armed struggle is the right path for our people to take. Violent revolt is simply not an intelligent and realistic approach to confronting the injustice we face, and it will not allow us to succeed in transforming the society from what it is to a state of peaceful coexistence. Anyway, I sense that even if my own strategic disagreement with, or some other people's moral judgements against, armed action did not solidify against a group's advocacy and use of violence, rejection and disapprobation by indigenous communities would surely come in the wake of armed revolt. Onkwehonwe would without a doubt be further abused and violated by repressive counter-violence that the state would use in retaliation.

Using violence to advance our objectives would lead to frustration and failure for political and military reasons, but it would also falter for deeper spiritual and cultural reasons. I find it very difficult to see any value in asking our future generations to form their identities on and live lives of aggression; would this not validate and maintain the enemy colonizer as an omnipresent and superior reality of our existence for generations to come? This is not the legacy we want to leave for our children. To remain true to a struggle conceived within Onkwehonwe values, the end goal of our Wasáse—our warrior's dance—must be formulated as a spiritual revolution, a culturally rooted *social* movement that transforms the whole of society and a *political* action that seeks to remake the entire landscape of power and relationship to reflect truly a liberated post-imperial vision.

Wasáse is spiritual revolution and contention. It is not a path of violence. And yet, this commitment to non-violence is not pacifism either. This is an important point to make clear: I believe there is a need for morally grounded defiance and non-violent agitation combined with the development of a collective capacity for self-defence, so as to generate within the Settler society a reason and incentive to negotiate constructively in the interest of achieving a respectful coexistence. The rest of this book will try to explain this concept (an effort the more academically inclined reader may be permitted to read as my theorizing the liberation of indigenous peoples).

My goal is to discover a real and deep notion of peace in the hope of moving us away from valuing simplistic notions of peace such as certainty and stability, for these are conceptions that point only to the value of order. Some readers may find themselves confused by the seeming contradictions in my logic and question how "peace" can be the orienting goal of this warrior-spirited book, wondering if perhaps a concept like "justice" may be more to the point and truer to the spirit of a book that takes a war dance as its emblem. But justice as a liberatory concept and as a would-be goal is limited by its necessary gaze to the politics, economics, and social relations of the past. However noble and necessary justice is to our struggles, its gaze will always be backward. By itself, the concept of justice is not capable of encompassing the broader transformations needed to ensure coexistence. Justice is one element of a good relationship; it is concerned with fairness and right and calculating moral balances, but it cannot be the end goal of a struggle, which must be conceived as a movement from injustice and conflict through and beyond the achievement of justice to the completion of the relationship and the achievement of peace.

The old slogan, "No justice, no peace," is a truism. We must move from injustice, through struggle, to a mutual respect founded on the achievement of justice and then onward towards peace. Step by step. Lacking struggle, omitting respect and justice, there can and will be no peace. Or happiness. Or freedom. These are the real goals of a truly human and fully realized philosophy of change.

Peace is hopeful, visionary, and forward-looking; it is not just the lack of violent conflict or rioting in the streets. That simple stability is what we call order, and order serves the powerful in an imperial situation. If peace continues to be strictly defined as the maintenance of order and the rule of law, we will be defeated in our struggle to survive as Onkwehonwe. Reconceptualized for our struggle, peace is being Onkwehonwe, breaking with the disfiguring and meaningless norms of our present reality, and recreating ourselves in a holistic sense. This conception of peace requires a rejection of the state's multifaceted oppression of our peoples simultaneously with and through the assertion of regenerated Onkwehonwe identities. Personal and collective transformation is not instrumental to the surging against state power, it is the very means of our struggle.

Memmi, who was so powerful in his exposure of colonial mentalities at play during the Algerian resistance against French colonialism, spoke of the fundamental need to cure white people, through revolution, of the disease of the European they have collectively inherited from their colonial forefathers. I believe his prescription of spiritual transformation channelled into a political action and social movement is the right medicine.

Following an awakening among the people and cultural redefinition, after social agitation, after engaging in a politics of contention, after creative confrontation, we will be free to determine our own existences. Wasáse, struggle in all of its forms, truly defines an authentic existence. This is the clearest statement on what I seek to cause with the ideas I am putting forward in this book. This is why I speak of warriors. To be Onkwehonwe, to be fully human, is to be living the ethic of courage and to be involved in a struggle for personal transformation and freedom from the dominance of imperial ideas and powers—especially facing the challenges in our lives today. Any other path or posture is surrender or complicity. And though I am speaking non-violently of a creative reinterpretation of what it is to be a warrior, I am doing so in full reverence and honour of the essence of the ancient warrior spirit, because a warrior makes a stand facing danger with courage and integrity. The warrior spirit is the strong medicine we need to cure the European disease. But, drawing on the old spirit, we need to create something new for ourselves and think through the reality of the present to design an appropriate strategy, use fresh tactics, and acquire new skills.

The new warriors make their own way in the world: they move forward heeding the teachings of the ancestors and carrying a creed that has been taken from the past and remade into a powerful way of being in their new world. In our actions, we show our respect for the heritage of our people by regenerating the spirit of our ancestors. We glorify the continuing existence of our peoples, and we act on the knowledge that our survival as Onkwehonwe depends on living the rites of resurgence. Fighting these battles in this kind of war, our nations will be recreated. The new warriors are committed in the first instance to self-transformation and self-defence against the insidious forms of control that the state and capitalism use to shape lives according to their needs—to fear, to obey, to consume.

When lies rule, warriors reveal new truths for the people to believe. Warriors battle against the political manipulation of their innate fears and repel the state's attempts to embed complacency inside of them. They counter-attack with a lived ethic of courage and seek to cause the reawakening of a culture of freedom.

Survival is bending and swaying but not breaking, adapting and accommodating without compromising what is core to one's being. Those who are emboldened by challenges and who sacrifice for the truth achieve freedom. Those who fail to find balance, who reject change, or who abandon their heritage altogether abandon themselves. They perish. The people who live on are those who have learned the lesson of survival: cherish your unique identity, protect your freedom, and defend your homeland.

Even from within a conservative viewpoint on politics, if self-government or self-determination are the goals, and if communities are seeking to restore a limited degree of autonomy for their people in relation to the state, it must be recognized that the cultural basis of our existence as Onkwehonwe has been nearly destroyed and that the cultural foundation of our nations must be restored or reimagined if there is going to be a successful assertion of political or economic rights. In other words, there certainly exists the moral right and the legal right for governance outside of assimilative or co-optive forms, but there is no capacity in our communities and there is no cultural basis on which to generate an effective movement against the further erosion of Onkwehonwe political authority. This has placed our continuing existence as *peoples,* or as nations and distinct cultures, in imminent danger of extinction.

I am not overstating the danger to make a point, or, as it may be suspected, for rhetorical purposes. Think of the pattern of societal decline described by Hannah Arendt: political authority falls after the loss of tradition and the weakening of religious beliefs. Spirituality breaks, there is a loss of traditional cultures and languages, and this is followed by political subjugation.[3] This pattern reduces the story of the 500-year conquest of *Anówarakowa Kawennote,* Great Turtle Island, to its essence. Imperialism has not been a totalizing, unknowable, and irresistible force of destruction, but a fluid confluence of politics, economics, psychology, and culture. It remains so.

What is the path to meaningful change in our lives? The most common answers to that question come in the form of big political or economic solutions to problems conceived of as *historical,* or past, injustices: self-government, land claims, economic development, and the legal recognition of our rights as nations. I recognize, of course, that these are crucial goals. In the long term, it will be absolutely necessary to redefine and reconstruct the governmental and economic relationships between Onkwehonwe and Settlers. Yet to the extent that self-government, land claims, and economic development agreements have been successfully negotiated and implemented, there is no evidence that they have done anything to make but a very small minority of our people happier and healthier.

In most cases, these agreements create new bureaucracies and put in place new levels and forms of government based on the colonial model, or new capitalist relationships with non-indigenous business partners. These new arrangements benefit a few people, mainly elected officials, entrepreneurs, lawyers, consultants, and, to a much lesser extent, the people who staff the various structures. Self-government, land claims, and economic development are abundantly positive for this fortunate minority. This is not to begrudge the fact that some of us have gained the education and skills needed to secure jobs or create businesses—these are the rewards of honest people who have worked hard to create strength for themselves. But in the midst of all of the apparent progress, there is a nagging sense among many people that something is wrong even with these supposed solutions. There is a dawning awareness among those of us who think outside ourselves, those who care about the not-so-fortunate and all-too-easily ignored 90 per cent of our people, those who get no benefit at all from the new political and economic orders being created by the collusion of interests that govern our communities today. It is the sinking feeling that political power and money, the things we've worked so hard to achieve, are still not going to be enough to liberate us from our present reality.

I am saying that the real reason most Onkwehonwe endure unhappy and unhealthy lives has nothing to do with governmental powers or money. The lack of these things only contributes to making a bad situation worse. The root of the problem is that we are living through a spiritual crisis, a time of darkness that descended on our people when we became disconnected from our lands and from our traditional ways of life. We are divided amongst ourselves and confused in our own minds about who we are and what kind of life we should be living. We depend on others to feed us and to teach us how to look, feel, live. We still turn to white men for the answers to our problems; worse yet, we have started to trust them. There are no more leaders and hardly a place left to go where we can just be *native*. We are the prophetic Seventh Generation: if we do not find a way out of the crises, we will be consumed by the darkness, and whether it is through self-destruction or assimilation, we will not survive.

Large-scale statist solutions like self-government and land claims are not so much lies as they are irrelevant to the root problem. For a long time now, we have been on a quest for governmental power and money; somewhere along the journey from the past to the future, we forgot that our goal was to reconnect with our lands and to preserve our harmonious cultures and respectful ways of life. It is these things that are the true guarantee of peace, health, strength, and happiness—of survival. Before we can start rebuilding ourselves and achieve meaningful change in the areas of law and government, of economies and development, we must start to remember one important thing: our communities are made up of people. Our concern about legal rights and empowering models of national self-government has led to the neglect of the fundamental building blocks of our peoples: the women and men, the youth and the elders.

Some people believe in the promise of what they call "traditional government" as the ultimate solution to our problems, as if just getting rid of the imposed corrupt band or tribal governments and resurrecting old laws and structures would solve everything. I used to believe that myself. But there is a problem with this way of thinking, too. The traditional governments and laws we hold out as the pure good alternatives to the imposed colonial systems were developed at a time when people were different than we are now; they were people who were confidently rooted in their culture, bodily and spiritually strong, and capable of surviving independently in their natural environments. We should ask ourselves if it makes any sense to try to bring back these forms of government and social organization without first regenerating our people so that we can support traditional government models. Regretfully, the levels of participation in social and political life, the physical fitness, and the cultural skills these models require are far beyond our weakened and dispirited people right now.

We will begin to make meaningful change in the lives of our communities when we start to focus on making real change in the lives of our people as individuals. It may sound clichéd, but it is still true that the first part of self-determination is the *self*. In our minds and in our souls, we need to reject the colonists' control and authority, their definition of who we are and what our rights are, their definition of what is worthwhile and how one should live, their hypocritical and pacifying moralities. We need to rebel against what they want us to become, start remembering the qualities of our ancestors, and act on those remembrances. This is the kind of spiritual revolution that will ensure our survival.

What are the first steps in this revolution of the spirit?

For a start, let's think about the most basic question: What does it mean to be Onkwehonwe? Many times, I have listened to Leroy Little Bear, one of the wisest people I know, speak on one of the real differences between Onkwehonwe and European languages. European languages, he explains, centre on nouns and are concerned with naming things, ascribing traits, and making judgements. Onkwehonwe languages are structured on verbs; they communicate through descriptions of movement and activity. Take my own name, for example. Taiaiake, in English, is a proper noun that labels me for identification. In Kanienkeha, it literally means, "he is crossing over from the other side." Struggling against and negotiating with the descendants of Europeans occupying our homelands for all these years, we have become very skilled, in the European way, at judging and naming everything, even ourselves—beliefs, rights, authorities, jurisdictions, land use areas, categories of membership in our communities, and so on—as if it were enough to speak these things to make them into a reality. In fighting for our future, we have been mislead into thinking that "Indigenous," or "First Nations," "Carrier," "Cree" or "Mohawk" (even if we use Kanien'kehaka, or Innu, or Wet'suwet'en), is something that is attached to us inherently and not a description of what we actually do with our lives.

The European way is to see the world organized in a system of names and titles that formalize their being. Onkwehonwe recall relationships and responsibilities through languages that symbolize doing. Apply this linguistic insight to our recent efforts to gain recognition and respect, and you start to get a sense of why we have fallen off the good path. We have mistaken the mere renaming of our situation for an actual reconnection with our lands and cultures. Living as Onkwehonwe means much more than applying a label to ourselves and saying that we are indigenous to the land. It means looking at the personal and political choices we make every day and applying an indigenous logic to those daily acts of creation. It means knowing and respecting Kanien'kehaka, Innu, and Wet'suwet'en teachings and thinking and behaving in a way that is consistent with the values passed down to us by our ancestors. My people speak of the coming generations as "faces who are yet to emerge from the Earth." We have a sacred responsibility to rise up and fight so that our people may live again as Onkwehonwe.

What is the way to restore meaning and dignity to our lives? This is another way of framing the question that guides us as we trace the path of truth and struggle from where we stand today. Too many of our peoples are disoriented, dissatisfied, fearful, and disconnected from each other and from the natural world. Onkwehonwe deserve a different state of being where there are real opportunities for us to finally realize justice and peace in our lives and where there is hope of creating a society in which it is possible to live a life of integrity and happiness.

The thoughts and vision I am offering through these words are rooted in the cultural heritage of Anówarakowa. And proudly so! They are not compromises between indigenous and non-indigenous perspectives; nor are they attempts to negotiate a reconciliation of Onkwehonwe and European cultures and values. These words are an attempt to bring forward an indigenously rooted voice of contention, unconstrained and uncompromised by colonial mentalities. A total commitment to the challenge of regenerating our indigeneity, to rootedness in indigenous cultures, to a fundamental commitment to the centrality of our truths—this book is an effort to work through the philosophical, spiritual, and practical implications of holding such commitments.

These commitments require the reader to challenge critically all of his or her artificial and emotional attachments to the oppressive colonial myths and symbols that we have come to know as our culture. I know that this is asking people to wander into dangerous territory; disentangling from these attachments can also feel like being banished, in a way. But stepping into our fear is crucial, because leaving the comfort zone of accepted truth is vital to creating the emotional and mental state that allows one to really learn.

It is a new approach to decolonization. Less intense, or less threatening, ideas about how to make change have proven ineffective from our perspective. I believe it is because they are bound up in and unable to break free from the limiting logic of the colonial myths that they claim to oppose. The myths' symbols and embedded beliefs force aboriginal thinking to remain in colonial mental, political, and legal frameworks, rendering these forms of writing and thinking less radical and powerless against imperialism. The reflections, meditations, teachings, and dialogues that form the core of this book are indigenous and organic: they emerge from inside Onkwehonwe experiences and reflect the ideas, concepts, and languages that have developed over millennia in the spaces we live, among our peoples. I want to bring the heritage and truth of Anówarakowa to a new generation and to engage passionately with indigenous truths to generate powerful dynamics of thought and action and change. I did not write this book *about* change, I wrote it from *within* change. I wrote it with the plain intent of instigating further contention. My hope is that people who read these words will take from them a different way of defining the problem at the core of our present existence, one that brings a radically principled and challenging set of ideas to bear on how to remake the relationship between Onkwehonwe and Settler.

A big part of the social and political resurgence will be the regeneration of Onkwehonwe existences free from colonial attitudes and behaviours. Regeneration means we will reference ourselves differently, both from the ways we did traditionally and under colonial dominion. We will self-consciously recreate our cultural practices and reform our political identities by drawing on tradition in a thoughtful process of reconstruction and a committed reorganization of our lives in a personal and collective sense. This will result in a new conception of what it is to live as Onkwehonwe. This book is my contribution to the larger effort to catalyze and galvanize the movements that have already begun among so many of our people. Restoring these connections is the force that will confront and defeat the defiant evil of imperialism in this land. We need to work together to cleanse our minds, our hearts, and our bodies of the colonial stain and reconnect our lives to the sources of our strength as Onkwehonwe. We need to find new and creative ways to express that heritage. I wrote this book as an Onkwehonwe believing in the fundamental commonality of indigenous values; yet I wrote it from within my own experience. I aim to speak most directly to other Onkwehonwe who share my commitments and who are travelling the same pathway. These words are offered in the spirit of the

TAIAIAKE ALFRED

ancient Wasáse, which was so eloquently captured by my friend Kahente when I asked her to tell me how she understood the meaning of the ritual:

There is a spiritual base that connects us all, and it is stimulated through ceremony. The songs and dances that we perform are like medicine, *Ononkwa*, invoking the power of the original instructions that lie within. In it, we dance, sing, and share our words of pain, joy, strength, and commitment. The essence of the ancestors' message reveals itself not only in these songs, speeches, and dances but also in the faces and bodies of all who are assembled. This visual manifestation shows us that we are not alone and that our survival depends on being part of the larger group and in this group working together. We are reminded to stay on the path laid out before us. This way it strengthens our resolve to keep going and to help each other along the way. It is a time to show each other how to step along that winding route in unison and harmony with one another. To know who your friends and allies are in such struggle is what is most important and is what keeps you going.

If non-indigenous readers are capable of listening, they will learn from these shared words, and they will discover that while we are envisioning a new relationship between Onkwehonwe and the land, we are at the same time offering a decolonized alternative to the Settler society by inviting them to share our vision of respect and peaceful coexistence.

The non-indigenous will be shown a new path and offered the chance to join in a renewed relationship between the peoples and places of this land, which we occupy together. I want to provoke. To cause reflection. To motivate people to creatively confront the social and spiritual forces that are preventing us from overcoming the divisive and painful legacies of our shared history as imperial subjects. The guiding question I asked earlier can be stated in another way: What is the meaning of self-determination? We have just now started on the journey together to find the full meaning of the answer to this question, but even so, I believe we all know that achieving freedom means overcoming the delusions, greeds, and hatreds that lie at the centre of colonial culture. This book is an expression of that common yearning for freedom, drawing on the inarticulate and unsettled energy that still resides in each of us.

Onkwehonwe have always fought for survival against imperialism and its drive to annihilate our existence. Our fight is no different from previous generations; it is a struggle to defend the lands, the communities, and the languages that are our heritage and our future. But the new imperialism that we experience has a special character. The close danger of a technological empire and co-optation is the insidious effort of the Settler society to erase us from the cultural and political landscape of the countries they have invaded and now claim as their own. Survival demands that we act on the love we have for this land and our people. This is the counter-imperative to empire. Our power is a courageous love. Our fight is to recognize, to expose, and to ultimately overcome the corrupt, colonized identities and irrational fears that have been bred into us. It is worth repeating that survival will require not only political or cultural resurgence against state power, but positive movement to overcome the defining features of imperialism on a personal and collective level. These resurgences, multiplicities of thought and action, must be founded on Onkwehonwe philosophies and lead us to reconnect with respectful and natural ways of being in the world.

I understand that not everyone realizes or accepts that Onkwehonwe are on the verge of extinction. There are many people, the majority in fact in any community, who still refuse to acknowledge and accept the fact of our perilous condition. The aboriginal "self-termination" movement is much stronger than any coordinated Onkwehonwe movement against imperialism and white dominion today. Most of our people are assimilated into the racist propagandas designed to rob them of their dignity and their lands and have normalized the destruction of their nations. That conclusion may seem harsh, but it is truth. The edge of extinction does not afford the luxury of mincing words.

You may be wondering how it is that I fail to appreciate the efforts to reform and reconcile social relations that are currently underway in the more progressive colonial countries. I do appreciate the nature of these reforms and reconciliations with colonialism only too well. Fifteen years of working in Onkwehonwe communities and organizations has taught me that continued cooperation with state power structures is morally unacceptable. Everyone involved in the Indian Industry knows that we are negotiating with our oppressor from a position of weakness. Organizations purport to speak for people who turn around and vehemently deny the legitimacy and authority of those very organizations and their so-called leaders. And the communities are disintegrating socially and culturally at a terrifying speed as alienation, social ills, and disease outpace efforts to stabilize our societies. In this environment, negotiation is futile. It is counter-productive to our survival. It is senseless to advocate for an accord with imperialism while there is a steady and intense ongoing attack by the Settler society on everything meaningful to us: our cultures, our communities, and our deep attachments to land. The framework of current reformist or reconciling negotiations are about handing us the scraps of history: self-government and jurisdictional authorities for state-created Indian governments within the larger colonial system and subjection of Onkwehonwe to the blunt force of capitalism by integrating them as wage slaves into the mainstream resource-exploitation economy. These surface reforms are being offered because they are useless to our survival as Onkwehonwe. This is not a coincidence, nor is it a result of our goals being obsolete. Self-government and economic development are being offered precisely *because* they are useless to us in the struggle to survive as peoples and so are no threat to the Settlers and, specifically, the interests of the people who control the Settler state. This is assimilation's end-game. Today, self-government and economic development signify the defeat of our peoples' struggles just as surely as, to our grandparents, residential schools, land dispossession, and police beatings signified the supposed supremacy of white power and the subjugation and humiliation of the first and real peoples of this land.

What it comes down to in confronting our imperial reality is that some of us want to reform colonial law and policy, to dull that monster's teeth so that we can't be ripped apart so easily. Some of us believe in reconciliation, forgetting that the monster has a genocidal appetite, a taste for our blood, and would sooner tear us apart than lick our hands. I think that the only thing that has changed since our ancestors first declared war on the invaders is that some of us have lost heart. Against history and against those who would submit to it, I am with the warriors who want to beat the beast into bloody submission and teach it to behave.

The time to change direction is now. Signs of defeat have been showing on the faces of our people for too long. Young people, those who have not yet learned to accommodate to the fact that they are expected to accept their lesser status quietly, are especially hard hit by defeatism and alienation. Youth in our communities and in urban centres are suffering. Suicide, alcohol and drug abuse, cultural confusion, sexual violence, obesity: they suffer these scourges worse than anyone else. It is not because they lack money or jobs in the mainstream society (we shouldn't forget that our people have always been "poor" as consumers in comparison to white people). It is because their identities, their cultures, and their rights are under attack by a racist government. The wounds suffered by young Onkwehonwe people in battle are given little succour by their own elders, and they find only scorn or condescension in the larger world. These young people are fighting raging battles for their own survival every day, and when they become convinced that to fight is futile and the battle likely to be lost, they retreat. Yet they have pride, and rather than submit to the enemy, they sacrifice themselves, sometimes using mercifully quick and sometimes painfully slow methods.

Some people may find it shocking or absurd for me to suggest that an Onkwehonwe community is a kind of war zone. But anyone who has actually lived on a reserve will agree with this tragic analogy on some level. Make no mistake about it, Brothers and Sisters: the war is on. There is no post-colonial situation; the invaders our ancestors fought against are still here, for they have not yet rooted themselves and been transformed into real people of this homeland. Onkwehonwe must find a way to triumph over notions of history that relegate our existence to the past by preserving ourselves in this hostile and disintegrating environment. To do so, we must regenerate ourselves through action because living the white man's vision of an Indian or an aboriginal will just not do for us.

We are each facing modernity's attempt to conquer our souls. The conquest is happening as weak, cowardly, stupid, petty, and greedy ways worm themselves into our lives and take the place of the beauty, sharing, and harmony that defined life in our communities for previous generations. Territorial losses and political disempowerment are secondary conquests compared to that first, spiritual cause of discontent. The challenge is to find a way to regenerate ourselves and take back our dignity. Then, meaningful change will be possible, and it will be a new existence, one of possibility, where Onkwehonwe will have the ability to make the kinds of choices we need to make concerning the quality of our lives and begin to recover a truly human way of life.

NOTES

1   Albert Memmi, *The Colonizer and the Colonized* (Boston, MA: Beacon Press, 1991) 120.

2   Memmi 127.

3   Hannah Arendt, *On Revolution* (New York, NY: Penguin, 1963).

rebellion of the truth

A Warrior is the one who can use words so that everyone knows they are part of the same family. A Warrior says what is in the people's hearts, talks about what the land means to them, brings them together to fight for it.[1]

— Bighorse, Diné

Onkwehonwe existences in all their diverse expressions and experiences are rooted in the recognition and respect of sensitivity to one's place in creation and awareness of one's place in a circle of integrity. Our goal, regenerating authentic Onkwehonwe lives, means finding ways to restore the connections that define indigenous consciousness and ways of being; it means individuals and communities seeking the re-achievement of the elements of integrity: strength, clarity, and commitment. There are many pathways to the achievement. The freedom and power that come with understanding and living a life of indigenous integrity are experienced by people in many different ways, and respect must be shown to the need for individuals to find their way according to their own vision. We who seek to bring about change in others and in society can only offer guidance out of shared concern and reflection based on our own experience, so that others anxious for the journey can listen and then embark on the challenge for themselves. Awakened to their own freedom and power-generating potential, people living colonial lives will rise to the challenge and move toward achieving integrity.

We cannot give people definitive answers to their problems, or hope to lay out predetermined steps for them to recover indigenous identities; colonialism has affected people in too many varied and complex ways for simple answers to suffice. There is no redemptive teaching or easy answers on how to be happy, only directions towards the truth and rough pathways to freedom. This is what we have to offer.

PATHS OF LEAST RESISTANCE

Before we speak of restrengthening, we should begin with an acknowledgement of how weakened Onkwehonwe have become: as a whole we have been dispossessed of land and culture and disempowered as peoples. The main implication of this disintegration of important aspects of indigenous integrity is the spiritual defeat of our people on an individual level. The culture of being colonized takes away a peoples' ability to resist the racist aggression and political, economic, and cultural pressures of the colonial state and Settler society to surrender remaining land and rights and to further assimilate culturally. This relation of culture and politics is the fact of our existence. There is no longer a culture that supports resistance in most Onkwehonwe communities; it has long been defeated by force, co-optation, and a relentless grinding-down of the strength that was manifested in the resistance of the leaders and families who held on to Onkwehonwe ideas and identities. Political culture, if it exists at all in Onkwehonwe communities, is centred around the accommodation of oppression and modes of cynical survival. Political life in Onkwehonwe communities today is a vast hypocrisy unhinged and cut off from the cultural roots of peoples' lives, and Onkwehonwe have become subjects of the Settler society's power and colonialist manipulation on all levels of our existence.

The most obvious sign of Onkwehonwe weakness is the fact that fear, corruption, and greed have become normalized as governing principles in so many of our communities. In too many First Nations, traditional ceremonies and practices have become nothing more than a cover for the cynical manipulation of our peoples' weakness by the state in collaboration with our own indigenous politicians. One recent high-profile example serves to illustrate the continuing trend toward a complete abandonment of any form of resistance on the part of First Nations politicians. In 2003, two First Nations band councils agreed to pay the province of British Columbia

$25,000 per year for the use of four acres of land in a resort town located in the First Nations' shared traditional territory. This was the first publicized case of Onkwehonwe paying white people for their own lands, of actually giving money to the people who stole their land in exchange for permission to use the very property that was stolen from them in the first place and which remains in legal limbo as far as its legal title goes, even in colonial courts. It would be easy to mock the band chiefs' cowardice, or shed tears over the loss of pride and culture that this represents, but this is the present reality of First Nations politics.[2]

This particular land deal was part of a band economic development scheme agreed to by the province. In exchange for the two band councils' participation in the City of Vancouver's successful bid to host the 2010 Winter Olympics, which is to take place in part in the resort town of Whistler, they were awarded the privilege of operating a cultural centre in the Olympic Village as a tourist attraction—to market their melanin and play the role of Friendly Indian for the otherwise white-washed Vancouver Olympic bid. The bid is a real estate developer's $850-million bonanza, bringing more jaded tourists, generic buildings, pollution-spewing resorts, and $387-million worth of paved roads and rail lines into the territory. The village of Whistler itself is one of the fastest growing winter playgrounds of the rich. Rather than dealing with land rights questions, the colonial government sought out Onkwehonwe politicians willing to speak in favour of the Olympic bid and offered them a partnership, making the deal one which money-minded band council chiefs could not refuse.

There are many questions being asked by Onkwehonwe communities about whether or not the band council chiefs should have accepted such a blatant pay-off for their support of the Olympic bid. Also, given the ongoing fight of Onkwehonwe in the area to protect their lands from predatory ski resort developers, and the fact that the planned Olympic facilities are to be situated on the pristine and unsurrendered lands of the Stl'atl'imx people (as is the resort town itself), there is much questioning of the sense and ethics of the band council's thrust toward an economic development agenda based on tourism. In justifying his council's actions, one of the band chiefs said that paying money to the provincial government in order to get involved in the tourist trade was the "path of least resistance." We can only suspect he believes this is a good thing.

Mimicking the masters of the money game, the chief informed the public that, "If you want to get into business, you've got to have the ability to go with the flow." How can anyone question that statement? But Onkwehonwe in the communities are probably asking themselves deeper questions than the chief is and wondering if "going with the flow" is the right thing to do when the mainstream is heading straight down the drain.

In colonized First Nations politics, principles don't mean a thing. Even moderate activism, the tame and constrained legalism of the current generation of leaders—futile court action to gain recognition of their rights and land title—is being rejected by the band council businessmen as too militant an approach. Further comments of the chief quoted above testify to a rejection of the responsibility to defend the peoples' ancestral rights in favour of embracing a capitalist ethic: "you know, we could spend a lot of money litigating, which would eat into the development dollars and profits." Going far beyond adopting the mentality of their colonizer, the new Onkwehonwe capitalists have taken to emulating the crass greed of their new partners in colonial crime. Said the chief of the deal, "this thing's going to give us the ability to shake all the dollars we can out of the tourists." Nice.

This deal is nothing more than a sell-out designed to benefit elite politicians on both sides of the colonial divide. It may be that some creative and (almost) credible arguments could be put forward if the package included skilled job training and long-term employment opportunities, as well as guaranteeing executive and management positions for band members. That at least would be justifiable in a materialist logic. But when questioned about the lack of experience and current capacity of people in their own communities to run even the cultural tourism centre, the chief responded, "That's the thing about having money, you can buy expertise, right?" Right. With that, it is clear that this deal is just another feeding frenzy for white consultants and band council politicians, who are collaborating to bury their faces in the government funding trough (which, it should be noted, provides the cash for the whole scheme). So much for the community development argument.

Aside from the common workaday corruption that continues to embed itself deeper in the lives of our communities through these types of deals, the most disturbing thing about the whole "cashing out" approach to decolonization—trying to buy freedom—is that the economic development agenda is founded on a basic concession to white power and the willing Onkwehonwe surrender of fundamental rights. In order to gain the benefit they expect from economic development partnerships, band council politicians have to accept the promise of money in exchange for protecting their people, lands, and cultures.

Situations such as this leave Onkwehonwe asking: Who is left to defend the land?

In the Whistler development deal, the band councils have sacrificed pristine valleys full of cultural memory, medicine, and spiritual power so that white people can build more ski runs for the Olympics and, later, turn them into tourist resorts. And they are promoting the land speculation that is already underway in the northwest corridor between the City of Vancouver and the resort area. The natural ecological balance will be disrupted and animal habitat will be lost as a result of huge increases in population and urban infrastructure. This will make it nearly impossible for people to use their lands for hunting, medicines, and ceremonial purposes. It is a sad claim to being Onkwehonwe when the identity being constructed is so closely associated with the destruction and not the love of nature.

What does it mean to be Onkwehonwe? The performance of dance shows and tourist "art" is not real culture. These are commodified artifices designed, packaged, and practised to entertain the rich and jaded bourgeois of the world, satisfying their craving for an "authentic" cultural experience—something completely out of reach in their own lives. Worse than just a pseudo-cultural sham, the tourist performance presents a false face of Onkwehonwe life to the world, one that is completely different from the politics, spirituality, and truth of lived Onkwehonwe existences. The messy complexity and aching conflicts of our real lives don't market well to people on vacation, so the First Nations businessmen market romantic lies.

The chief who promoted the village deal was also quoted as saying that "we're setting a trail for the other First Nations. That's how I see it anyways." He sees the path to the future as a forest trail freshly paved over with money. It's plain and obvious by their actions that his band councillors also see it this way. From a true Onkwehonwe perspective, it's difficult to grasp the crude materialism and total disregard for our heritage and cultural values exhibited by these colonized band council chiefs—it's as if they're looking at the world through big 1970s-era sunglasses with dollar signs on the lenses that make everything look moneyed! Yet, I must grudgingly admit that these unfortunate glasses are in vogue; the weak-kneed "least resistance" mentality is, in fact, the dominant ethic in First Nations political circles today.

What about taking an honest and principled stand for what is right, working together and sacrificing to force change on the path of maximum resistance? Those words are a joke to most leaders in the band council system, who believe that any alternative to selling-out (or "paying-out," in this case) has been discredited. At political meetings and conferences, you can hear chiefs saying it all the time: "Nobody wants to fight anymore." Or, "We

43

tried being adversarial in the 1960s and look where it got us!" So, was the short-lived radical phase of the American Indian and First Nations organizations responsible for poisoning the waters of integrity? It is not that simple. The path of least resistance I am pointing to is corrupted by greed. The majority of band chiefs don't care about community accountability and questions of integrity because the colonial gravy train keeps dropping loads of cash into their coffers. As a result, they continue to play their designated and essential role in the colonial system. Even when the endemic corruption of the Indian Affairs system is exposed and broadcast in the media, as has repeatedly occurred in both Canada and the United States, nothing of consequence happens to those involved.[3]

What kind of game are these band council chiefs playing? Onkwehonwe are seriously thinking about the future and the costs of continuing the charade that giving more authority and money to band and tribal councils— the very instruments put in place by the Settlers to divide and conquer their nations—will solve the problems and change the injustices faced by the masses of indigenous people on reserves and in the cities. Only people who have become dependent upon the state for their survival can possibly see a brighter future for their children in the bureaucratic notion of decolonization; enhanced governmental accountability mechanisms coupled with increased jurisdictional authority and more diverse governmental revenue streams are hardly an inspiring vision. When people who are *not* working for Indian Affairs hear that kind of language, they wonder what it means to anybody but government agents and colonial cooperators.

We must cut through the political rhetoric and legal double-talk. People need to think hard about the problems in their community and what is at stake in their children's lives and then ask themselves if the economic development and self-government agenda promoted by colonial authorities and cooperators is at all relevant to reality. The problems faced by Onkwehonwe have very little to do with the jurisdiction and financing of band councils or even with high unemployment rates. The real problems are the disunity of our people, the alienation of our youth, our men disrespecting our women, the deculturing of our societies, epidemic mental and physical sicknesses, the lack of employment in meaningful and self-determining indigenous ways of working, the widespread corruption of our governments, and the exploitation of our lands and peoples—all of which most of our current leaders participate in, rather than resist. Thinking this way, most Onkwehonwe will agree with me that against the fearsome enormity of this spiritual crisis, the chiefs' money-minded "path of least resistance" makes these men seem pale, small, and weak.

THE ETHICS OF COURAGE

Not all of us have been conquered. There are still strong Onkwehonwe who persevere in their struggle for an authentic existence and who are capable of redefining, regenerating, and reimagining our collective existences. If we are willing to put our words into action and transform our rhetoric into practice, we too can achieve the fundamental goal of the indigenous warrior: to live life as an act of indigeneity, to move across life's landscapes in an indigenous way, as my people say, *Onkwehonweneha*. A warrior confronts colonialism with the truth in order to regenerate authenticity and recreate a life worth living and principles worth dying for. The struggle is to restore connections severed by the colonial machine. The victory is an integrated personality, a cohesive community, and the restoration of respectful and harmonious relationships.

Translating this ethical sense and idea on a way of being into a concise political philosophy is difficult, for it resists institutionalization. I might suggest, as a starting point, conceptualizing *anarcho-indigenism*. Why? And why this term? Conveyance of the indigenous warrior ethic will require its codification in some form—a creed and an ethical framework for thinking through challenges. To take root in people's minds the new ethic will have to capture the spirit of a warrior in battle and bring it to politics. How might this spirit be described in contemporary terms relating to political thought and movement? The two elements that come to my mind are *indigenous*, evoking cultural and spiritual rootedness in this land and the Onkwehonwe struggle for justice and freedom, and the political philosophy and movement that is fundamentally anti-institutional, radically democratic, and committed to taking action to force change: *anarchism*.

This philosophical outlook is close to what Vaclav Havel described as his utopia—in his terms, a decentralized economy, local decision-making, government based on direct election of political leaders, and the elimination of political parties as governing institutions, a sort of a spiritual socialism:

> It's hard to imagine the kind of system I've tried to describe here coming about unless man, as I've said, "comes to his senses." This

45

is something no revolutionary or reformer can bring about; it can only be the natural expression of a more general state of mind, the state of mind in which man can see beyond the tip of his own nose and prove capable of taking on—under the aspect of eternity—responsibility even for the things that don't immediately concern him, and relinquish something of his private interest in favor of the interest of the community, the general interest. Without such a mentality, even the most carefully considered project aimed at altering systems will be for naught.[4]

There are philosophical connections between indigenous and some strains of anarchist thought on the spirit of freedom and the ideals of a good society. Parallel critical ideas and visions of post-imperial futures have been noted by a few thinkers, but something that may be called anarcho-indigenism has yet to develop into a coherent philosophy.[5] There are also important strategic commonalities between indigenous and anarchist ways of seeing and being in the world: a rejection of alliances with legalized systems of oppression, non-participation in the institutions that structure the colonial relationship, and a belief in bringing about change through direct action, physical resistance, and confrontations with state power. It is on this last point that connections have already been made between Onkwehonwe groups and non-indigenous activist groups, especially in collaborations between anarchists and Onkwehonwe in the anti-globalization movement.

But even before this, and without explicit linkages in theory or politically, resurgences of Onkwehonwe self-determination have been seen by the state in the same way as anarchist challenges to state authority: direct defence of rights and freedoms in a physical sense has been met with extremes of repression by the state.

The so-called "Oka Stand-off" in 1990 saw a surge of indigenous power in the resistance of the Kanien'kehaka communities (located around the city of Montréal) to the Canadian state's attempt to expropriate lands and impose its police authority on them. The determination and disciplined tactics of the *Kahnawakero:non*—people of Kahnawake, women and men alike and together—stymied the Canadian army's efforts to occupy the Kanien'kehaka village, and their ferocious but non-lethal defence of their lands and homes forced the army, trained and equipped only to confront other military forces in conventional armed combat, to withdraw after a prolonged effort. This incident, which happened at the end of a wearying 78-day stand-off between the Kanien'kehaka and Canadian police and military forces, is an unappreciated benchmark of indigenous resistance struggles.[6] Its lessons were reinforced by the so-called "Gustafsen Lake stand-off," where a serious paramilitary force was brought to bear by the Canadian state (this time in interior British Columbia) against a small group of Onkwehonwe who had occupied a sacred ceremonial site and refused to vacate the premises when ordered to do so by the Settler who held legal title to the land. Splitting-the-Sky, one of the defiant Onkwehonwe leaders in the conflict, describes what happened:

> We were unarmed. But then when they brought in arms, we weren't too far out to get some rifles, because everybody up there in the Cariboo hunts. I mean, everybody has shotguns and it's no big secret. So we ended up with about 17 shotguns to defend ourselves. I was asked at that time, "What should be the stance we make?" "Well," I said, "According to Canadian law, if somebody puts a gun in your face, you have a right to pick up a gun and defend yourself from being attacked or killed." That is Canadian law. Every citizen has that right according to due process of law—the Canadian law. And so it was a question of self-defence.[7]

These two incidents illustrate how immediate the issue of violence and self-defence is to any serious conception of resurgent indigenous power. The logic of contending with state power is inescapable. If contention is necessary to make change, if contention leads necessarily to confrontation, and if confrontation has an inherent element of potential or real violence, as the experiences in Oka and Gustafsen Lake demonstrate, then we must be prepared to accept violence and to deal with it. To continue advancing, the intelligent course of action is contention. Dogmatically pacifist movements have only succeeded in making change when they are backed by the support of the threat of violence—either explicit in the form of organized armed resistance movements subsumed within the larger non-violent movement or implicit in the fear the state and Settler society have of the potential of unorganized violence coming out of frustration. Thus we must contend, and we must confront, and we must be prepared to shoulder the burden of conflict. But how?

Governments will always use violence, and it is a responsibility to recognize this. How do we resist the power of violence and prevent it from becoming a way of life as it has become in places like Israel, Northern Ireland,

and Sri Lanka? In a sense, the question could be framed as: What is our theory of violence?

In treading this ground, we must proceed cautiously. It is crucial to understand the difference between courageously standing up to violence employed in the service of oppression and using violence to advance our own political objectives. We can take sobering insights from the words of suicide bombers from al-Qassam, the military arm of Hamas, the Palestinian Islamist organization. One of the Hamas planners said, in an interview questioning why they had implemented the suicide bomber strategy, "We paid a high price when we used only slingshots and stones. We need to exert more pressure, make the cost of the occupation that much more expensive in human lives, that much more unbearable."[8] They clearly planned the suicide bomber strategy as an effort to draw their oppressors (Israelis) into the world of pain experienced by the Palestinians, to make the price of the Israeli occupation of Palestine high for everyone. But is it possible to use violence and fear to create a new consciousness? Ultimately, the Hamas planner said, they recognize that the "battles for Islam are won not through the gun but by striking fear into the enemy's heart."

This candid exposition of the terrorist logic (which could be applied to the strategies of both sides of the Israeli-Palestinian conflict) illustrates the push, in violent conflicts, to ever-escalating levels and intensities. The rationale is always there, and within the ethical and ideological frame of force as a legitimate strategy, a moral justification can always be found. But our questions must be asked from within the foundations of our spiritual teachings and cultures as Onkwehonwe. Our question centres on an indigenous logic and the struggle for Onkwehonwe strength and freedom. Is it acceptable to move against the aggressor/oppressor using armed resistance? The best way to find an answer to that question is by delving into the experience of other colonized peoples who have contended with imperial power and sought to rid themselves from foreign occupation and who have resisted violent oppression.

In the contemporary era, one of the best known and most instructive cases of anti-colonial resistance is that of Vietnam. In the Onkwehonwe view, what were the underlying reasons for a Vietnamese revolution against French colonial rule? Essentially, it was a rebellion by the Vietnamese against economic exploitation by European and Euroamerican imperialism and for control of their own land and resources. It was not the Europeans' civilizing mission that was intolerable to the Vietnamese; many appreciated the advances in transportation, communication, education, political institutions, and physical infrastructure, all of which they needed and wanted. They had endured, for generations, a corrupt and ineffective "indigenous" government. In the final analysis what made colonial rule intolerable—and what must be seen as the major cause of the revolution—was French racism and abuse towards the Vietnamese people and the French exploitation of the economic resources of that country. Vietnamese intellectuals reacted strongly to the French attempt to undermine indigenous social institutions, and the average person reacted strongly to the imposition of French taxes and the unfair demands by and advantages given to French businesses operating in Vietnam.[9]

But, given the other options that existed then as now, why did the Vietnamese peoples' movements develop and begin to carry out campaigns of armed resistance against the French and, eventually, the United States? The rationale was voiced in different ways by the revolutionary hero of Vietnam, Ho Chi Minh, and Nguyen Thuang Huyen, one of Vietnam's "patriotic scholars." Nguyen Thuang Huyen believed that the I Ching defined revolution in reformist terms as dynastic change within an established system of rule; a regime clinging to power would crush any attempt at reform, leaving those who wished for change no choice but to resort to a corresponding violence to defeat and replace their rulers.

Ho Chi Minh believed instead in a more systemic, Western, notion of revolution. Reform, he thought, is what happens *within* an institution; whether it is successful or not, some of the old regime remains. Revolution, on the other hand, *replaces* one system with another. He concluded that there was no accommodating the French regime, which had shown itself unable to accept Vietnamese national independence and to abandon its interests in the colony of "Indochina." Thus, a movement that preserved the imperial system was unacceptable; the only way the Vietnamese people could achieve real change was through an armed revolutionary movement to replace imperial rule with a self-determining Vietnamese state.

When interviewed by an American intelligence agent in 1945 in the wake of Japan's defeat, shortly after he had declared the independence of Vietnam and had begun the military campaign against the French imperial re-occupation, Ho revealed that his primary ideology was Vietnamese nationalism and that communism, with its call for mass struggle, was instrumental to that cause:

> First, you must understand that to gain independence from a great power like France is a formidable task that cannot be

achieved without some outside help, not necessarily in things like arms, but in the nature of advice and contacts. One doesn't in fact gain independence by throwing bombs and such. That was the mistake the early revolutionaries all too often made. One must gain it through organization, propaganda, training and discipline. One also needs... a set of beliefs, a gospel, a practical analysis, you might even say a bible. Marxism-Leninism gave me that framework.

Thus, Ho's adoption of Marxism/Leninism, with its implicit theory of revolutionary violence, was not simply expedient (in that he could approach the Soviet Union and China for cash and arms and training) but was influenced by considerations of the Vietnamese peoples' necessity of survival in the face of a humbling and divisive colonial power. Imperialism was the oppressor, so an alliance with the anti-capitalist/anti-colonial communist bloc was the answer. Armed struggle was seen in this frame as necessary and unavoidable.

Focusing on the same ideological frame, the thoughts and methods of the Argentinean guerrilla leader, Che Guevara, offer great insights into the practices of armed revolution from an insurgent or minority position.[10] Guevara argued that the colonial enemy will fight to remain in power, that feudalism is globalized and mutually supportive, and that the anti-imperial struggle was continental in nature given the extent of the influence of the United States over North and South America. This prescient analysis is no longer questionable in the age of globalization. His Leninist assessment of imperialism still holds:

> We must bear in mind that imperialism is a world system, the last stages of capitalism—and it must be defeated in a world confrontation. The strategic end of this struggle should be the destruction of imperialism. Our share, the responsibility of the exploited and underdeveloped of the world, is to eliminate the foundations of imperialism: our oppressed nations, from where they extract capitals, raw materials—instruments of domination—arms and all kinds of articles...[11]

However, there is a fundamental problem with Guevara's logic when he makes the shift from diagnosis to prescription: revolutionary struggles using direct armed confrontation have failed to stop capitalism's expansion. Everywhere except in the local struggles in Vietnam and Cuba, armed struggle, peasant uprisings or *foco*, and militant international socialist solidarity have failed to produce long-term or generally successful resistances. The question for us today is: What kind of "world confrontation" is necessary to bring about not the Guevarian military "defeat" (which has proven impossible to achieve) but the transformation of imperialism?

An emblem of the "revolutionary" person and spirit, Guevara was uncompromising in his belief in the necessity of armed struggle and his hatred of imperialists. These are, in fact, the essences of the revolutionary spirit: violence and hatred. But the experience of revolutionary action in world history points to a fatal flaw (aside from the truth of living and dying by the sword): revolution and armed resistance theories with their simplistic materialist notions ignore the inextricable bonds between means and ends.

Even the inspiring Frantz Fanon, whose theory was layered with meaning, combining deep psychological insight with political-economic analysis, did not recognize the inability of a strategy of decolonization based on violence to transcend violence in the society and state which it achieves.[12]

There is also a basic question to be put to the Onkwehonwe contemplating different ways of bringing about change: Are we ready to kill and to die for the cause of self-determination? If the answer is no—and I believe most Onkwehonwe would say no—then our strategy and tactics must be shaped instead to reflect the level of conflict tolerance and willingness to engage in direct action that actually exists among our people. Yet the spirit of resistance of the old revolutionaries is worth emulating. Guevara wrote: "We cannot foresee the future, but we should never give in to the defeatist temptation of being the vanguard of a nation which yearns for freedom, but abhors the struggle it entails and awaits its freedom as a crumb of victory."[13] To honour the spirit and yet have an approach that respects our values and is effective against our adversaries and enemies, we need to define "struggle" in a way that makes sense for us in our circumstances. This means finding a theoretical logic that rejects violence as a means of liberation.

Before that is possible we must recognize the attraction of violence. It is a powerful strategic weapon. Violence gets attention, it consumes state resources, people have a morbid attraction to its effects, and it is perhaps the easiest means of resistance. But the drawbacks to violence are serious. Violence forces people to choose sides, and because it is repugnant to so many people, it causes them to disavow the cause; it limits potential allies; and it is as addictive as a drug—its immediacy and paraphernalia are seductive and intoxicating in the short term, and in the long term, the inevitable cycle of repression creates a situation justifying further violence.[14]

There are arguments in any movement both for and against violence that make sense. Western notions of non-violence are rooted in a counter-historical reading of Jesus' teachings (given that Judeo-Christian societies are among the most violent the world has ever known) and are advocated as a moral choice. But, in fact, this reading is unnecessary; non-violent action coupled with a capacity for physical self-defence is a strategic choice, not a moral choice. It is simply the best way of prevailing in a struggle. In a state context, rather than attempting to destroy or displace state authority, non-violence offers a sound strategic vision that will mobilize a movement to deny rulers control of community life and will undermine the legitimacy of the state both domestically and internationally. Because the practices and theories of politics today are so permeated with the logic of armed force, my argument here will seem counterintuitive to most people. But in fact, non-violent resistance, as the foundation of a movement made up of many different tactics responding to the demands of circumstance, has been historically widespread and effective against all types of repressive regimes.[15]

So resurgence raises the question of ethics in terms of maintaining a connection to Onkwehonwe values and ways of living while fighting in creative ways and preserving the ideas and values that are the foundation of Onkwehonwe existence.

It is a warrior's definition of courage that most concerns us, as it will be individuals who will contend against the state. Willpower and determination are the elements of courage. They are not a finite reserve and must be nurtured, fed, and developed if Onkwehonwe are to be able to stand up to state authority in any way—whether it be protest, contention, or more aggressive assertions. People who engage in battle in whatever form are not "fearless." Ninety-eight per cent of combat soldiers break down mentally in wartime situations, and for military commanders, the question is not if, but when will the men's well of courage run dry?[16] Onkwehonwe, like all warriors in battle, will realize our collective courage from sharing in others' wells of strength and determination and building up our collective store of mental and emotional strength by supporting each other in struggle and achieving victories along the way to our goals. And it is the warrior's question that is our challenge: How to shore up courage? The answer is that we, like any warrior in battle, need to realize that our collective fortitude consists in sharing in others' courage, as leaders inspire and motivate us to persevere when we feel like quitting the fight, and by building up our collective store of mental and emotional strength through the uplifting and cumulative effects that victory provides a people.

Courage in facing adversity is one part of the ethical question; the other centres on not *suffering* harm but *causing* harm. Being in contention with state power will, without a doubt, cause human harm or some form of suffering due to the strong reaction it will provoke among the conservative defenders of the colonial status quo. This much is undeniable: white society, through the agencies of the state, will use violence in the attempt to suppress any serious threat to the colonial order. Given this fact, some may argue that causing any disruption in society that causes any form of human suffering is wrong in the first instance. This is a false logic on two grounds: first, Onkwehonwe are *already* suffering in the status quo; and secondly, the state does not *have* to respond violently to Onkwehonwe challenges, it *chooses* to do so. The responsibility for violence begins and ends with the state, not with the people who are challenging the inherent injustices perpetrated by the state and who are seeking to alleviate their own present suffering under the state's existing institutions and practices. But behind the logic of this attitude of "I am doing something people don't like, therefore I am a bad person" is the totally misguided rumination of a colonial mentality, the source of the reluctance, fear, and inability of oppressed people to take action in support of their rights. Change necessitates conflict, but a violent form of conflict is a strategic choice of the state supported by colonial elites and by public opinion as well. We understand the implications of our actions in a rational ethical frame, not on emotion or judged by a Judeo-Christian guilt complex. Some people's interests and property or emotional attachments to evil colonial institutions and symbols may be affected or harmed; there is the potential for wrong to be done in the context of any movement. This is true, but the focus of our ethical reasoning must be in justifying our actions by putting them in context, in focusing on the details and implications of the actions we promote, and in forcing the state and other political actors to justify their actions and the implications of their choices. We can thus work through the ethical dilemma of promoting contention and being responsible for engendering a response from the state that is likely to turn violent. Careful thought—and the mental discipline of a true warrior—leads to the ethical consideration of the consequences, the intent, and the nature of the actions we take in the course of our struggle against the state. Yet these are all less important ethically than the main consideration, which is the motivation we bring to the struggle and the spirit of our actions.

53

In the case of actions conducted as part of indigenous resurgences, "causing harm" would be an accidental and unintended result of creative engagements with the state and social forces of our oppression. Contrast this with simplistically reasoned Western ethics (which comes out of the proscriptive orders of Judeo-Christianity and which is embedded within the liberal tradition so central to justifying colonialism) where the focus is on acts themselves. Onkwehonwe and other non-Western cultures are not shackled to the monotheistic delusion and put acts in context of a situation. This is at once dangerously liberating ("Thou Shalt Not Kill" provides moral security, even if it is broken with impunity by Jews and Christians, compared to the Onkwehonwe pronouncement "Don't Kill, Unless You Have To and the Circumstance Requires It"), cumbersome, and constraining—because it depends on human reason negotiating the complexity of the real world.

This is an ethics of spiritual and physical courage, of restraint, and of mental discipline. Everything has to be thought through, there are no moral absolutes or set rules for guiding human behaviours either in the personal or political realms. Even in regard to the "Golden Rule" basic principles that transcend moral systems and cultures (do not lie, kill, steal, commit adultery), to which the Buddhist and Onkwehonwe philosophical systems add proscription against alcohol, these should be understood as rational, intelligent guidelines, or the wisdom of the ages, rather than divine orders.

The Dalai Lama, in *Ancient Wisdom, Modern World*, has defined ethics as, "the indispensable interface between my desire to be happy and yours."[17] How do we determine if something we are doing is wrong? We can take our cue from Buddhist teachings: you are wrong when you consciously do something to cause unhappiness and harm to others for selfish ends. So for Onkwehonwe, as for Buddhists, the central question of ethics doesn't involve simply proving something was done and labelling the doer evil or wrong because of his role in conducting an act that has been objectively defined as such. Instead, the crucial process is contextualizing the whole experience and trying to figure out why the act was done and what made the person do it, so as to determine whether the act was evil or not.

For our contentious actions to be properly considered, they must be put into context, and the motivation of the vision driving the act needs to be understood. It is true that in situations of extreme contention there is a deep disregard by some people of the basic human impulse towards care and affection for others—this is the colonialists' position en masse. But the fact that Settler society is "evil" in the sense that it has inherited not rights but wrongs from its forefathers, does not mean that we can justify any action taken against the evil based on an eye-for-an-eye ethic. We want and desire peaceful coexistence, and we must advance our cause against the evil of colonialism accordingly.

The real question facing Onkwehonwe is how to counter the evil of imperialism ethically. Raw anger against the Settler society is potentially a good thing because it is a force capable of driving us to action—altruistic action. Yet anger must be investigated to discover its roots and to discern its appropriate focus. It should not be denied—either suppressed out of fear or for a show of stereotypical stoicism—but it must be restrained and channelled through a deliberate and voluntary discipline. This is "patient forbearance" in Buddhist teachings. In terms of our discussion here, it may be that the most suitable term is *non-violent militancy*, meaning remaining firm in the face of fear, doing what is necessary for what is right, yet not allowing negative thoughts and emotions to control us.

For sure, this is different from do-nothing passivity and the total loss of confidence that is cowardice. The middle path between raging violence and complacency is akin to the Gandhian strategy of non-cooperation.[18]

The Indian mass movement against British colonization was not passive, but militantly pacifist, and it actively confronted power in a strategic, creative, and tactically diverse manner without using violence. It was built on the spiritual strengthening of the people; the development of personal and community capacity for self-sufficiency; non-cooperation with the institutions of domination; and the disruption of oppressive systems by using strategies of militant non-violence, such as civil disobedience, boycotts, strikes, sit-downs and sit-ins of all kinds, protest marches, and rallies. There are, of course, differences between the situation in imperially occupied India and the situations of our peoples, but for cultural, political, and strategic reasons the basic Gandhian approach is a solid conceptual foundation for Onkwehonwe resurgences.

The beauty and strength of this approach to confronting imperialism is that it goes straight to the core of state power in its assault on injustice. The basic structure of the state as a system of power is tripartite: it has power, or force, in a physical or military sense; it has authority, or laws, which it uses to regulate and discipline people to its power; and it has legitimacy, which it manufactures and manipulates to create and maintain support. These facets of power create a reality in which the state's capacity for and use of force is unquestioned. The state cannot be defeated militarily because it has too much physical force at its disposal. To this kind of power we must defer. But the authority of the state is something we *can* contest. The legal and bureaucratic structures that manage the state's power are vulnerable because they rely on people's cooperation in order to function. This kind of power we must defy. And state legitimacy is the most imperceptible yet crucial form of power. It relies on the psychological and social conditioning of people to create an acceptance of the state and the forms of power it normalizes: imperatives to obey the state's offices and authorities and to fear the state's ability to enforce its rules with violent repression of serious dissent and disobedience. The first and most important objective of movements against state power must be to deny the state's legitimacy in theoretical and concrete ways. In the long term, legitimacy is the most important form of power the state possesses. Regimes cannot survive without the legitimation by subjects of their authority and consequent acceptance of their right to use force to maintain the social, political, and economic order represented by the institutions that make up the state.

In colonial relationships, impositions of power and authority can probably be absorbed, tolerated, or accommodated by indigenous populations in various ways over time, but true conquest becomes inevitable when the Settlers' imperial claims to legitimacy are accepted and normalized by Onkwehonwe. Legitimation (acceptance and support for colonial institutions) is the fundamental battlefield. Imperialists and colonial governments know this from their long history of scourge and defilement of non-white countries. This is why, for the colonizers, the most important and immediate imperative is to assimilate indigenous peoples culturally: without an indigenous cultural foundation or root there is no memory store or intellectual base upon which to build a challenge to the empire.

It is the capacity of action premised on indigenous authenticity that is most important and immediately imperative for anti-imperial struggle. Culture exists in communities and in the lives of people; culture is the foundation of indigenous resurgences—contrary to the institutional-organizational approach to confronting state power, which structures resistance in forms of counter-imperial organizations that mimic the state in order to confront it on its own terms.

The Gandhian movement was not formed on organizations at all. It was centred on inspired leadership-by-example, by leaders convincing people to stand up and take action and to coordinate their various and autonomous demonstrations of courage. This is the same leadership model which is the foundation of Onkwehonwe political systems.

So far in this line of thinking, we have the beginnings of a conceptual vocabulary for our movement: the tactics of militant non-violence and anti-institutional strategies are key. Add to these the politics of contention. This brings us to the question of forms of contentious action against the state. What is action? Is it a demonstration of courage to throw out strong words and to oppose the state verbally? Antonio Gramsci coined the term, "contradictory consciousness," for a situation in which the oppressed both reject and accept their subjugation at the same time.[19] This is most definitely a character of aboriginalist mentality and rhetoric; piercing this crippling hypocrisy is the first step to our reawakening as peoples. Words can, in fact, be powerful shocks to the system and are capable of causing people to rethink their identity and their place within colonialism. But if they are to be powerful enough to cause crises in the contradictory consciousness of the colonized individual, the words must be dangerous and must push people outside the bounds of their comfort zone and beyond acceptability. The test of whether one's words are contentious in this sense is this question: How much guts does it take to say what you are thinking and to be who you are?

What separates the warrior from the cooperator is this dangerous engagement with power. Passivity shifts resistance to the less dangerous spheres that the dominant power has designated/created as areas for negotiation or reform—after all, it does not take any courage to *negotiate*, to *advocate*, or to *reform*. Rhetorical power is dangerously contentious when it seeks to provoke a response outside of the accepted, normalized, and sanctioned patterns of interaction that form the colonial status quo. And to be truly dangerous, words and ideas must be convincing in their logic and so grounded in social, cultural, and political reality that there is imminent possibility of their affecting and shaping the actions of people. Overblown rhetoric and fantastic pronouncements that resonate with no one and have no possibility of forming the basis of action are not warrior words at all. They are only small acts of blustery cowardice, rhetorical withdrawals from dangerous realities that are just as condemnable as bodily withdrawals in the face of physical danger.

Some people, no doubt, would consider Gandhi's pacifism as a lesser form of contention than struggles founded on revolutionary materialist theories. Compared to the spirited agitation on Gandhian principles Ward Churchill's "libratory praxis," for example, may seem radical and extremely courageous. He rejects non-violence (specifically, the unwillingness to kill) as an "illness" and argues for the necessity of a violent socialist revolution to supplant the capitalist state. He focuses his approach on efforts to deprogram people's aversions to the tools of violence; therapeutic discussions, spending time with oppressed people as "reality therapy," and hands-on sessions to demystify weaponry are some of the tactical suggestions offered.[20] There are very few, if any, Onkwehonwe (and others) who would even consider adopting his approach and program, so that his ideas appear ludicrous, not dangerous. No one is seriously considering these ideas as a platform for a real movement; they are therefore rendered safe. So Gandhi's more moderate sounding but more attractive and viable ideas can be seen for what they are in comparison: truly dangerous and really revolutionary.

The fact that there are people like Ward Churchill who do fantasize about carrying out acts of violent revolution—and I will admit from personal experience and from many conversations that this fantasy is widespread among Onkwehonwe and harboured by many frustrated warriors—highlights that anger is a very strong force in contemporary Onkwehonwe societies. We must understand that raging violence is always more of a reaction to the internal and external hypocrisy of colonial relations than to injustices in economic or political forms.[21] But for Onkwehonwe resurgences, this path of raging anger is overly emotional, and it replicates the exact wrong that we are trying to confront. Yet it continues to energize young males especially; they are the frustrated warriors acting out against state oppression and not channelling it internally.[22] This is a useless waste of energy. The revolutionary guerrilla model of change is clearly a gendered concept rooted in machismo and valorizations of violence—the common and unexamined male approach to the universal need to prove a strength which comes to women naturally through their capacity to bear pain and especially to endure childbirth (which explains why there is such a mocking distaste for this approach among females).

The joke on the guerrilla mentality is even crueller today than at times when empires were in fact vulnerable to attacks in a physical sense. Oppression has become increasingly invisible; no longer constituted in conventional terms of military occupation, onerous taxation burdens, blatant land thefts, etc. In this post-modern imperial context, rather than engaging in futile (albeit glorious!) military confrontation with the armies of the empire, latter-day armed guerrillas find themselves punching at air, thus compounding the frustration factor. The forces that oppress us today are beyond elusive. The power of empire is not in machines, bayonets, barbed wire, or even soldiers. Its effects have become ever more present and damaging to be sure, but as a military or protest action target, it is almost invisible. Doubly frustrated warriors soon come to realize what the social theorist C. Wright Mills observed in the 1950s, the "movement from authority to manipulation":

No longer can the problem of power be set forth as the simple one of changing the processes of coercion into those of consent. The engineering of consent to authority has moved into the realm of manipulation where the powerful are anonymous. Impersonal manipulation is more insidious than coercion precisely because it is hidden; one cannot locate the enemy and declare war upon him. Targets for aggression are unavailable, and certainty is taken from men.[23]

If this is so, whom do we attack? What building do we capture? At whom do we direct our hatred when the empire is dispersed and more of an infusion that flavours our lives than an obstacle to be overcome? It seems impossible, facing a post-modern imperialist state, to isolate a discrete target for direct resistance actions, so we must continue our struggle by engaging its corrupting power *at all times* and *in all ways*, as perpetual warriors. The only way to do this is in creative contention.

Violence, or at least the guerrilla posture, does remain attractive for emotional and cultural reasons. To prevent people from being drawn to useless strategies of resistance, the Onkwehonwe movement requires discipline. By discipline I mean the development of a resurgent power and culture of resistance that channels our angry and potentially deadly and self-destructive energies into a positive force for change. This strength lies in Onkwehonwe communities and people being decultured and disabused of the colonial mentalities and various colonial myths and recultured to support the resurgence of action against state manipulations of their identity. Strong people and strong, united communities can provide the support and validation for serious actions; we need authentic ideas and intellectual tools drawn from the heritage of Onkwehonwe peoples, physical infrastructure, and reinforcement of community cohesion in communications and media and education. It is a major problem that we are, for the most part, lacking these sources of strength in ourselves and in our Onkwehonwe communities. Outside of the Zapatista army and other indigenous Mexican people currently supporting rebellions of indigenous truth against capitalism,[24] there is no cultural base for mass action, nor is there a crucial mass of strong people to support actions and strategy that have any hope of challenging state power in any form. This must change if we are to survive.

Lacking a resurgent warrior culture, we need to consider the ways in which, outside of futile raging against the symbols of state power, we can effectively act against state power in psychological terms to generate the required strength.

Psychologically, we can cope with battle stress and take action against it in two basic ways: through direct action we can alter the relationships between ourselves and the sources of our stress; and through "palliation," a technical term meaning that there is no change in our relationship with the sources of our stress, we can do things to make us feel better.[25] The choices fall on the continuum between change and palliation. Yet the myriad palliation tactics and processes evident in our communities and politics today are losing their ability to make us feel better about our colonial oppression. This is the psychology of deep denial, using religiosity and chemical aids— drugs, alcohol, sugar, tobacco, and processed junk food—to distance and medicate the pain. There is no fundamental difference between the subversion of pain inherent in alcoholism and the psychological denial of the obvious corruption inherent in the politics of assimilation. If we are concerned about addressing our relationships with the sources of our stress, and not only with medicating the pains caused by that stress, direct action is the only solution.

The target of direct action must be the most immediate danger and cause of our collective stress: the racism that is still rampant in Settler society. Violent, degrading, and belittling white attitudes and behaviours are systemically woven into the fabric of Settler culture. This racism manifests itself in every facet of colonial society. There are intellectually false premises that form the bases for beliefs about national identities. There are denials of truth that are the foundations of colonial politics. There are legal fictions masquerading as justice. And there are economic deprivations rationalized to form capitalist economic theories and policies.

Yet it is the bold and unchallenged white arrogance and racial prejudice against indigenous peoples that is the first and most important target of action. The personal and mundane maintenance of colonialism and colonial power relations through words and behaviours on a one-to-one level, conversationally and socially, must be stopped. Psychological research has conclusively proven that the racism of white society manifest in its most basic form, hostility and aggression, more than anything else assaults the sense of self-control and affects the health and well-being of people who are discriminated against.[26] The constant hostility of white people and lack of acceptance on a societal level has been proven in studies of African-Americans in the United States to have a direct effect on the rates of high blood pressure in that population, for example. So racism is expressed on all levels in many forms as a personal relationship, and it is embedded systemically in colonial relations. This must be acted against if our people are to survive and restrengthen. This is the orienting first goal of the Onkwehonwe struggle for freedom.

There is a real question here on how we would inoculate people from fear to allow them to act with courage against this root cause of Onkwehonwe stress, suffering, and premature death. I believe it must be a primary belief in all of our leaders and peoples' minds that the racism of white society *can* be overcome; our people must be reoriented culturally and politically so that their conscious and subconscious minds learn that stress and hate can be defeated and that they have a responsibility to act against racism. In doing so, they will be truly living the ethic of courage as warriors for the next generations.

REGARDLESS OF THE CONSEQUENCES

We turn now to the strategic and tactical questions of how to carry the fight to the adversary, by taking a long view on the struggles of people who have sought to free themselves from colonial oppression. All successful anti-colonial wars have been based on the existence of three factors favouring the indigenous people. First, the conditions must be ripe, meaning that domination was a present and onerous fact and that there was a focused colonial assault on the national and social aspects of the indigenous people's existence. Second, anti-colonial forces were organized to endure over the long term and to grow. And, third, the anti-colonial forces had disciplined organizations that were connected to other resisting organizations. The defeat of colonialism has always been essentially political and caused by a few key factors being made into realities by the indigenous people: the continuing organizational strength of the indigenous people as distinct from any battlefield or other tactical successes or failures; the growth and maintenance of the support of the people; the imposition of what eventually becomes unbearable costs on the colonial government and economic systems; internal divisions in Settler society; spiritual and financial weariness among the Settlers over time; and attacks on the position and power of co-opted comprador politicians who work with the colonial regime to ensure, or to participate directly in, their own people's oppression.[27]

It cannot be denied that these factors apply in the description of Onkwehonwe situations. But it is rare, due to widespread intellectual and moral cowardice among aboriginal elites and supposedly progressive

Settlers, to apply the remedy that is so obviously applicable as well to the situation of Onkwehonwe.

But there may be cause for caution in following the anti-colonial line all the way to its logical conclusion. The pattern of revolutionary struggles has historically been one of a cycle of futility. As peoples have sought the long-term objective of achieving their freedom, their movements have been paired with the rhetoric and politics of anti-imperialism. This has led to the development of nationalism, an ideology of anti-colonialism geared toward regaining control of resources and imposing socially and culturally conservative cultures as a counter to colonial corruptions. In fact, this has been the experience of the limited resurgences undertaken by Onkwehonwe thus far, except for the notable exception of the Zapatista movement in Mexico. Even in the context of the small-scale localized struggles of the past generation on Turtle Island, *Anówara Kawennote*, consider how the radical potential has been co-opted by the inherent conservatism of nationalist ideologies and agendas. Out of the Oka Crisis and the military stand-off in 1990 between the Kanien'kehaka and the governments of Québec and Canada came the entrenchment and growth of the co-optive band councils in the Kanien'kehaka communities that had fought to protect their lands from further encroachment by Settlers. Out of the Burnt Church resistance in the mid-1990s to defend inherent and treaty rights to fish came the co-optive fishing agreements recognizing colonial authority signed by all of the Mi'kmaq band council governments. Our experience thus far demonstrates that "revolutionary" conditions as described above do exist in our communities, but that we completely lack the structural capacity to carry our movement beyond actions that leverage political advantage to comprador politicians operating within colonial systems. There is no indigenous organizational capacity for taking advantage of the oppressive conditions that do exist and for channelling Onkwehonwe stresses into an effective action strategy against the colonial system itself. Action in our current frame leads, ironically, to further entrenchment of the colonial system. As the state represses radical direct action by funding conservative, legal negotiation accommodations, nations and the movement are divided, thus ensuring the continuing role of colonial law, which is supported by the ideology of "Aboriginal" nationalism constructed within the frame of colonialism. Such a nationalism is actually a cover for accommodation and surrender.

The most difficult question facing us is: How do we break from the cycle of assertion/co-optation and become a credible threat to the colonial state? How do we end passivity and natural human inertia and get people to activate and engage in organization and direct action in the social, cultural, and political spheres of society? In this, it is important to grasp the insight, pointed out by the political scientist Sidney Tarrow, that the causes of any political action are not the *conditions* endured by people, who can always find ways to live with much deprivation, but the *opportunities* to and limits placed on their collective action. This is even more so when the people believe that doing nothing is even more dangerous than taking action. So, in getting Onkwehonwe to become involved and take on the challenges and sacrifices needed to build a movement for change, on a collective basis, three important things must be realized in concrete ways, as Tarrow discovered in his own research:[28]

+ *self-sufficiency*: people must have access to the resources that will allow them to defy the state and the control of colonial institutions;
+ *reorganization*: new channels for people's energy must be created for them to take part in contentious action against state structures and colonial power; and,
+ *reculturation*: people and communities must come to understand that cooperating with colonial authorities is wrong and must be acted against.

All of these are at the same time material and spiritual processes, as much internal and psychological as external and strategic. Getting people moving, and moving together in the same direction, starts with waking them up or shaking them up. Awakening the people is both a spiritual movement and a political mobilization. Individual and collective militancy is generated and deepened when people are exposed to experiences by leaders who seek to provoke a heightened sense of reality through collective action. The leadership's acts of resistance are designed and conducted to inspire and set an example, and to directly challenge the world-view and mentalities of the colonized peoples. Resurgence also involves changing social conditions so that even within unaltered mind frames, new rationales for action emerge. The combination of both of these has proven to be an explosive approach, especially in the Miskito Nation's self-defence against the Nicaraguan state in the 1980s and 1990s.[29] This model of cultural regeneration and political resurgence to create change depends, in strategic terms, on the presence of certain institutional resources or political opportunities. Thus, it is the task of people seeking to bring about change in their communities and nations to recognize the existence of, or to create, these conditions, in order to have any chance of generating a mobilization of people to act against their previously unquestioned oppression.

These are the conditions that must be met:

1. the movement must have access to institutional power, such as government organizations and the media;
2. there must be political and social divisions among the Settler elite, in terms of either political parties, economic classes, or ideologies;
3. the movement must have the support and cooperation of allies in the Settler society;
4. the state's ability or capacity for repression must be in decline, in either physical terms or due to legal constraints or the political or social context; and,
5. the movement must be capable of advancing its claims and delegitimizing the state in the mass media.[30]

Once awakened and organized potentially, the inevitable question in this politics of contention is that of the eventual conflict. When and how does one fight the forces of state power? In the long run, radical education and transformation of the fundamental beliefs and attitudes of the Settler society is the objective. Adolfo Pérez Esquival, the Argentinean Nobel Peace Prize laureate, cut to the core of what resurgence against imperialism is about when he said that a movement must achieve "an organized set of ruptures in the civil order so as to disturb the system responsible for the injustices we see around us...."[31] This can only be achieved through the steady challenging of the intellectual and cultural foundations of Settler society in the media, schools, popular culture, and the arts. But to move people from one level of understanding to another requires the stimulus of direct action in the political, economic, and social spheres to generate both the attention and reflection needed to force a furtherance of self-awareness and critical thinking in the colonial society. Education is both words and action. Thus, consideration must be given to the political and strategic environment to gauge the appropriate type and level of intensity of direct actions that should be taken to supplement the ongoing "soft" educational process to force a breakthrough to a new, heightened level of awareness and understanding. Leadership and foresight are imperative to success in this process. It is crucial to employ a direct action strategy and a set of tactics that are appropriate to the political landscape and strategic terrain. The "terrain," in this case, is more than a geographic location, it is the historical, situational, and psychological reality of the people and of the adversary. And the terrain we inhabit as Onkwehonwe surging against 500 years of colonization is one that is ideal in strategic terms for engaging with the adversary to test, learn about, and discern the true limits of Settler power. It is also good ground to start strengthening alliances in anticipation of a coming intensity of struggle.[32] But the primary goal, given the basic lay of the land (our peoples being disorganized for struggle and divided amongst ourselves) is for a strategy of direct action with the intent of unifying Onkwehonwe and demonstrating the necessity of further solidarity. This is the positive lesson to be drawn from the incidents of assertion that took place in the Oka Stand-off and at Burnt Church: action brings Onkwehonwe together and teaches us the true nature of colonial power.

This crisis solidarity can be transformed into momentum for a resurgence if the cycle of co-optation is broken and if the positive energy that flows from people working together in resistance against injustice is channelled by leaders and organizations toward positive ends as opposed to being leveraged as bargaining power in existing colonial processes to accommodate the Settlers' power. Just imagine how different things would be in Canada today if band councils had seized the opportunity to make meaningful change during the most recent era of confrontation that culminated with the Oka Crisis in 1990. They could have focused on spreading the wave of assertion and linked the reserve-based communities' capacity to resist land incursions with the disruptive potential of urban Onkwehonwe. Or they could have started promoting education as a way to reduce people's dependency on the colonial infrastructure and white-owned businesses. They had the option of turning away from the bureaucratic models of community government imposed through land claims and self-government processes and could have reinvigorated indigenous governments. If instead of flying in airplanes to collect cheques and sit at meeting tables with white lawyers, they had instead stayed home and walked on their lands with their people, learning and working with them to create healthier communities, might our people be better off now? These kinds of things are all it would take for a resurgence to happen and for that movement to transform the country.

Not only are there enormous challenges to building this kind of resurgent Onkwehonwe movement, but there is a strong likelihood of setbacks or outright failure. The natural inertia of people and the active opposition of organizations and persons serving the colonial authorities, both within and outside of our communities, virtually ensure that the first phase of contention will be in the construction of a movement, not in that movement's conflict with the state. A realistic and responsible leader seeks to understand not only the reasons for such movement failure, which is, again, a probable outcome and the likely immediate result of engagement with state forces, but also the failure of people seeking change to heed the laws of contention as learned from generations of anti-imperial struggle in other times and places. Think of the ways our less radical movements have failed and led to the entrenchment of colonialism in our lives, such as the virtual internal exile of band council elites in First Nations communities. Other movements, such as the attempt by band and tribal leaders to create representative bodies to advocate for their interests in the federal government system (the National Indian Brotherhood, later renamed the Assembly of First Nations, in Canada and the National Congress of American Indians in the United States), have been cut off from people or made irrelevant by accommodation and cooperation with government. Think also of the aboriginals, the incidentally indigenous, scholars, and government-appointed mediators who do not even know the people they are paid to speak for. Consider also the traditional tribalists who constantly fail to see beyond their own local, tribal, or family interests to realize a more general Onkwehonwe identity and who ignore the connection of their struggles against the state with others'. Think also of the sparsely populated pocket movements, organized around one individual or one strictly local concern, who fail to attract enough people into their organizations to make them viable. Think of these things, relate them to your own community experience, and you have a theory of failure.

It is not only our own doing that makes failure such an imminent threat to a movement for Onkwehonwe freedom, but there are also serious factors of intransigence related to being a minority population, surrounded by a majority society. In a basic sense, our existence depends on the majority's tacit acceptance; the government enjoys the support or at least the neutrality of the majority, and there is a natural illegitimacy to our cause in the eyes of the unenlightened mainstream of Settler society. These are the huge hurdles facing anyone who seeks to engage the state in a confrontation to liberate us from imperialism. To truly understand this, we need to depart from analysis and theorizing to engage with direct experience in standing up to the power of government authority in order to reflect on the realities of resistance and resurgence.

Sakej is a Mi'kmaq warrior who has led direct actions to defend his territory and the rights of his people. He is both trained in military methods and university-educated, and is experienced in both cultural politics and political contention. He is pure physical presence, thoughtful and committed to the ethic of courage and the defeat of imperialism through direct action and physical resistance to state authorities that unjustly control Onkwehonwe lands and lives. Sakej's objective is to build a militarized movement of Onkwehonwe youth to promote revolutionary action and to advance intellectually and politically a radical concept of Onkwehonwe nationhood. He is a powerful speaker, a charismatic personality, especially for alienated and angry Onkwehonwe, and he is a compelling figure who represents the most radical pathway to indigenous freedom.[33]

As the head of the East Coast Warrior Society and an influential figure in direct actions across the northern part of Anówara, his vision should be taken seriously by anyone hoping to understand the spirit and calculus of this path, which is increasingly attractive for Onkwehonwe youth. In conversation with Sakej, I focused on his role as one of the main strategists and organizers behind the post-Oka Warrior Society movements in the east and west coast fishing disputes between Onkwehonwe nations and the government of Canada.[34] I wanted to get a clear sense of what motivated Sakej, a father and grandfather from the well-established Mi'kmaq community of Burnt Church, New Brunswick, to take up the life of a warrior. I wanted to know why, and then how, someone could live as a revolutionary within the centre of imperial power and move about with a guerrilla mentality in the midst of the Settler society he was intent on confronting and defeating.

TA: *Sakej, how do we become the kind of people you envision us to be?*
S: We are a warrior race. A lot of our people fail to realize that and think of themselves as colonized subjects of Canada; we do not acknowledge that part of our past. We try to bring back roles and responsibilities, but we always fail to bring back the traditional role that encompasses half of our people: the male population.

TA: *Why do you think that is?*
S: It's definitely because of the colonized attitude to begin with. But on top of that, we seem to have adopted, within this colonization, two big influences that have led to the pacification of our mentality. The first is Christianity. As long as we have the pacification from within the Christian religion, we always have this mentality of "turn the other cheek," "forgive and forget," that "in the end there will be a reward for us somewhere in the white man's heaven." Then, I really think that the 1960s and 70s, with all that social upheaval, created what I always refer to as a "hippy influence…"

(Laughter.) There is a certain hippy influence that is extremely passive. As long as we have our own people, even the traditionalists, coming out with this hippy influence and telling our young people to not be warriors, in the sense of taking up action against the state, then they're feeding into the colonization themselves. They're perpetuating the colonization upon us— they are doing the job of the colonizer.

TA: *But Gandhi believed in nonviolence and he was pretty effective in breaking the hold of that colonial mentality in India...*
S: In his time, Gandhi could use civil disobedience for the sake of nationalism in a place where Natives made up the majority of the population. They were 99 per cent of the population. So when you do something like civil disobedience—when you martyr yourself and victimize yourself—that action appeals to 99 per cent of the population of that country. You can cause social mobilization on civil disobedience when your target audience makes up the vast majority of the population.

TA: *You mean by "target audience" those people who are sympathetic and tied to you through kinship and shared identity or ethnicity?*
S: Ethnic identity, struggle identity, whatever it may be. As long as they see you as one of them being persecuted for the exact same ideas that you have, you could create social movement on that model. However, in a political environment where we make up maybe 3 per cent of the population, we can't use that model, because as indigenous people in North America, we have, potentially, only 3 per cent of the people who will identify with our struggle. We'd be lucky to get even a tiny fraction of that population to identify with what's going on. So for us, civil disobedience cannot create the effect of social mobilization as you saw with Gandhi. It just could not happen here.

There's something else too, it's what I call "sympathy with consequence." The problem is this: if you're asking a colonizer who lives right here on your land to completely sympathize with your cause, you're going to ask him to go through the period of decolonization and to admit that his ownership of his private property is wrong; that his job is based on exploitation of your resources and is wrong; that his whole social, political, and economic structure is wrong. How many non-native people in Canada are going to turn around and sympathize to that degree? So, civil disobedience will go nowhere in Canada because our population is too small and because of the non-native population's inability to sympathize with our cause.

TA: *How does that analysis apply to the African-American situation with the civil rights movement in the United States? They were a minority population too, and they succeeded in achieving their aims.*
S: They were able to appeal to a common ground with the whites. They used Christian rhetoric, and a white person at that time could have a religious identification with the black struggle. Plus, in that movement, they were fighting for civil rights. That's not a very large goal in terms of a movement— they were just looking for reform, not revolution. When you start talking about self-determination and nationhood, you start to create a bigger gap between you and the colonizer. You're calling that entire colonizing country into question.[35]

TA: *Are there any other movements with whom we have something in common in terms of our struggle, or goals, and the revolutionary spirit?*
S: Absolutely: with Subcommandante Marcos and the Zapatista revolutionaries in Mexico. What we are seeing there is the emergence of a brand new model for revolution. Revolution up to this point, at least since the 1800s, has been a conflict between communism and capitalism. Revolution was based on putting communist governments in place. It was revolution against Western *capitalism*, but it wasn't revolution against Western *colonialism*, even though the rhetoric was against imperialism as the force behind capitalism. But it wasn't the means to try to get the Westerners out of power, it was just a particular style of governance that they wanted to get rid of. With the fall of communism in 1990-91, and with the Zapatista rebellion in 1994, we're seeing an indigenous revolution that does not seek to empower a communist state—not some Marxist or Maoist type, or even along the lines of Che Guevara. It's not trying to put a political party into power; they are creating political space so that people can determine their own type of governing structures.

Inherently, they already have what they are seeking; it's just a matter of empowering it. They have liberated zones that are within Zapatista control, and they are creating the emergence of an indigenous government within those areas. They are practising indigenous revolution, but they are not going for the one big ultimate goal of nationhood—they are not saying that those liberated zones are sovereign. They say that the liberated zones are autonomous. I do think that they have the chance now to start pursuing that bigger goal. They are far ahead of us, because the only way you're going to get sovereignty is to fight for it, and they have. No nation-state has ever given up part of its own sovereign power willingly.

TA: *But outside of Cuba and cases like Vietnam, where the struggle became a conventional or proxy war between bigger powers, no guerrilla movement has ever been successful in the attempt to defeat a state militarily.*

S: They already have it half beat. The hardest part is militarily to liberate areas of territory. They have already got that done! Granted, they are still surrounded by Mexican troops, and what they have is a sort of contested sovereignty. Still, I think they are far ahead of other guerrilla movements that have fought against states.

TA: *Is it these kinds of autonomous, liberated indigenous governance zones that you're looking to achieve?*

S: I do see that as a goal. What I don't see is it happening in my lifetime. I recognize the fact that this is going to be a very long struggle. What myself and the people I work with are hoping for is that we can be catalysts to kick things off and get things started. If we don't, the rate of assimilation is so great that we won't have any thinkers or people willing to put themselves on the line any more. We're all getting so canadianized that we can't even stop to think about taking some kind of action against the colonial state. We've been so assimilated into that state that we can only look for redress within the parameters already established by that state. I don't know if it's going to be this generation or the next, but I don't believe there is a lot of time left for those who are thinking in terms of revolution and resistance and creating the liberated zones for indigenous people to survive in.

TA: *Do you see any prospect for decolonizing the Settlers' mentality?*

S: If you play by the colonizer's rules, how are you going to win the game? I see decolonizing intellectual effort as positive so long as it can accept the fact that we will need at some point to move past political resistance into military resistance. That is what it all comes down to in the end, if you're serious about it.

TA: *What about people who say that other non-violent avenues—like political, social, cultural, or legal and economic means of struggle—haven't so much failed, but that they are in the process of succeeding and that you are too impatient?*

S: To that I would say that they should look at the youth in our communities, which have the highest suicide rate in the world. I consider those youth to be casualties of war. A lot of people say, "If you take up arms and take action, people are going to get killed!" Well, they're dying every day right now, and when are we going to put a stop to it? The erosion of our rights and who we are is getting worse, and the problem of the highest suicide rates in the world is going to get worse too. Right now, in our politics, we're helping to improve colonial control over us, and it's proving to be extremely detrimental to our people.

TA: *Dying in an armed confrontation with the state is preferable to suicide?*
S: I'd rather live my life as a warrior, even though it means I'm going to be frustrated with fight after fight and defeat after defeat and have to make all kinds of sacrifices, than to live my entire life as some kind of economic slave to a colonial empire knowing that all I have is welfare from cradle to grave. That is not living.

TA: *Is your own life important to you?*
S: It is. But, the next seven generations are far more important. We have to start taking on a sense of urgency, and we have to come to realize that we have one lifetime to change 500 years of colonialism. If we don't want our next generation to experience these same or worse high rates of suicide, high incarceration rates, drug and alcohol dependency... something drastic has to be done.

TA: *I understand this motivation, Brother. But what about having a real effect, making change, decolonizing? What's your strategy?*
S: We have to look at a wide spectrum, and in that, it's extremely important to think in terms of physical resistance. We need to create a cohesive strategy of political, social, economic, and legal resistance. But, from my point of view, physical resistance has to be at the forefront.

TA: *Why?*
S: The colonial state will jealously guard its own sovereignty and economic interests with the use of force. This puts us in a situation where it's almost like a game of chess. We're in check right now. The question is: Are we going to do something about it? Are we going to be willing to face force with force? If, after pursuing all other avenues for change, they resort to the use of force to maintain their power, are we going to just give up right there? It's like we've been checked, and are we going to say, "Okay, you guys win"? Or are we going to fight back and start playing tough and try to get them in checkmate.

TA: *How are you preparing yourself for confrontation?*

S: We are rebuilding and re-empowering warrior societies. We know what the threat is, and based on that knowledge, it's clear that we have to redevelop warrior societies—build them, recruit, train, organize—so that they can be capable of conducting physical resistance against the colonizing state. That's the process we're in now.

TA: *The kind of "empowerment" you're talking about is, well... illegal. Does this cause you difficulties in your life?*
S: Sure it does. Almost everything we do is on the run. What happens is that our activities become like shadow activity—almost like a guerrilla movement. The Canadian state sees us as a threat and rightly so: we contest their sovereignty and dominion. Think about it: Is organized crime really a threat to national security? It's a threat to the social environment, for sure, but not national security. Whereas we have far less resources than the Hell's Angels, for example, but we're even more of a threat. It's not our resources that make us powerful—we don't have any—it's the cause that we're fighting for. We're talking about immorality and injustices at the very foundation of the Canadian state's legitimacy, and we can bring these truths out in the open. That's more threatening to the Canadian government than the Hell's Angels ever will be.

TA: *When you use the word "fighting," what exactly do you mean?*
S: An actual physical fight. At Burnt Church, we were in the middle of a firefight with non-native fishermen. They came into our area with the intent of cutting our traps. There were 55 of their large 50-foot boats, and we responded with seven dories—little home-made wooden boats. They immediately shot at us when we got within 100 metres of their flotilla. There were eight shots taken at the boat I was on, and the other boats were being shot at also. So we said to ourselves, "Our people are in danger here, we're being shot at, and this is going to change." So there was returned fire, and about an hour of fire exchanged back and forth—the RCMP emergency response team just sat around and watched the whole thing. Before the night was over, one of their boats had chased one of our little boats, and their boat grounded on shore. The occupants were removed from that boat, and, somehow, it ended up in flames. That type of consequence was exactly what was needed at that time.

TA: *I like how you said that, "somehow, it ended up in flames..." (Laughter.)*

S: I don't know how it happened! And they were drunk too, so who knows what was happening on that boat. (Laughter.) So anyway, there was a consequence to their actions because of our physical resistance. The demonstration of our ability to defend our traps, our people, and our rights was a real victory.

TA: *So it seems obvious from that example that there's a direct connection between taking action and the preservation of your rights, something that's just not there in conventional forms of protest?*
S: You know, there was a plea from some of our people that we should just pursue the politics of pity and try to get Canadian society to somehow identify with our issues so much so that they would put a stop to their government's actions against us. Obviously, it didn't work. In fact, the reason we made such a huge stand against the non-native fishermen was because on every Sunday, right after Mass, they'd come in to try to destroy our traps. There would be no consequence for them. The idea of appealing to their morality just did not work. We tried civil disobedience and protest and arguing with them, but that didn't work. They did not stop until the day there was a consequence imposed on their actions, the day we shot back, and the day their boat ended up in flames. From that day on, there were never any non-native boats trying to come in and cut our traps again.

TA: *Do you see any limitations that may constrain your strategy? I'm thinking that it's one thing to take on some fishermen, and a whole other game to confront the force of the Canadian military.*
S: Yeah, it's easy to take on a small, untrained, and not very well-equipped force. And it's easy to create fear amongst them too. Taking on police forces and the Canadian military is a much harder task.

TA: *Are you addressing this problem?*
S: Obviously we're not going to have 60,000 warriors ready to go any time soon. I'm recruiting, but I just don't see it happening in the near future! So, we're looking at quality, and we're looking at training our guys to be better than the average Canadian soldier coming out of boot camp. We can never let ourselves become psychologically defeated, no matter how small our numbers are. It's all a question of strategy and the best way to fight.

TA: *So, it's your belief that indigenous people can train and equip a fighting force to physically confront the state as a means of advancing our cause, which is forcing the colonials to recognize our nationhood and to respect our rights?*
S: Yes it is. And to dispel the fear-mongering and the delusion that we can't take on the military, all you have to do is conduct a simple analysis of the Canadian Forces as an actual fighting force. Right now, there are 57,000 soldiers in the Canadian military, of which there are 24,000 in the army, and only 4,500 of those are infantry soldiers. At any one time, many of those infantry soldiers, roughly one-third, are deployed overseas. Another one-third is always on the rest-refit-recovery cycle. That leaves only 1,500 soldiers, a brigade size element...

TA: *That's what the Canadians used against the Mohawk Nation in 1990.*
S: That's right. Now, think about it, if we had multiple "Okas" happening simultaneously, how are they going to handle that? That would be military overstretch. They couldn't handle it.

TA: *What's your sense of the potential for building an effective resistance movement that draws in large enough numbers of people not only to stand up to, but in the longer term take advantage of liberated spaces to transform our relationship to society as a whole, socially, politically, and culturally?*
S: I definitely see some potential in this new generation. They've seen that all the cooperative avenues have been tried and that's it's led us nowhere. They're all starting to realize that we have a connection to each other and that we have obligations to each other and to our ancestors. You see among them an unconscious rejection of the colonial reality. I have a lot of faith in the youth. The question is how do we direct and shape all of that to create the force we need to stand as a deterrent to the colonial enterprise. I don't see us having a strong enough military power to *conquer* Canada, but I do see us having the strength to create a condition of *deterrence* where colonial domination becomes very difficult for Canada to continue. This will create the physical and political space for us to pursue our own definition of our rights and our ways of life.

TA: *So what is it going to take to organize the youth into this kind of movement?*
S: It's just a matter of time. It's happening as we speak. We're going through a process right now of growing political awareness, of social and political organization, of making people realize that they have obligations and duties as warriors. Our ancestors are just waiting to see us retake these roles and

revitalize these obligations. The youth understand that completely. They want to take their place of honour beside their ancestors.

Sakej is the most serious person I know who is developing and practising the ideal of the warrior in contemporary Onkwehonwe society. But is he Quixotic? It is the question we must all face, because whether we are committed, as Sakej is, to a military struggle or whether we are fighting intellectual battles, the spirit and the challenge of the warrior are the same. Anyone who is provoked by Sakej's words to cast judgements on him or to ascribe to him a death-wish should reflect instead on the words of the great nineteenth-century African-American orator, Frederick Douglass, a militant abolitionist and himself an escaped slave, who wrote in 1850:

> Those who profess to favour freedom, yet deprecate agitation, are men who want crops without ploughing up the ground. They want rain without thunder and lightning. They want the ocean without the awful wrath of its many waters. Power concedes nothing without demands—it never did and it never will. Find out just what any people will quietly submit to, and you have the exact measure of injustice and wrong which will be imposed upon them. And these will continue until they are resisted with either words or blows, or with both. The limits of tyrants are prescribed by the endurance of those whom they oppress.[36]

People like Sakej and the warrior societies of Anówara don't do submission. And a growing number of Onkwehonwe youth are following their lead. Pushing the colonial tyrant to his limits takes both strong words and courageous blows against his coercion. Hence the necessity of a physical capacity for resistance and a practised politics of contention to supplement education and growing enlightenment. The Chinese classic Taoist teaching, I Ching, advances that, "In contention there is sincerity."[37] Trouble doesn't start without reason, contention arises because of a need for change. Contention flows from a manifested unwavering commitment to the truth: sincerity. The Chinese hexagram for "contention" shows both internal desire and outward strength; the etymology of the Chinese hexagram shows how, in Chinese philosophy as in Onkwehonwe teachings, contention is natural and organic to human relations. The wisdom here is deep: the symbol evolved from divinations traced as far back as 1300 BCE, through narrative descriptions, or stories, of observed changes in the natural world; for at least 2,000 years, the hexagrams have been explicit and specific in this teaching. Philosophically, contention can be seen as the dialectical unity of polar energies bringing together opposed forces that need to and must be reconciled if life is to continue. It is not something to be feared or avoided—people seeking balance and harmony *must* embrace the process of contention. The *I Ching* also teaches that contention is related to the concept of impermanence, that struggle is constant and that it is only the form of contention that changes over time. This is an obvious truth, too, in our experience as Onkwehonwe. We can choose to live with colonial conflict inside of ourselves and our families, or we can redirect that negative force through contention toward its source, which is the injustice of the state towards our people.

Contention is always justified when it challenges oppression as an opposition to suffering caused by others' greed and aggression. There is no valid argument for complacency or tolerance of colonial injustice that is not based on moral failure or sheer cowardice. As becomes clear in my discussion with Sakej, the only real question is *how* to fight.

How to fight against colonialism? There is, as one conceivable path, a well-established spectrum of contention that is rooted in the experience of peoples all over the world. *Conflict is contention* taken to its limit; *war is conflict* taken to the extreme—always considered as a last resort and in just cause, but always the end result nonetheless. This idea of struggle, founded on the base power of violence, is in fact a cycle of futility. Feelings of pride rise in the people, who begin to assert themselves, raising voices in protest, causing disruption, eventually acting violently against injustice, causing inevitable counter-violence, spurring warfare, repression, and again, subjugation (whether the subjugated become the powerful matters little as the cycle of violence's continuation is guaranteed). This is repeated perpetually in cycles of conflict between human communities until it is broken by the establishment of a peaceful coexistence that follows the transcendence of the psychological, spiritual, and socio-economic bases of the relationship between the peoples who are in conflict. The transcendence can happen when the critical period of heightened attention caused by a disruption of normality opens a door to new understandings and before it is shut again in the closed-minded and hard oppositional environment that accompanies violence and counter-violence's march to subjugation of one of the parties in the relationship.

Our people knew how to fight, and they knew how to break the cycle of conflict. For our people, real treaty-making, those ensuring peaceful coex-

istence and founded on mutual respect and the shared goals of peace and friendship, occurred in the context of *potential* mutually destructive warfare with
colonial powers. From a position of strength and rooted in philosophies of
peace, they negotiated new relationships and regimes of respect and sharing
when first confronted by the new reality of European peoples in their territories. Contrast these achievements with the false "treaties," surrenders,
and subjugations in law, which happened later and are happening today.
These are possible when defeat is evidenced and admitted by one party—
the Onkwehonwe—in the Onkwehonwe-Settler relationship. Real treaties
ensured peaceful coexistence and created *new* relationships that removed our
people from cycles of violence. Surrenders and subjugations embed *old* relationships and ensure the continuation of cycles of conflict and suffering.

We need to take our direction from the achievements of our Onkwehonwe
ancestors in creating balanced and respectful relationships. In advocating
a strategy of contention, what I am acknowledging is that peace and harmony are only possible if we take the possibility of contention to its limit.
That limit is reached by developing a renewed sense of pride in bold and
serious disruptions of the status quo. Reaching that limit is only possible
if we discipline ourselves to reject the promotion of offensive violence as the
means of advancing our struggle; if we commit to using words, symbols, and
direct non-violent action as the offensive weapons of our fight on a battlefield that is the critical juncture of contention and conflict; if we push disruptive direct action tactics right up to the point that they will become a
means of violent attack on our adversaries. Arms are certainly necessary, only
because we must protect ourselves from violent attack and survive in a physical sense, but we should have faith in the power of our ideas and in our abilities to communicate our ideas without resorting to the mute force of violence
to bring our message to people. We should seek to contend, to inform our agitating direct actions with ideas, and to use the effects of this contention to defeat
colonialism by convincing people of the need to abandon the cycle of subjugation and conflict and join us in a relationship of respect and sharing.

SACRED PROTECTORS

Reconnection to our heritage and the sources of our strength as
Onkwehonwe will not happen just because we need it or wish it to be so.
In laying out an essentially non-violent theory of resistance, I should make

clear again that I am not saying that we should avoid engaging the adversary in battle. Make no mistake: Onkwehonwe will have to fight to recover our dignity, and we will need to sacrifice and struggle to make the connections that are crucial to our survival.

We need to become warriors again. When we think of those people who take on the responsibility to act against threats to the people, we think of the word, "warrior." But, obviously, the way that word is understood is just one of the meanings of the term. It is European in origin and quite a male-gendered and soldierly image in most people's minds; it doesn't reflect real Onkwehonwe notions from any of our cultures, especially that of the ideal we are seeking to understand and apply here, of men and women involved in a spiritually rooted resurgence of Onkwehonwe strength. Trying to gain a deeper understanding of the various Onkwehonwe senses of being a warrior, let us consider the different ways of thinking about being a warrior in the framework of our own languages. My friend Thohahoken helped me understand the Kanien'kehaka meaning and concept of a warrior. Right away we noticed how interesting it was that the English word "warriors" and the self-referent Kanienkeha word for someone who is a fighter, *wateriyos*, sounds almost the same![38]

The most common English-Kanienkeha translation for the word "warrior" is *rotiskenhrakete*, which literally means, "carrying the burden of peace." The word is made up of *roti*, connoting "he"; *sken* in relation to *skennen*, or "peace"; and *hrakete*, which is a suffix that combines the connotations of a burden and carrying. Many of our people say that the concepts built into the word *rotiskenhrakete* form the contemporary Kanien'kehaka cultural basis for the militant action in our communities for the last couple of generations. It was one of the founding ideas of the Mohawk Warrior Societies that emerged in Kanien'kehaka communities in the 1970s and 1980s and a strong link between the traditional teachings and the contemporary movement ideology. But the word has a much broader usage in Rotinoshonni traditional culture relating to warriors: in the Condolence ceremony, in which grief is assuaged and new chiefs are raised up by clans, young men of the nation are referred to as *Rotiskenhraketakwa*; in the traditional Thanksgiving Address, in which gratitude for our place in creation is expressed, the sun is called *Rotiskenhraketekowa*. So the word has a deeper meaning than the simple equivalent to "warrior" in English.

In fact, Thohahoken told me that he had spoken with elders about this question many times. They said that the concept of a warrior in our "real old" traditional culture has no relation to *rotiskenhrakete* and that the name for warriors that more closely reflects the notion of warriors of the people living the values and principles of the *Kaienerekowa*, the Great Law of Peace, is *Oyenko:ohntoh*, which means "the tobacco hanging." As Thohahoken put it:

> *Rotiskenhraketakwa* are like conscript fighters, men who would normally not be fighting except when conscripted to defend the peace, *Oyenko:ohntoh* are more akin to the Japanese samurai. One of our more sacred protection medicines is tobacco, *oyenkwe-honwe*, and in the old days it was cured by hanging it up in the rafters of the longhouse, *arhenton*, "in the shadows." Thus, hanging tobacco in the longhouse rafters protects the house. *Oyenko:ohntoh* are not conscripts, but sacred protectors; they are anonymous shadow warriors in a secret society whose duty it is to protect the house.

This is the depth of understanding and appreciation of the warrior's role that is lacking from less culturally grounded notions. Thohahoken's teaching on the traditional Rotinoshonni ideas of the warrior as sacred protector is a good place to begin a further exploration of the modern concept of the warrior in Onkwehonwe societies. The great Lakota scholar Vine Deloria, Jr. has written on the qualities of warriors like Tecumseh, Crazy Horse, and other old war chiefs:

> they had a sense of personal worth, of a mission to be accomplished, and of a relationship with the life forces of the greater cosmos in a measure that we have not seen since. Fighting overwhelming odds, suffering the loneliness of knowing the situation was hopeless, and maintaining their sense of person was an achievement few of us can conceive and none of us can match.[39]

This description of the warrior spirit resonates with the response I received from a long-time Onkwehonwe activist, who commented on the theme of restoration that I developed in my last book, *Peace, Power, Righteousness*.[40] The comments reflect the spiritual need for this kind of inspirational and courageous individual among Onkwehonwe today:

> Condolence cannot happen if we are all in grief. The healthy ones, the bright-eyed ones, must accept their responsibility to restore those in grief, temporarily in dysfunction, so to speak, to

health, to accept, recognize, restore, ameliorate, admonish, and provide the new mentor, model and inspiration. In today's context, that is a primary task and responsibility of the warrior. We need a new statement, a creed, almost, which sets out some near-universal (at least North American) concept of the traditional person, the traditional life, the traditional society—what it is we are aspiring to be.[41]

From ancient teachings embedded in our indigenous languages, to the most thoughtful of modern reflections, there seems to be a great consistency among Onkwehonwe about the idea of the warrior.[42] To get at this notion beyond my own people's cultural heritage, I asked a number of people from different nations to tell me what the *warrior* word was in their own language:[43]

+ for the Kuna: there is no literal equivalent for the English term (it should be noted that they interact mostly with Panamanians, Spanish-speaking Settlers), and the closest approximation is *napa-sapgued*, meaning "One who protects or guards the land, or nature."
+ for the Dakota: *akicita* generally refers to those who have engaged in war combat, though linguistically the word is related to *akita*, which means "to seek" (as in something lost) or to hunt for something, generally in reference to hunting animals.
+ for the Wsanec: *stomish* means those who protect the territory and defend the names with honour and discipline.
+ for the Dakelh: the word for soldier is *lhudughan*, meaning "he who kills" and includes the notion that he is in the midst of killing (the word for war is *lhadughan*, meaning "they kill one another"). I was told that these words came about only recently, as until recent years most Dakelh spoke only their own language, and that they had to formulate such words to talk about what was happening in Europe.
+ for the Pawnee: there is no particular word for warrior, although *Ootakissh*, the phonetic spelling of "young man," is a word mentioned frequently in war dance songs. A more familiar word is *heluska*: the warrior, the war dance, the war, battle, struggle.

A Pawnee friend summarized beautifully for me the unified Onkwehonwe concept of warrior and the struggle of our peoples when she further explained her people's idea of *heluska*:

> One of my most favourite sayings is *tu-da-he*, "the war, the battle, the struggle is good, sacred, right." In other words, life and the everyday struggles of living, good or bad, is the epitome of life. It is how you know you are living. Nothing is easy, and because it isn't easy, one should truly value the blessings. Of course, in a warrior society the warrior ideal is how life is lived. It is what you do, it is who you are—you fight. Defeat is painful, but it is only temporary because you still live to get yourself up and see the dawn.

After hearing her teaching, my earlier framing of the question of how to fight seemed superficial. Faced with the thought of struggle as an identity, the more appropriate question becomes not *how to* fight but, *what is* the fight? We often talk in radical political circles of the need to take action. But what is "action"? Is it movement with purpose? Decision put into practice? Is it constituted in moral, physical, or cultural acts? This is difficult to grasp.

We can be sure that action is not reaction. It is not declarations or statements or rhetoric by which people are affected and then decide to plan to take action. Action is spirit and energy made into a driving force for change. Action is the manifestation in physicality of the spiritual energy of the warrior. It is behaviours, methods, goals, desires, and beliefs, all expressed in real ways in relationships with other people and forces.

In the context of colonialism and the Onkwehonwe struggle, proactive and protective actions are the elements of a resurgence. Actions—thinking, feeling, and behaving indigenously—are the things that make our movement Onkwehonwe, not simply what we might name it. Our indigeneity is observable as a personal quality. Are we living culturally as Onkwehonwe? This kind of authenticity is a powerful melding of renewal and continuity. It can be figured with reference to history, drawing on indigenous values and teachings, and from recent cultural developments that respect indigenous principles. Such a combination creates a cultural foundation for contemporary forms of resistance, making in effect new cultural practices to shape authentically indigenous movements which are both outgrowths from historic forms and organic expressions of timeless indigenous values. There are five main characteristics, both authentically indigenous and effective as a means of confronting colonial dominion, which are evident in Onkwehonwe movements from the Mohawk Warrior Societies to the Zapatistas to the recent mass movements against governmental corruption in Ecuador:

- They depend on and are led by women.
- They protect communities and defend land.
- They seek freedom and self-sufficiency.
- They are founded on unity and mutual support.
- They are continuous.

It is a much easier task to describe the qualities of a real indigenous movement than it is to point out examples of their emergence in Onkwehonwe societies. An authentic movement for change that is true to Onkwehonwe values and effective at engaging unjust power is very rare because there are so few Onkwehonwe who have remained connected to their traditional cultures and fewer still who have preserved within their culture and philosophies the ethic and practice of the sacred protector—the warrior spirit. There are no movements for change among indigenous peoples generally because the sad fact is that there are hardly any more warriors, sacred or otherwise. Are we fearful of the consequences of contentious action? This may be so, but the fact is that, whether we realize it or not, as Onkwehonwe nations today we have a stark choice: organize or die.

Onkwehonwe resurgences in the past and in their rare instance today have shown that in order to survive as peoples, we must have a well-thought strategy, strong belief in principles of justice, and the unwavering courage to act on these principles.

Today's leaders face the challenge of reinvigorating a warrior heritage that is deeply rooted yet hidden under the weight of many fears and delusions piled high by colonial rulers. Even among those who recognize the necessity of battle to protect our rights and our land, there is a confusion of many voices, different calls for different kinds of action, reflecting levels of commitment and degrees of frustration. Our modern day warriors are not part of a unified struggle, our battles are fought either on fronts that are inside our own communities or in a clannish fashion as small outnumbered groups. Where does this leave us in trying to understand the new warrior way? Perhaps even more importantly, where does this take us in terms of protecting the people and the land as a collective effort?

I think that the lesson of the past and of contemporary struggles is that we need to conceptualize our struggle as the practice of freedom and of applied indigenous intelligence in order to gain a realistic appraisal of whom and where we are. We need not so much a confrontation in the way that word is normally understood, but an awakening, a rising up, a restrengthening. It will be necessary to overcome fear in the first instance; the main concern of an Onkwehonwe warrior in today's world is to strive to overcome the oppressive force of the state, to persevere to maintain one's indigenous existence, to practise forbearance and fortitude. It is to make the movement continual, to embrace the struggle and challenge of a way of life for its inherent value, not as a temporary or instrumental process or posture in the service of some other goal. The ethos and ethic of the new warrior is to be a free speaker, an independent and creative thinker, and to live direct and radical action. This is a new way of thinking of what it is to be a "revolutionary" or "radical." Of course, in refocusing the present challenge, we shouldn't forget that some things have not changed.

Traditionally, for Onkwehonwe, the main objectives of war were to preserve territories, cultures, and the independence of our peoples.[44] In a basic way, this remains so. Yet we do not live in the ancient societies of our ancestors. The social and political institutions that used to govern warriors' conduct and structure their role in society have fallen into disuse. How do we resurrect the ideals of a warrior in Onkwehonwe societies that are so different from the ancient ones? The need for people who do the things warriors do is still there, but the people who do them, the way they do them, and how they fit within the society all have to be rethought to be brought back to life. Think of the societies and cultures of our ancestors and the integrity of the spiritual, social, and political fabric of their lives. For them, the main characteristic of a warrior was to embody the power that the ethic of sacrifice, restraint, and social unity produced. How was that restraint and unity achieved for ancient warriors? What I have called a "culture of resistance" combined with discipline, courage, and spirituality was the norm among ancient peoples. Human beings haven't changed in any fundamental way; what has changed is that we have been colonized.

Colonization has changed everything about the way we live our lives. Our nations were made up of strong families that supported each other by intense extended affiliations and the supportive networks of clans. Our people put a priority on knowledge and indigenous intelligence; they were always thinking and constantly assessing the possibilities of growth and adaptation to new realities. They possessed spiritual power and were guided in the conduct of their lives by their indigenous customs and religious beliefs. They were unified in their communities and in their actions. This

83

sense of unity was especially important to them because they understood that disunity degraded not only their existence as collectives but also their spiritual power as persons. Reciprocity and mutual obligation were the foundations of human interactions and of relationships with other elements of creation. This created the kind of solidarity that allowed them to withstand the challenges of survival in harsh physical environments and against evil forces—that allowed them to survive intact as people and as nations. Most clearly different from the way we live our lives, our ancestors lived in a culture and society of warriors; there was social pressure for men to walk the warrior's path, and women's roles were defined in accordance with their power and responsibility to maintain the culture and care for the families and to enable the men to defend the nation.

The culture and old patterns of society and of warfare are no longer in effect. Colonization decultured us. Euroamerican values of materialism, patriarchy, and individualism have been embraced by most of our people and have broken down any semblance of traditional governance in our communities. As the reader will see from the conversations with the female warriors that follow in this book, we cannot hold on to a concept of the warrior that is gendered in the way it once was and that is located in an obsolete view of men's and women's roles. The battles we are fighting are no longer primarily physical; thus, any idea of the indigenous warrior framed solely in masculine terms is outdated and must be rethought and recast from the solely masculine view of the old traditional ways to a new concept of the warrior that is freed from colonial gender constructions and articulated instead with reference to what really counts in our struggles: the qualities and the actions of a person, man or woman, in battle.

Aside from using our knowledge of the past to try to shape our identities from this heritage, is there anything we can draw on, tactically, from the way our ancestors embodied indigeneity and conducted themselves in battle? Until our peoples were overwhelmed by the numbers of European immigrants and by the microbiological holocaust that obliterated our collective strength, Onkwehonwe warriors were successful on the battlefield against colonial military forces and were sought after as military allies because they uniformly possessed the characteristics of great combat fighters. They were *adaptable*, independent thinkers and flexible in responding to changes in plans and in situations. They had *skills*, were well-trained, and possessed the specific knowledge required to be effective in various types of battles and environments. They were *disciplined*, tough and stoic in the face of the extreme deprivations of war, including harsh mental and physical conditions. And they were motivated by the martial attitudes pervading Onkwehonwe societies. Is it possible to recover and rebuild this kind of warrior ethic among our people today? I think it is.

Onkwehonwe ancients were not the only people who were strong warriors. There are many cultures which have and continue to produce people capable of carrying the burden of contention. The challenge for today is not how to restore ancient societies, but how to regenerate our culture and revitalize our people as warriors. We must find a way to reorient ourselves, our ways of thinking and behaviours, so that the next generation of Onkwehonwe is capable of standing up and throwing off the weight of colonial oppression and shouldering the responsibilities of a dangerous freedom-seeking struggle for dignity.

Revitalizing these Onkwehonwe traits is crucial for successful engagement with the colonial adversary today, whether in a physical, intellectual, or spiritual struggle. In our battles, knowledge connected to direct action is the real power that makes change, and we are most likely to find ourselves engaging the adversary in contests in the realm of ideas. Knowledge holds power, but it is the kind of knowledge that one holds that is the important determinant of whether our movement's warriors will be successful in dislodging the colonizer. We all possess knowledge, but today this knowledge perpetuates our colonized status as subservient and debased parts of the colonial structure, knowledge that has trained us to be dominated by others. We need to empower ourselves for the contest with colonial authority by retooling and retraining ourselves for freedom. The same independence and flexibility, skills and training, discipline and motivation that were the marks of our warrior ancestors are the very things that we need to recreate and channel among our people today.

It begins with attitude. If we find a way to shed the defeatism of colonial identities and take on instead the outlook of the proud warrior, we would be able to regenerate ourselves as free people. I recall reading in one of the anthropologist Carlos Castaneda's dialogues with a Yaqui elder a simple definition of a warrior that frames well what we are trying to understand: "a warrior is one who leads a warrior's life!"[45] This straightforward statement points us towards two important lessons on being a warrior: the importance of *belief*, which provides emotional stability in the face of constant conflict and danger, and the necessity of consistency between belief, thought, words, and behaviour.

Warriorism is a way of life and a philosophy that is capable of carrying our people through their lives in resistance to the sources of their pain and discord, no matter where and who they are, much more so than the weak, defeatist, and victim-producing coping strategies that are commonly promoted among our people and so dismally failing to provide hope and strength. Clearly, real warriors can be distinguished from those normally functioning but ordinary people who seek simply to carry a warrior ethos into their everyday lives by the conflict situations in which they place themselves. Both are necessary, the fighters and those who create the cultures that produce and sustain fighters and honour their actions. Yet we must distinguish the banal from the heroic as the battleground shifts from the mundane to sites and situations of crucial contention where more immediate and dangerous costs are attached. We make the transition from warrior ethics to warrior, from normal to heroic, by placing ourselves in situations of dangerous contention and serious challenge to the imperial authority and to the adversaries of our people. So we can understand the need both for a pervasive warrior ethic to inform all of our identities and actions as nations of people in struggle against colonialism and the dominion of Euroamerican Settler society and for warriors modelled on the idea of sacred protectors, who put themselves forward to confront the danger actively.

Given the fractured and unhealthy social environments we live in, where do we begin this process of regeneration? Again, it is clear that we need to focus on spiritual foundations and provide ourselves with a new psychological and mental framework for decision-making in our own lives and in that of our communities. Directly challenging the most un-indigenous of cultural traits imposed through assimilation in the colonial era, we need to do some very simple yet profoundly important things to re-indigenize our existences. We must shift our perceptions of the world and our experiences in it away from ourselves and towards others in order to create meaningful communities and solidarity between our peoples. We need to avoid extremes and always seek to achieve balance in an emotional and physical sense in our lives, in order to restore our psychological and physical health. We need to start disciplining our lives to toughen up our minds and our bodies. And we need to practise humility and modesty as an antidote to the personality of entitlement and arrogance that is so common everywhere today.[46]

If there is an Onkwehonwe warrior creed, it is that he or she is motivated in action by an instinctual sense of responsibility to alleviate suffering and to recreate the conditions of peace and happiness. The warrior's first battle is with himself or herself; having fought that battle his or her responsibilities are extended to immediate family and other human beings. The warrior takes action to change the conditions that cause suffering for the people in both the immediate (self-defence) and long-term (self-determination) sense. The warrior does not focus on abstract or historical injustices and believes wholeheartedly that the ability to generate change is within the power of the people.

What kind of people do we need to become in our personal transformations into warriors? There are myriad examples of cultures bringing to reality the universal concept of devotion to service, self-discipline, and the ethic of courage. The ideal was expressed most elegantly, perhaps, in the fourteenth-century Japanese Samurai prayer that has come to be widely known among practitioners of the martial arts as the Warrior's Creed:

I have no divine power.
I make honesty my divine power.
I have no magic secrets.
I make character my magic secret.
I have no sword.
I make absence of self my sword.

The way of the new warrior is as much a tactical battle against the patterns of our modern existence as a philosophical and political struggle. The warrior will be reborn inside and among us if we simply do the things that make and have always made a warrior:

+ *mental awakening* through the promotion of knowledge and the reassertion of a social environment where children and youth are encouraged to seek out and listen to knowledge, to learn from it, and to practise it;
+ *emotional fortitude* and the instilling of emotional and psychological stability leading to the generalized state of courage where Onkwehonwe can again persevere against the fears that are used so cynically to oppress us;
+ *purifying and strengthening* our bodies by returning to traditional diets and regular hard physical labour and exercise so that we can be rid of the scourges of diabetes and obesity that create total dependence on the colonial state's health bureaucracy; and
+ *rediscovering meaning* outside of shallow materialism and our hollowed-out existences as consumers by reviving ceremonial and ritual cycles as a means of restoring social connection and spiritual rootedness, thus making life sacred again.

The process is definitely one of experience, risk, experiment, and exploration of new-found psychological, intellectual, and emotional terrains. And, in addition to the effort, strain, and aches that are the natural effects of all change processes—where friction accompanies movement there is turmoil on an internal as well as external level—there is also a cost to be paid for an individual's movement away from colonial mentalities and behaviours because not all Onkwehonwe are involved in struggle or care to be, nor does everyone move at the same pace or in the same way even when they are committed to change. There are relationship costs to be paid by the warrior on the path of truth. The ignorance, hostility, jealousy, scorn, and even aggression of still-colonized Indians and aboriginals are very real factors. But to persevere in spite of these negative attitudes is to break through to the freedom to recreate our persons, identities, and relationships.

To illustrate this facet of the warrior ethos, rather than embarrass people by naming them exemplary beings, I offer this list of questions that I trust can serve as the basis for productive reflection on what it is to achieve decolonization in a real personal and practical sense. Here I am thinking of a way both to recognize the kind of warrior I am talking about and to distinguish the character of true warriors from shallow users and selfish posers.

- Are these people who call themselves warriors simple and austere, or dependent on and attached to material things, living unnecessarily complicated lives? Simple lifestyles, disciplined surroundings, and a healthy existence characterized by cleanliness and organization are the traits of a warrior.
- Are they kind and generous, living for others, especially the poor, in what Buddhist teachers call accepting responsibility for being "the strength of the weak" instead of living a showy, braggart, and arrogant life?
- Are they accustomed to self-sacrifice? Do they have a fit body, do physical training, and eat a moderate and healthy diet of natural foods, as opposed to living the slovenly and poisoned lives expected of colonized beings?
- Do they benefit from some form of spiritual introspection that deepens their existence beyond the fast-paced, frenetic, and essentially meaningless modern lifestyle of the mainstream?
- Do they have self-control and self-discipline?

+ Have they conquered their rage and do they engage challenges without anger but with non-violence, forbearance, and the oft-derided but very warrior-like trait of stoicism?

+ Are they honest people who keep their word? Do they believe in and practise integrity and democracy in all dealings with other people?

+ Are they incorruptible in public affairs and sincere in their private lives? In contrast to the hypocritical self-serving ethic of contemporary politics, do they truly serve the people?

+ Do they understand and respect the power of words? Or do they tell lies, speak maliciously, use sharp or harsh words, or engage in useless gossip? Colonial beings use words to harm, destroy, and divide; warriors use words to restore harmony to situations.

+ Are they moral? Or are they, like far too many of our people, abusive or prone to stealing? Does their use of drugs or alcohol cause them to lose control, leading to further abuses of their senses and a crazed or obsessively damaging sexuality?

+ Are they humble? Warriors are students in search of knowledge and recognize that the world is full of teachers and mentors. Warriors seek to place themselves as humble learners in the care of learned elders and mentors, recognizing that the mentor knows more than they do. Unlike the precocious, the know-it-all, and the smart-ass, the knowledge-seekers lead exemplary lives based on their growing understanding and do not hoard or profit from what they have gained on the warrior's journey.

+ Is their life-goal spiritual enlightenment and empowerment? Not money, not revenge, not prestige and status, but the cultivation of the ability to bring enlightenment and power to others, to have the capacity to bring back balance in the world and in people.

These are ideas drawn from many teachings. They are, in a sense, a simple theory to guide the very real and infinitely more complicated personal struggles we all face in breaking out of the colonial cage.

To give one voice to this process, we turn now to the experience of someone who has attempted and continues to attempt to confront colonization on a personal level, as a reality in his own and his family's life, and to organize a movement of young Onkwehonwe men to agitate for change on a broader, societal level.

David Dennis was instrumental in the formation of the Native Youth Movement in the City of Vancouver and other urban centres in British Columbia. He went on to become the founder of the Westcoast Warrior Society, a group committed to direct action and the physical defence of First Nation lands and people when they decide to engage the state in contention or are attacked by police forces when they are asserting their rights as indigenous peoples. He represents a new generation of intelligent and angry young Onkwehonwe mainly from urban centres and to a lesser extent from reserves. These warriors are dedicated to agitating from within and projecting Onkwehonwe resurgence into the realm of politics and into the culture of their nations and that of mainstream society. The Native Youth Movement, and particularly the Westcoast Warrior Society, are two of the very few examples we have in Anówara of Onkwehonwe consciously attempting the resurrection of traditional identities and the concepts of the warrior to construct a movement for internal community reform and as a basis on which to contend with state power.

My conversation with David began with my trying to get a basic grasp on what they see as his fundamental objective for engaging in political struggle.[47]

TA: *What is the Westcoast Warrior Society all about?*
DD: There have been examples in the past of organizations that stood for our peoples' rights, but none of them, in the opinion of young Native people today, had a fine enough edge to them. They didn't clearly define things and say, "This is the way you can live. This is the way you should live." So in our eyes, this is why we have to redefine what a warrior is today, in terms of our standards. In the 1960s, the Red Power movement, with their bandanas and raising their fists in the air, had their definition of what a warrior was and of resistance. Ours is completely different.

TA: *Do you see that 1960s-style activism as something that turned into a dead end for our people?*
DD: That's difficult to say. Despite the circumstances, they exercised bravery. The police harassment, in terms of the brutality, was extreme against those groups. People were killed by the police. So in terms of their bravery, it's definitely something to build upon. But the movement that they went into, with the confrontational style of politics and whatnot, that's not us. With our movement, we'd rather show people that we can live and provide for our own families and still maintain a set of principles. That's the difference between our movement and mainstream politics now too: we have princi-

ples. And our principles are the character of our lives, right? It's impossible for us to sell out; we can't. We have principles; we made our house on a strong foundation.

TA: *What are you trying to protect and to preserve?*
DD: We have to have a clear definition, and preserve a clear idea of, who our enemy is. I think most of our people have lost that idea because of our bastardized sense of identity and from always trying to get along, you know? It's important for us to maintain the belief that we live amongst our enemies. That's a big part of becoming a warrior.

TA: *A way of looking at the world...?*
DD: It's not the camouflage that makes the warrior, it's the person inside. To be honest, it's hard to maintain. With all these other influences in your life—and I hate to say it—but it's easy to take down your camp and just go home. To say, "Just forget it, to hell with it!" That's why you need to have the discipline of those principles; you need to be able to maintain.

TA: *It is a constant battle with oneself to maintain focus in the face of the pressures to, as you said, fold camp and go home. I think having a strong bond with other like-minded people is important in this. Is this anything like what you mean by "warrior society"?*
DD: Our relationship with the police is a hostile one. So in order for us to feel worthwhile in doing our job, and to reassure ourselves that we're going down the right path, we have to find our peers.

TA: *You used the word "hostile." Is it anger that moves you to action?*
DD: There is a spirit among young people today that is motivated by hate and that is motivated by anger. There's a big sense of injustice coming from our young people. We're pissed off because we've been shit on and we've been abused. It's like waking up from a sleep and then noticing that you've been messed with, you know? And when you wake up out of that sleep, you're like a bear, you're fuckin' angry. But in terms of our approach, and I wouldn't want to use the word "refined" here, but it is a responsibility to carry on and to conduct ourselves properly—we're always being watched by the people, heh? So yeah, there is hatred, anger, and destructiveness, all coming from our sense of belonging in history and our sense of where these conflicts come from. It also comes from a sober understanding of our relationship with the Canadian government: we don't bullshit ourselves into believing that Canada has the best intentions for our people.

TA: *Where did that understanding come from?*
DD: We understand that Canada has under no circumstances ever tried to exercise any good faith with us. They have never, at any time or at any moment in history, extended any peaceful means towards us—aside from when they needed our military help to be allies in wars against the French or the Americans.

TA: *You've had a good reading of history.*
DD: I've immersed myself in it. And I'm pretty happy that in BC, there's a keen sense of militancy among the young people.

TA: *Why is it then that not every young Native wants to join your movement?*
DD: Nobody *has* to. You can live your life entirely provided for by the government—you may not be totally content, but you will be provided with welfare or whatever. Living right beside the enemy, "hanging around the fort," like you said before, it has its benefits! Everybody likes to be a winner.

TA: *You think fear has anything to do with it?*
DD: That's the biggest thing. Residential schools have instilled a fear of authority in our people. They instilled a fear of going against the grain in any way. Every aspect of life that existed prior to the residential school era was erased, almost to the point of no return. In terms of restoring what a government looked like prior to the residential schools, it's impossible. And that's a big point, because it separates us from most older people. Young people these days have a better grip on the reality of our situation, so in our idea of rebuilding our nations, we know it's not going to look the same as before. Our ideas about injustice might even possess and lead us to fight our own people and the injustice they are bringing on through the instrument of their form of government. There's a lot of fear in our leaders, and that leads to an unwillingness to engage the government or to see it as an enemy. It's because of the residential schools and the fears they created. Adding to that, there's all of the benefits put in front of us so that we can live our entire lives without ever having to do a thing.

TA: *How come you're not affected by that?*
DD: Once you begin to unravel history and what the government has done to us, you can start to trace the genesis of our fears. You start at the root, which is the fear of authority, and you understand that the starting point was a priest yelling at these little children, our parents. They passed that fear onto us. It's

like when kids are scared of friggin' rats and spiders. Ninety-nine out of 100 times, it's because they had a bad experience with those things when they were younger. It's the same thing with us: a bad, bad, experience with the federal government and the churches. When you trace that fear back, you find out where it's coming from, and when you find out it was just a weak-minded and evil person at the root of it, the fear dissipates.

TA: *What if it's not a weak man, but a strong and well-armed man facing you?*
DD: Even then, your understanding gives you strength. You understand that there is an economic purpose to the residential school; there's an economic purpose to the Department of Indian Affairs; there's an economic purpose for the RCMP. They are all there for one purpose: to protect the fort. When you understand that concept, you come to understand that the man of the cloth is the same thing as the RCMP, and the prime minister is the same thing as your local mayor. All of those people are there for the same purpose, which is the occupation of your territory, the stealing of your resources, and to lie and cheat you into the history books. Once you conquer the fear of one of those things, the strength builds in you to overcome the other things.

TA: *What about the pull of materialism or the temptation of a cozy government job that's always there for any Native who wants to sell-out?*
DD: Getting involved in the tribal council, or becoming a forestry officer, or taking part in government programs set up on your reserve, those things are not going to bring any solutions to our problems. Those things are not ever going to bring any resolution to our social and economic situation. If you break it down and understand it, you see that the "pull of materialism" is not leading to greener pastures. It's pretty easy once you've made up your mind and you are determined. The old people talk about "finding your way"—every man, woman, and child has a way for them. It's up to each person to find it, but once they've determined what their way is, nothing can change it.

TA: *So there's no turning back once you're on the warrior's path?*
DD: There is no turning back. It's not as if five years from now I'm going to see the light and start working for the tribal council! (Laughing.)

TA: *The government does a damn good job of undermining the movement, heh?*

DD: We didn't join the fight for young people to be recognized so that one person could get a position on a board of directors with an organization that is selling our people down the drain. I've seen a lot of my peers, who I still consider friends and loved ones, now working for these government-sponsored youth programs. In their mind, they're still creating some sort of change, "Well, there are some programs that deal with street kids…," but they don't see it the way those of us who are against that type of thing see it. We see it as, like it or not, you're doing what the federal government wants you to do.

TA: *What makes the difference between these two ways of seeing things?*
DD: Some people have deep-seated personal issues. I find that a lot of the people who conform are scared. A lot of them come from homes where there is a lot of physical and sexual abuse, and a lot of that gets piled on to the fact that, you know, they're getting paid! It just shifts their thinking and they start to cooperate. But it doesn't mean that their fighting spirit can't be re-empowered.

The need to strengthen the culture of resistance to support those who do choose the path of contention with the state is clearly evident. Soon after our conversation, David Dennis himself chose to move into the arena of institutionalized electoral politics in his nation's tribal council. The lack of an organizational framework and institutional base for radical action is the most common factor in people rationalizing a more "insider" approach to change than one rooted in confrontation with colonial institutions. Nonetheless, Dennis's own analysis of the personal motivation for those who choose to work with the system rather than fight against it unavoidably points right to the other component: personal calculations of interest.

I followed up our earlier conversation by asking David in the fall of 2004 if he could explain to me how he ended up working for the tribal council after all, and to reflect on the experience he has had working in that position.

DD: In early 2003 our warrior society began attending the Nuu-Chah-Nulth war council. This endeavour proved to be valuable to us because this group organized several public speaking engagements focusing on the events surrounding Burnt Church. It also provided an opportunity for some of us to connect back with the community. The war council has not been active since then, other than providing financial support for some of our community work, but it brought activists from both sides of the treaty chasm together.

The person who was most notable to us was a rising tribal council technician, Clifford Atleo, Jr. Cliff, who is a treaty manager, was by far the most broad-minded amongst the minions of youth that had been recruited and pushed forward to contrast the demagogues, such as those in the Native Youth Movement and the Westcoast Warriors. Clifford immediately began to identify with our movement because of his experiences in the treaty process. For months we had tried to recruit him into the warrior society. He was reluctant at first, but we ended up striking a deal: he would join the warriors if I would accept the nomination for the recently vacated seat of co-chairman of the Nuu-Chah-Nulth Tribal Council. I immediately agreed. I figured, What chance did I have in getting elected anyway? Unfortunately I was elected.

TA: *So has being the chairman of the tribal council and working inside the system changed anything about the way you see politics or the relations between our people and white governments?*
DD: I have been a tribal "leader" for more than two years now. This experience has confirmed some of the conclusions I had made in the past, but it has changed my view on others. My experience as chairman has reinforced my belief that meaningful progress for our people cannot occur in this system. This system, which is dependent upon the same people it intends to fight, is not conducive to the necessary overthrow of established powers and politics. It is an antiquated system that is not organized to contemplate such things as national conscience, much less revolution. It is organized in such a fashion so that economic development and integration are interdependent ideas.

TA: *So it's just reinforced what you already knew, or suspected, about trying to work within the system?*
DD: I can no longer say that the tribal council is *totally* incapable of doing good. This tribal council has been instrumental in bringing forward knowledge of the crimes that have been committed in the residential school epic. This tribal council has commissioned a book on the Alberni, Christie, and Ahousaht residential schools that expose the government crimes against our people at the hands of white clergy, officials, and politicians. It was also the motivating factor in which an RCMP investigative team was formed to root out the abusers. It has also organized many meetings in which the survivors themselves have given direction to the leaders on how to pursue these crimes on their behalf, and it is pursuing an apology from the prime minister.

TA: *Those are positive things, for sure.*

DD: But I must confess that beyond affecting social issues, I have zero confidence in this form of organizing.

TA: *So I take it that you're not planning on making a career out of this?*
DD: I intend to serve out my mandate, which ends in September 2005, and then step aside for someone more ambitious than myself.

TA: *So what comes next for you and the Warrior Society, after the fall of 2005?*
DD: I feel that that we can and should organize instead around ideas of indigenous nationalism. If we're going to be successful in organizing in such a way, it must be done independent of government funding. I hope that we can get to a place where our people can challenge the legitimacy of tribal and band councils and to get the councils to stop acting on their behalf and to do their proper job of being social agencies. From my perspective, that is all the councils are capable of after all.

TA: *I definitely agree with you there...*
DD: And I should say too, Taiaiake, that money was not a factor in my decision-making on this. Having the steady income from this job has helped the movement in some ways; but I met someone recently who made more money selling hotdogs than I do selling out. (Laughter.)

Consider the changes our societies have undergone and the pressing current needs in Onkwehonwe communities expressed in Dennis's words and experience. To be realistic and to insulate against co-optation in a psychological and economic sense, the transformation must be more fundamental than merely organizational. The movement, if it is to be effective and sustainable, must be founded on strong people, and it must address in realistic ways three concerns: dispelling fear, providing a compelling rationale for sacrifice, redirecting youthful energy, and supporting the activities and role of warriors so that they are not alienated or drawn away from the movement because of practical concerns of providing for themselves and their families.

As we seek restrengthening and embark on pathways to recover the personal and collective ethic of the warrior, we should hearken back to the spirit of the teachings that do survive, like that of the Kiowa nation's Dog Warriors, whose founder had a dream in which warriors were led into battle by a dog singing the *Ka-itsenko* song. Ten men only, the bravest in the nation, wore a ceremonial sash and carried a sacred arrow, and, as described famously by the writer N. Scott Momaday, "In times of battle he must by means of this arrow impale the end of his sash to the earth and stand his ground to the death."[48]

In most people's minds, the words "North American Indian warrior" invoke images of futile angry violence or of noble sacrifice in the face of the white march of triumph over this continent. To Euroamericans, the descendents and beneficiaries of conquest, "Indian warriors" are artefacts of the past; they are icons of colonization, that version of history in which the original people of this land have been defiant but defeated by Euroamerican land greed and the unstoppable advance of Euroamerican civilization. But history has not ended. There are still Onkwehonwe lands, souls, and minds that have not been conquered. For them, a warrior is what a warrior has always been: one who protects the people, who stands with dignity and courage in the face of danger. When lies rule, a warrior creates new truths for the people to believe.

NOTES

1 Tiana Bighorse, *Bighorse the Warrior*, ed. Noel Bennett (Tucson, AZ: University of Arizona Press, 1990) xxiv.

2 This section was previously published as an article entitled, "The Path of Least Resistance," archived on my Website, <http://www.taiaiake.com>. The article was based on information originally reported in Joan Taillon, "First Nations Team Up for Economic Opportunities," *Raven's Eye* (July 7, 2003), from which all of the direct quotes attributed to the band council chief in this section are taken.

3 The best sources of information on these issues are on the Internet. On management problems with the Canadian Department of Indian Affairs, see Chapter 8 of the 2003 Auditor General of Canada report <http://www.oag-bvg.gc.ca/domino/reports.nsf/html/20031108ce.html>; on the Samson Cree Nation's breach of trust suit against the Government of Canada in relation to the Department of Indian Affairs' mismanagement of the Nation's oil and gas revenues, *Buffalo v. The Queen*, see the Website set up to provide information on the case <http://www.samsoncree.org>; and on the suit against the United States for Bureau of Indian Affairs trust fund misappropriations, *Cobell v. Norton*, see an overview report from the *Boulder Weekly*, online at <http://www.monitor.net/monitor>.

4 Vaclav Havel, *Disturbing the Peace*, trans. Paul Wilson (New York, NY: Vintage, 1991) 17.

5 See Hakim Bey, *T.A.Z.* (San Francisco, CA: AK Press, 1985) and *Immediatism* (San Francisco, CA: 1994). See also Richard Day, "Who is This We That Gives the Gift? Native American Political Theory and *The Western Tradition*," *Critical Horizons* 2:2 (2001): 173-201; Richard Day and Tonio Sadik, "The BC Land Questions, Liberal Multiculturalism, and the Spectre of Aboriginal Nationhood," *BC Studies* 143 (Summer 2002): 5-34.

6 Sean M. Maloney, "Domestic Operations: The Canadian Approach," *Parameters*, US Army War College Quarterly (Autumn 1997). See also Sandra Lambertus, *Wartime Images, Peacetime Wounds: The Media and the Gustafsen Lake Stand-off* (Toronto, ON: University of Toronto Press, 2004).

7   *Monday Brownbagger*, 25 March 2002, Co-Op Radio, CFRO, Vancouver, BC.

8   Nasra Hassam, "An Arsenal of Believers," *The New Yorker* (19 November 2001). For an interrogation of the notion of non-lethal physical resistance or "limited violence," as well as an excellent analysis of the strategic shift from limited violence to armed struggle as the primary means of resistance to Israeli occupation by Palestinians, see Edy Kaufman, "Limited Violence and the Palestinian Struggle," *Unarmed Forces: Non-violent Action in Central America and the Middle East*, ed. Graeme MacQueen, Canadian Papers in Peace Studies 1 (Toronto, ON: Science for Peace, 1992).

9   The most authoritative source on the ideological foundations of the Vietnamese revolutionary resistance is Duiker's biography of the communist leader, from which the quotations below are drawn. See William J. Duiker, *Ho Chi Minh: A Life* (London, UK: Allen and Unwin, 2000).

10   For an excellent analysis of the life and mythology of Che Guevara, see Jorge Casteñeda, *Compagñero: The Life and Death of Che Guevara* (New York: Random House, 1997).

11   Che Guevara, *Guerrilla Warfare* (New York, NY: Monthly Review Press, 1961) 171.

12   This is most clearly evident in Frantz Fanon, *The Wretched of the Earth* (New York, NY: Grove Press, 1963). For a full explanation and discussion of Frantz Fanon's ideas, see Nigel C. Gibson, *Fanon: The Postcolonial Imagination* (Cambridge, UK: Polity 2003).

13   Guevara, *Guerrilla Warfare* 171.

14   Sidney Tarrow, *Power in Movement: Social Movements and Contentious Politics*, 2nd ed. (Cambridge, UK: Cambridge University Press, 1998) 93-105.

15   Peter Ackerman and Jack DuVall, *A Force More Powerful: A Century of Nonviolent Conflict* (New York, NY: Palgrave, 2000) 5. Also, for solid arguments for non-violence as a strategic option based on the success of Latin American social movements in forcing change in those societies, see Philip McManus and Gerald Schlabach, eds., *Relentless Persistence: Nonviolent Action in Latin America* (Santa Cruz, CA: New Society Publishers, 1991). And for an argument against the notion that violence is the most powerful means of political action, see Gene Sharp's "Non-violent Struggle Today," *Unarmed Forces: Non-violent Action in Central America and the Middle East*, ed. Graeme MacQueen, Canadian Papers in Peace Studies 1 (Toronto, ON: Science for Peace, 1992).

16   Dave Grossman, *On Killing: The Psychological Cost of Learning to Kill in War and Society* (Toronto, ON: Little, Brown and Company, 1995) 83–85.

17   Tenzin Gyatso, the Fourteenth Dalai Lama of Tibet, *Ancient Wisdom, Modern World: Ethics for the New Millennium* (Toronto, ON: Little, Brown and Company, 1999), 48.

18   For a description and explanation of the Indian anti-imperial struggle, see Mahatma K. Gandhi, *Non-Violent Resistance, Satyagraha* (New York, NY: Schocken Books, 1961) and his *An Autobiography, or The Story of My Experiments With Truth*, trans. M. Desai (1927, 1929; New York, NY: Penguin 2001); also see Krishnalal Shridharani, *War Without Violence* (Belmont, CA: Harcourt Brace, 1939).

19   The Gramscian approach to theorizing indigenous struggles is best developed in Charles R. Hale, *Resistance and Contradiction* (Stanford, CA: Stanford University Press, 1994) 31.

20   Ward Churchill and Mike Ryan, *Pacifism as Pathology* (Winnipeg, MB: Arbeiter Ring Publishing, 1998) 93–101.

21   Hannah Arendt, *On Violence* (Belmont, CA: Harcourt Brace, 1969) 65.

22   The frustrated warrior concept and its link to violence is developed in B. Duran and E. Duran, *Native American Post-Colonial Psychology* (Albany, NY: State University of New York Press, 1995).

23 C. Wright Mills, *White Collar: The American Middle Classes* (New York, NY: Oxford University Press, 1956) 110.

24 See Tom Hayden, ed. *The Zapatista Reader* (New York, NY: Avalon, 2002).

25 Richard Holmes, *Acts of War* (New York, NY: The Free Press, 1985) 29.

26 Grossman, *On Killing* 77–84.

27 Gérard Chaliand, *Revolution in the Third World*, rev.ed. (New York, NY: Penguin, 1989) 37–49.

28 Tarrow, *Power in Movement* 71.

29 Charles R. Hale, *Resistance and Contradiction* (Stanford, CA: Stanford University Press, 1994) 27.

30 Drawing on Chaliand, *Revolution in the Third World* 181.

31 Esquival quoted in McManus and Schlabach, *Relentless Persistence* 6.

32 Here I am drawing on the "Nine Grounds" concept from Sun Tzu's *The Art of War*, trans. Thomas Cleary (Boston, MA: Shambhala, 1991) 27. And for an excellent discussion of how language and geographic place names are tied to cultural memory in indigenous landscapes, see Keith H. Basso, *Wisdom Sits in Places: Landscape and Language Among the Western Apache* (Albuquerque, NM: University of New Mexico Press, 1996).

33 Sakej was interviewed by the author in Victoria, BC, in the spring of 2002.

34 On the 1990 Oka conflict, see Geoffrey York and Loreen Pindera, *People of the Pines: The Warriors and the Legacy of Oka* (Toronto, ON: Little, Brown and Company, 1991) and Taiaiake (Gerald) Alfred, "From Bad to Worse: Internal Politics in the 1990 Crisis at Kahnawake," *Northeast Indian Quarterly* 8,1 (Spring 1991): 23–32. And for background and context on the Mi'kmaq fishing conflict, see Ken Coates, *The Marshall Decision and Native Rights* (Montréal, QC: McGill-Queen's University Press, 2001).

35 A note of dissent from Sakej's assertion here: I believe that there was in fact significant diversity within the American civil rights movement in terms of strategies and overall objectives. On this, see the American historian Taylor Branch's monumental trilogy on the movement, especially the volume entitled, *Pillar of Fire: American in the King Years, 1963–65* (New York, NY: Simon and Schuster, 1998). Also, to locate the philosophical points I am discussing with Sakej in a larger intellectual context, see Robert Young, *Postcolonialism: A Very Short Introduction* (Oxford, UK: Oxford University Press, 2003).

36 Quoted in Michael Rosen and David Widgery, *The Vintage Book of Dissent* (New York, NY: Vintage, 1996) 81.

37 Thomas Cleary, *Classics of Strategy and Counsel* (Boston, MA: Shambhala, 2000) 194.

38 Similarities in the concept of the warrior as Sacred Protector as explained by Thohahoken can be found in Tibetan Buddhism as explained in Chögyam Trungpa, *Shambhala: The Sacred Path of the Warrior* (Boston, MA: Shambhala, 1998).

39 Frank Waters, *Brave are My People: Indian Heroes Not Forgotten* (Athens, OH: Ohio University Press, 1993) xiv.

40 Taiaiake Alfred, *Peace, Power, Righteousness: An Indigenous Manifesto* (Don Mills, ON: Oxford University Press, 1999).

41 Rarihokwats to Taiaiake, personal communication, 2003.

42 For an additional appreciation of the traditional warrior's view of the meaning of resistance, see Jon W. Parmenter, "Dragging Canoe: Chickamauga Cherokee Patriot," *The Human Tradition in the American Revolution*, ed. Nancy Rhoden and Ian Steele (Lanham, MD: SR Books, 2000) 117–37.

43 The definitions and explanations of the various Onkwehonwe words were provided by Brock Pitawanakwat (Spanish and Kuna), Nick Claxton (Sencoten), Angela Wilson (Dakota), Patty Loew (Ojibway), and Lyana Patrick (Dakelh/Carrier).

44 Carl Benn, *The Iroquois in the War of 1812* (Toronto, ON: University of Toronto Press, 1998) 5–13 and 70–73.

45 Carlos Castaneda, *The Teachings of Don Juan: A Yaqui Way of Knowledge* (New York, NY: Washington Square Press, 1998) 24.

46 Here I am drawing on Tenzin Gyatso, the Fourteenth Dalai Lama, *Ancient Wisdom, Modern World* (Toronto, ON: Little, Brown and Company, 1999) 106.

47 David Dennis was interviewed by the author at the Cactus Club in Vancouver in March 2002.

48 N. Scott Momaday, *The Way to Rainy Mountain* (Albuquerque, NM: University of New Mexico Press, 1969) 21.

colonial stains on our existence

One who would take away our rights is, of course, our enemy.[1]
— Deskaheh, Rotinoshonni

A surge of strength, when it is disconnected from the other elements of the circle of integrity, is nothing more than an act of defiance: proud, bold, and possibly a signal of the stirring of a new movement. But without clarity on the full meaning and depth of our situation, understanding the landscape of our colonial existence and achieving a clear-eyed and sober vision of our goals, all of the rage and acting out against our adversaries will be for nothing. Our energies, unchannelled or misdirected, will fall short of an effective challenge to the status quo. Worse still, the frustration of failure may cause us to turn our energy inward and begin to devour ourselves, thus perpetuating imperialism and furthering the domination of Onkwehonwe.

IMPERIAL ARROGANCES

If Onkwehonwe movements are to force Settler societies to transcend colonialism, we need to understand clearly who and what constitutes our enemy. The "problem" or "challenge" we face has been explained in many ways, but to move our discussion forward I will state it in a blunt and forcefully true way: the problem we face is Euroamerican arrogance, the institutional and attitudinal expressions of the prejudicial biases inherent in European and Euroamerican cultures. This is not the abstract concept it may appear to be on first reading; it is the fundamental source of stress, discord, and injustice and capitalizes on the ubiquitous nature of imperialism and the threat it presents. The challenge we face is made up of specific patterns of behaviour among Settlers and our own people: choices made to support mentalities that developed in serving the colonization of our lands as well as the unrestrained greed and selfishness of mainstream society. We must add to this the superficial monotheistic justifications for the unnatural and misunderstood place and purpose of human beings in the world, an emphatic refusal to look inward, and an aggressive denial of the value of nature.

Forcefully stating this theme in much of his own work, Onkwehonwe scholar Jack Forbes has written that Western "civilization" is no such thing. European philosophies have always been much less concerned about the search for truth than with providing intellectual covers for the exercise of brute power by white rulers.[2] There always has been an apparent separation between the ethical principles and the philosophies and practice of government in the Western tradition. Take, for example, the profundity of some of the original texts of the Western tradition, subtract the sum of their practical application throughout the history of European empires and states, and you are left with little that is substantial and real; hardly anything of lasting worth for the betterment of the human race has resulted from European exercises in imperial self-justification. The celebration and defence of imperialism and its intellectual underpinnings is the worst sickness of the colonial mind, and all Euroamericans are affected by this disease of the colonizer to one degree or another.

To be sure, some have found their way out from under the burden of their intellectual heritage of empire and understand what the truth is: they have embraced alternative ways of living and seek to create a balanced, respectful set of relations with other peoples and the earth. So, from the perspective of the Onkwehonwe struggle, the enemy is not the "white man" in racial terms, it is a certain way of thinking with an imperialist's mind. We should ask ourselves if it is possible to blame or hold accountable people in Settler society who tacitly support the colonial regime by inheriting their rights, and wrongs, and continue their lives in ignorance of the colonial state they live within (it is certainly possible to do so in this age of blatantly manipulative media and educational systems). Can we blame those who are simply humanly weak and suffering from insatiable addiction to the material goods of contemporary society? These are difficult questions to answer.

I believe that true culpability implies a more active participation in the core processes of colonialism. What marks a person as guilty is taking part in territorial dispossession, the political denial of Onkwehonwe existences, racialized violence and coercion, cultural disruption, and economic exploitation. We need some precision on these questions, because what good does it do to hate everyone, and what strategic advantage can be gained for us in targeting the whole of Settler society?

The *enemy* imperialists are personified as those who are aware of their unjust power and informed of the effects of their choices, but still choose to do harm and commit rapacious crimes against people and the earth; they are the players in the political economy of Euroamerican arrogance and the intellectual framework that supports its continuing existence. On a theoretical level, the enemy of our struggle is the noxious mix of monotheistic religiosity, liberal political theory, neoliberal capitalist economics and their supportive theories of racial superiority, and the false assumption of Euroamerican cultural superiority.[3]

It is impossible to defeat the institutional or physical manifestations of this enemy, or to challenge our adversaries to do better, so long as the cultural, psychological, and spiritual foundations of Euroamerican arrogance remain intact. A clear-eyed analyst of political relations in Central and South America has remarked, when considering the failed efforts to bring justice to the former Spanish colonies through the armed revolutionary struggles of the 1980s and 1990s: "Given that the dominant groups are disinclined to concede these groups their rights, being more interested in keeping them true 'internal colonies,' the socio-political premises for their recognition can be established only through their own struggles."[4] In seeking to transform colonial society totally, it is a cold fact that *struggle* is necessary to bring *justice* and, eventually, *peace*. The three cannot be conceived or achieved separately, especially in countries whose social, political, and economic relations are colonial at root and remain colonial. The question for us centres not on whether struggle is needed to achieve justice and peace, but on the best way to conduct that struggle. In this context, people who reject or deny the necessity of struggle and contention are in fact defending the privilege of empire and acceding to the continuance of colonial society in all its arrogance.

We are concerned here with clarity, with logic and rationality, and though the necessity of struggle may be difficult to accept on an emotional level and frightening in its implications, a strong, clear mind will recognize that struggle is a necessary conclusion. The failed course of non-contentious, rights-based Onkwehonwe movements proves that contention is necessary to take us forward. The conventional legalist approach to making change, focusing as it does on civil and constitutional rights, or rights parity, or fair treatment for Onkwehonwe within the legal and constitutional structure of one or another colonial state, is basically a moral appeal to the high ideals of the religious foundation of imperialism, Christianity. Rather than being a liberatory struggle, such a legalist approach has led to the constitution of movements and political identities firmly rooted in European cultural vocabulary and Christian symbolism. Aside from the obvious problem that the Western state is based on a vast hypocrisy and has never adhered to the principles it espouses and to which indigenous movements have appealed, the legalist approach has created within indigenous struggles an inauthentic, guilt-ridden, condescending, and degrading agenda full of cries for redemption, grovelling for pity, and begging for a merciful end to mistreatment at white hands. At the same time, appeals to the higher ideals of an arrogantly secure Euroamerican culture buttresses the moral foundation of Christianity so that the legalist approach depends on non-indigenous values and ethics.

The Onkwehonwe alternative to this weak and ineffective approach is a challenging and powerful attack on the very foundations of colonial mentality and Settler society. Euroamerican confidence in their own rectitude and the security of the moral rightness of their civilizing mission must be attacked and destroyed. Onkwehonwe must put forward an alternative rationale for relationships between Settlers and indigenous peoples, rationales which must reflect universal humanistic principles. And we must advance an agenda of social equality and political pluralism by shining the light of radical truth through the fog of racial prejudice and overwrought emotional attachments to colonial institutions that make up the state and culture of colonial society.

Settlers will react to such a movement in a personal, visceral, and emotional way; even those with little to lose, materially, from the changes being promoted will defend their cherished delusions. The inherent conservatism of any human community is strengthened further in a colonial situation by manipulation by elites that have much to lose through any change in the status quo. This conservatism is manifest in personal and public ways and underscores the stronghold colonial myths and identities have on people and how deeply entrenched the psychological bases of imperialism actually are in the public mind. People, not the system, must be the focus of the movement for change because, after all, it is people who make empires; systems and structures are only the theoretical constructions we use to understand the dynamics of psychology manifesting and people interacting in public and private ways.

So, in the framework of this struggle, what kinds of people make up Settler societies today? From the position of a movement for change, it is very important to distinguish between the various elements of the Settler population and to develop appropriate strategies of contention for each of the adversaries and enemies. There are those whom Albert Memmi called the "colonizers who refuse" to accept their position and role in the unjust state, usually left-wing intellectuals.[5] These are people whose indignation at the theoretical injustices of imperialism as an historical process (usually thought of as happening in foreign countries rather than their own beloved backyards) is not accompanied by action. They may be progressive politically, but they usually hold a strong attachment to the colonial state and to their own privileges within Settler society. They are effectively silenced by being caught in the squeeze between their intellectual deconstructions of power and their moral cowardice when it comes to doing something about injustice in a real sense. The colonizers who refuse to acknowledge their privilege and inheritance of wrongs are practising another form of selfishness and hypocrisy—they claim the right and privilege of indignation and the power to judge those cruder colonizers among them and attempt to use this rhetorical posture to release themselves of their own responsibility for the colonial enterprise, both historically and in the way it has affected their own lives, their families' privileges, and their communities' formation. These people are paralyzed by fear. Their guilt renders them useless to our struggle and paradoxically makes them one of the strongest blocs of hard-core conservatism in Settler society. Put so eloquently by the African-American writer Audre Lorde, "guilt is just another name for impotence, for defensiveness destructive of communication, it becomes a device to protect ignorance ... the ultimate protection for changelessness."[6]

Another arm of the colonial body is the colonizer who accepts his or her role, who has internalized colonial myths, mainly racist histories, notions of white superiority, and the lie of progress (or the immigrants' hope that material accumulation and expansion of wealth is indeed the formula for happiness, acceptability by the white man, and legitimacy as citizens). This posture is simple enough to understand and hardly needs further elaboration, except to acknowledge that the majority of the Settler population is in this category, an indication of the vastness of the challenge ahead of us.

Characteristic of colonial societies is the entrenchment by Settlers of irrational notions of racial and cultural superiority (especially among economic elites and the politicians and academics who serve them). Even among those exhibiting signs of fully developed humanity—writers, artists, spiritual people—the powerful psychological process inherent and necessary to the solidity of their identity maintains a hold on their psyche. The psychology of imperial arrogance is displayed in word and deed in myriad ways; colonial society is infused with the flavour of ill-gotten privilege and audacious lies. In terms of government and law, arrogance is manifested in strategies to pass off white people's usurpation, and a feigned legitimacy is constructed to normalize the structure of racism built into notions of indigenous peoples' land tenure and political rights. As an intellectual project, imperial arrogance takes the form of literature, scholarship, and art to demonstrate the eminent merits and to replicate the simple fabricated facts and narratives needed to justify colonial privilege. In case this is not obvious to the reader, here are some examples of these myths:

1. the supposed superiority of Canada over the United States as a place to live, measured in levels of violence, universal health care status, and "non-violent" histories;
2. in the North American popular press and in general attitudes in that society, excessive self-extolling by white people and the moral debasement and disciplining by verbal and physical violence of Onkwehonwe;
3. generally accepted police brutality against non-whites and especially against Onkwehonwe;
4. the prevalence and normalcy of the murder of Onkwehonwe women by white men;
5. the perpetuation in television and film of colonial lies like the glorification of the pioneer spirit, the glorification of the genocide of indigenous peoples, and false stereotypes of Onkwehonwe.

Need I go on…?

Obscurantism is another central psychological and cultural process in colonial societies. Among Settlers speaking of their own countries and situations, decolonization is not admitted as a necessity, at least not in terms of true decolonization as has been mandated morally and politically in Africa and Asia. Their own countries are considered special cases, different in a fundamental way from the colonialism that occurred in Africa and Asia. Why?

It is difficult to figure out because, although many convoluted rationales are offered, the only consistency among their arguments is that their forebears were born *here* and that therefore European settlement *here* is different than in Africa or Asia. The only consistency among the legion of excuses for various family legacies of colonial privilege is moral cowardice on the part of contemporary Settlers. The implication of this obscurantism (historical and moral) is that what is happening *here* in the United States, Canada, Australia, and New Zealand is not as serious as what happened *there* in South Africa and India; and, of course, *we* Americans, Canadians, and Australians *are* not as bad as *they were* in Indochina and the Congo. The larger implication of this attitude is that contemporary Settlers and their situations (i.e., their property and power) are shielded from the full logic of colonization/decolonization as it has been and is understood elsewhere. Giving back stolen lands, paying recompense, and respecting Onkwehonwe autonomy are outside the realm of possibility for Settlers who have thus far escaped the hideous possibility of reckoning with their forefathers' evil misdeeds. I am convinced that most Settlers are in denial. They know that the foundations of their countries are corrupt, and they know that their countries are "colonial" in historical terms, but still they refuse to see and accept the fact that there can be no rhetorical transcendence and retelling of the past to make it right without making fundamental changes to their government, society, and the way they live. For no other reason than a selfish attachment to the economic and political privileges they have collectively inherited as the dominant people in a colonial relationship, they, by cultural instinct and imperative, deny the truth. The disjuncture between knowledge and its acceptance is baffling and grating to anyone who doesn't understand the absolute need to deny in the colonial mind.

To deny the truth is an essential cultural and psychological process in Settler society. Try to understand how even the *Globe and Mail*, a staunchly conservative Canadian financial and news journal, can admit the following, in commenting on the exploitative economic relationship between northern "territories" and the other, wealthier, mainly Euroamerican parts of Canada, and still maintain that Canada itself is a legitimate and just state: "Either our territories will eventually become provinces, or the Canadian government will have to acknowledge that these territories are, in fact, colonial possessions."[7] Whether called a territory or a province, the area remains a colony of Canada, and neither the problems nor the rights of its colonized population, which is largely indigenous, are addressed, and the colonizers

107

themselves never have to face the unsavoury task of acknowledging the truth about themselves.

There are deep roots to the racism and intolerance at the core of Settler cultures. Euroamerican arrogance comes from the monotheistic tradition of Judeo-Christian religions, which preach the "one right way." Biblical scholar Donald Akenson has written extensively against the notion of a "good" Christianity, or Judaism, or Islam for that matter:

> There is no such thing as nice monotheism. How could there be? Monotheism associates the One True God with one set of people, its tribe or converts, and the god of any other people is *traif* (non-kosher). It either has to be destroyed (by destroying its adherents) or, at a minimum, marked down as misled, mistaken, or non-existent.[8]

Monotheism, by transporting a certain spiritual orientation and worldview into cultural forms and projecting those onto the political realm, suffuses patterns of Western thought and modes of governance.[9] Consequently, the depth of the required change is daunting; it would be even more discouraging if monotheism had to be completely defeated for freedom to emerge. But, it is the *institutions* of society that created this reading of the myths and prophets of the peoples' heritage, and *they* are the proper foci of our efforts. The recent and growing trend of American-based Protestant fundamentalist churches proselytizing in Onkwehonwe communities is the most evident of these institutional enemies. Our born-again Christian relatives, who love their people and are otherwise caring, are swept up in a mission to wipe out the remnants of indigenous spirituality in themselves and their communities, some going so far as labelling Onkwehonwe spiritual practices as "satanic."

It is mostly forgotten by monotheists today that Jesus himself was a radical who challenged accepted wisdom and the power of established Jewish and imperial institutions. Jesus' message was co-opted over time by authorities and patterned for a singular truth: theological and political. Christianity became the state religion of the Roman Empire and thence the spiritual font and justification of imperial dominion worldwide in the British and American empires. The monotheistic belief system and worldview is ideally suited to be the justification for subjugation and genocide. It trumpets one right way; singularity; judgement and condemnation; the righteousness of believers, who are chosen people by birth or through conversion; the doctrine of suffering in the here and now for heavenly reward in the afterlife; and strictures against questioning authority. Empire, the root and source of the world system confronting us today, needed a doctrine, and in the xenophobic, retributive, monotheist tradition, it found its perfect match.

The big mistake of Christian church-oriented reformers acting in the political realm to make change has been to convince themselves that there is a higher ethical and moral potential in Christian and Jewish colonizers than is evidenced in their behaviours over the last millennia and in their construction of regimes of destruction and hatred all over the world. The first transcendence must be of the mentality of the "one right way" inherent in the monotheistic tradition, a recognition that there is no wisdom that is detached from nature in all of its diversity and complexity. This is a self-conscious intellectual process of deconstructing the religious and philosophical justifications for imperialism. Rather than being liberatory possibilities, their true function in the world is to pacify and discipline populations and to generate the mentalities that are necessary preconditions for maintaining dominion: subservience to authority, denial of obvious facts, and normalizing discipline by coercive violence.[10]

As a clash of "cultures," "civilizations," etc., this problem could be discussed in more objective theoretical terms to avoid the discomfort of personal responsibility, but, in reality, the injustices we live with are a matter of choices and behaviours committed within a worldview defined by a mental framework of Euroamerican arrogance and self-justifying political ideologies set in opposition to Onkwehonwe peoples and our worldviews. The basic substance of the problem of colonialism is the belief in the superiority and universality of Euroamerican culture, especially the concepts of individual rights as the highest expression of human freedom, representative democracy as being the best guarantor of peace and order, and capitalism as the only means to achieve the satisfaction of human material needs.

It is this "liberal dogma"[11] that is the clearest and most present manifestation of Euroamerican arrogance, and it displays itself across the political spectrum and colonial class structure as racism, conservatism, and liberalism. This is evident in the knee-jerk and dogmatic reactions to the challenge to established order that emanate from the intellectual defenders of imperialism and most vehemently in the predictable scholarly and political backlash to movements for fundamental change.[12]

At base, the liberal, conservative, and racist reactions across the political spectrum are the same and distinguish themselves from each other only in their varying intensities and styles. There is complete unity around the basics, though, and it is possible to outline the framework of the imperial/colonial mentality, which has come to form the parameters of the Euroamerican worldview and the far limits of normal political and social thought in contemporary Settler societies.

+ *Sharing and equality are wrong.* This is made clear in the Settlers' rejection of all forms of real socialism.
+ *Selfishness and competitiveness are good.* This is evident in the Settlers' sacred attachment to money, material goods, and competition.
+ *Science and technology are "progressive" and therefore good, whereas humans (being cursed with Original Sin or just being unwieldy) are bad and nature is fearsome.* This is plain to see in the unremitting drive of white people to conquer the natural world and exploit it to impose the predictability and order needed for capitalism to function smoothly.
+ *Order is of higher value than truth and justice.*
+ *Euroamerican culture is the perfect form of human existence,* and every other way of life is a threat to civilization and freedom. This is made clear in the disrespect, denial, and outright hostility to other peoples' ways of seeing and being in the world.

It is the unquestioned normalcy of these beliefs and assumptions that must be problematized for decolonization to occur. The behaviours that flow from them must be linked to their roots as a way of tracing the imperial mentality to its source. As it stands, within the paradigms of Euroamerican arrogance, injustices are explained away through deflective strategies of denial, projection, or misappropriation. Racial discord, physical violence, and all manner of conflict are attributable to strictly material causes or to differences within Onkwehonwe cultures or dysfunction in the non-white population.

The vast hypocrisy of Western "civilization" is an attempt to obscure the various truths of Euroamerican life. If we could ignore all the self-justifications not rooted in any observable reality, what would Euroamerican values consist of? Through their critical reflection, vocal opponents of liberal orthodoxy and the growth of corporate power in Western societies have exposed for us the foundational values of Euroamerican society. Media critic Jerry Mander has even created a list that captures what we might call the essence of whiteness as cultural and social construct: profit, growth, competition, aggression, amorality (consciously masked by a faux altruism), hierarchy, quantification, dehumanization, exploitation, anti-nature, and homogenization.[13]

Being so ingrained and so amorphous, the "whiteness" of the way we live our lives is difficult to analyze or criticize because the values Mander lists are the overwhelming cultural reality of life in Western societies. The core and unique nature of the Euroamerican worldview are easier to grasp when they are considered as a set of practices, or principles, in the context of relations between colonial states and Onkwehonwe.[14] Euroamerican arrogance and its cultural assumptions have operated in the context of political domination and economic dependency to produce pure expressions of white power and project them onto the lives of Onkwehonwe. This arrogance is the root cause of the massive problems affecting our societies and creating such a financial and moral burden on the Settlers: social and psychological suffering in Onkwehonwe communities, unstable political relations between Onkwehonwe nations and state governments, and land dispossession and environmental pollution. Yet, Euroamerican society still displays the persistence of arrogance in confronting these problems by attempting to design solutions from within the same intellectual and moral framework that created the problems in the first place! In the processes that have been implemented to attempt the decolonization of internal colony states not only in Central and South America, but also in Canada, New Zealand, and Australia, Settlers have steadfastly refused to remove themselves from the foundations of their colonial enterprise. They prefer to lazily observe and address the problem from within the comfort zone of their own imperial cultural heritage.

For instance, technical and bureaucratic reforms always take precedence over political questions. One example in Canada is the establishment of the British Columbia Treaty Commission negotiation framework, which is the main process for resolving the issue of the nearly total lack of treaties transferring ownership of the land from Onkwehonwe to colonial governments in what is now known as British Columbia. It was determined at the outset that the negotiations could not consider questions of principle on indigenous land ownership or questions on the state's claims of ownership or jurisdictional legitimacy. In the realm of Canadian law, reform of the Onkwehonwe-state relationship is discussed and negotiated as a reinterpretation of existing constitutional provisions and of federal and provincial statutes, not as a constitutional rearrangement.[15]

Myths of national identity and prejudicial attachments to colonial structures and symbols as the guarantors of social peace and "national unity" are

111

sacred and always remain unexamined and unquestioned. This leads to a political climate in which radical notions of justice are seen as a threat to the very existence of the countries supposedly seeking to transcend the legacy of colonialism. These myths and attachments are rooted in a simplistic liberal ideology that has as one of its core premises that unity requires homogeneity: we can all get along only if we are all made to be the same. Hence, the rejection of pluralistic notions of relationship and the inherent institutional-statist bias in all discussions of reforming relations between Onkwehonwe and Settlers.[16]

If the mere idea of difference threatens colonial societies and the liberal state in an existential sense, the capacity to act on collective differences is definitely seen as a very real threat to be suppressed. Any notion of indigenous autonomy is rejected by states as a threat to "national sovereignty"[17] based on the fiction of preserving national unity and an explicit rejection of inherent culturally rooted Onkwehonwe collective rights and freedoms. Indigeneity is legitimized and negotiated only as a set of state-derived individual rights aggregated into a community social context—a very different concept than that of collective rights pre-existing and independent of the state. This position, held by the populace and government representatives, holds that Onkwehonwe rights are incompatible with liberal legal guarantees of civil and human rights and freedoms for all citizens within the state, a position founded on the unproven and unobservable assumption of the superiority of Euroamerican concepts of rights and freedoms.

Onkwehonwe rights and freedoms are always falsely identified in the mass media and public commentary (which are tacitly supported by the government) as the instruments by which Settlers are victimized. Recognizing and respecting Onkwehonwe rights is played off against white people's property values and their personal and emotional security, which are all at base an assertion of convenience and entitlement to continue in the benefit of crimes by earlier generations without recompense to the actual people who suffered in the relationship. The convenience of this assertion as justification for the unwillingness of the white population to take serious stands against injustice should not be lost on anyone; the pronouncement that Onkwehonwe rights harm white people is simply not true and cannot be supported with evidence. It is nothing but a Rhodesian projection of white power onto a framework of potential Onkwehonwe achievement and reempowerment.

These false decolonization processes also all demand clear demarcations of the territorial bounds of the concept of Onkwehonwe nationhood.

This may not sound like such a problem at first glance, but it is in fact a conscious tactic designed to ensure the failure of meaningful negotiations. The demand for territorial clarity and non-overlapping negotiations on land issues is predicated on an acceptance of the Euroamerican way of viewing land, demarking and dividing the land and environment and relationships between peoples on the basis of European-derived notions of property, ownership, and jurisdiction.[18]

These are the fundamentals of Euroamerican arrogance projected onto the politics of decolonization. This is what Memmi's disease of the European looks like to us today. Is there a cure? Is there a way to break the grip of this powerful sickness in the hearts and minds of Settler society?

These questions are of enormous significance. How do we make their history and their country mean something different to people who feel entitled to the symbolic and real monopoly they enjoy on the social dynamics of our relationship and on the cultural landscape?[19] It seems that if we are to move beyond the charitable racism of current policies or paternalist progressivism of liberal reconciliation models, justice must become a *duty* of, not a *gift* from, the Settler.[20] And for this to happen, Settler society must be forced into a reckoning with its past, its present, its future, and itself. White people who are not yet decolonized must come to admit they were and are wrong. They must admit that Onkwehonwe have rights that are collective and inherent to their indigeneity and that are autonomous from the Settler society—rights to land, to culture, and to community. The Settlers' inability to comprehend justice for Onkwehonwe from within their own cultural frame is simple, really. Why are the Settlers' supposed gifts and concessions, stingy and reluctant though they are, toward Onkwehonwe not seen as duties? Because that would mean the Settlers must admit that they were and are wrong and would imply a set of rights for Onkwehonwe.

THE OTHER SIDE OF FEAR

The colonial relationship is a dynamic relation of arrogance, complacency, and complicity. Aboriginalist complicity with the injustice and Onkwehonwe complacency toward our rights and freedoms enable the arrogance. Euroamerican pretensions are empowered and emboldened by the unwillingness of Onkwehonwe to defend the truth and by people's participation in the white man's lies. As Onkwehonwe who are committed to the Original

Teachings, there is not supposed to be any space between the principles we hold and the practice of our lives. This is the very meaning of integrity: having the mental toughness and emotional strength to stand up for what we believe is right. The challenge is to master, not conquer, fear and to engage in the constant fight to resist both the corrupting effects of the financial, sensual, and psychological weapons used by the colonial authorities to undermine Onkwehonwe people and the corrosive effect on the Onkwehonwe mind and soul of Euroamerican culture and society. The question here is a real and immediate one for Onkwehonwe who enter the struggle actively: How do we deal with the psychological and physical battle fatigue which in most cases leads to eventual despair and defeatism?

Tahehsoomca voices deep experience of this question. She expresses not only the frustrations of dealing with the Euroamerican attitude on a daily basis, but also the fulfilment that can be achieved in standing against the tide, even in a quiet and (mostly) non-confrontational way. A former elected band chief of a small Nuu-Chah-Nulth community on northern Vancouver Island,[21] she is a woman of immense strength and integrity who has persevered in the pursuit of her own personal transcendence of colonialism's realities in her life, racial prejudice against her, violence, and community suffering. Beyond this, she has been consistent in her efforts to bring her people together and to bring dignity to their lives, in spite of many personal betrayals and political setbacks and continuing community discord. She is unwilling to accept her people's colonized situation. She is repelled by the disgustingly selfish and destructive attitudes of people who are in positions of power in the Indian Affairs system. Yet she is unable to turn away; she is drawn to fight against further losses and shaming.

I invited Tahehsoomca to talk with me about her personal struggle and that of her community. At the time we spoke, she was engaged on all levels in the battle to confront the realities of Canada's control over her people and the effects that the loss of control and dignity have had on her family and community.

TA: *We always hear people talk about how oppressive the dysfunction and violence is on isolated Indian reserves. You've lived there; is it really that bad?*
T: Yes, it is. I went to my home community ten years ago, after having lived on a reserve outside of Victoria all of my life, and the difference between this urban reserve and my home reserve was obvious in the oppression that people there experienced. When I first went home, there were ten houses and none of them were sober. Now there are 12 houses, and three of them

are sober homes—people know that there isn't any drinking in those three houses. Now I can see, ten years later, a bit of a difference. People are starting to take responsibility and stop blaming everybody else for their problems. But that's only a small percentage.

But still, you don't see any singing or dancing or any of that when you go into our community. When I was the chief, I asked people from elsewhere to come in and do those things, because we didn't have anything. We had to bring people in from the outside. That meant a lot for our community: getting something back that we had lost. I'll tell you, I was so surprised to see drummers and singers, and people saying, "Who are the women that danced?" Ten years ago, it was gone. Now it's coming back. It's all coming back, but in a different kind of way. Before I was chief, our meeting would start with, "Our Father, who art in heaven…"

TA: *The Lord's Prayer, at a band council meeting? You're kidding?*
T: The whole thing! So I was like, "We gotta change that. If there's anything we're going to change, that's going to be the first thing!" So after that, my grandfather, Grandpa Moses, our Elder, or whoever was there that could speak our language, was asked to say a few things to open the meeting. That was one of the first changes that we made when I became chief. Before that, Moses was never asked to say a prayer in our language. That's something that we started, and that's something that still continues. And if we don't have somebody there who can do it in our language, we'll say in English what Moses meant to say in Indian.

TA: *It sounds like not only land and money were stolen from your people, but memory and history too.*
T: The reason we're having to undo so much damage is because our leaders don't know how to be chiefs. They don't know their roles and responsibilities like a chief a long time ago would have known. We're having a clash of hereditary chiefs right now. Everybody wants to be a chief; but they don't actually want to take the responsibility that goes along with it. They just want a title.

Traditionally, we had 21 hereditary chiefs, ranked in terms of their responsibilities, based on the leadership a chief had demonstrated. That's how my family held the first seat; it was because our family had the leadership skills that the people required and valued. But when the Department of Indian Affairs came into our community, they appointed another chief to take a place in our seat. Now our family does not hold a seat at all, ever since the Department

115

came in years ago and said to some guy, "You're a chief," just because that man knew how to speak English. Our number one chief, the one they call *Tyee*, is a fellow from another community who's not registered on our band list and who doesn't live in our community. He is chief because his great-grandfather was the one appointed by the Indian Department.

TA: *It seems like such a screwed-up idea of traditional or hereditary "leadership."*
T: That's the debate that Grandpa Moses and I used to have before he passed away. He wasn't very happy with the way that I thought about leadership and about being a chief in my own way. If you ever talked to Moses about it, it was all heredity. He'd say, "It's just blood, that's the important thing." To me, it all just boiled down to the ability to show leadership. But for him it was all bloodline, and that's still kind of the way people look at it now. They don't look at it in terms of responsibility at all.

TA: *What would it mean to you for somebody to show leadership in your community?*
T: People always talk about what needs to be done, but never do it. My uncle was the chief of our band for 15 years. We heard him talk about tradition, but it wasn't actually happening. Everything he wanted to show off to the world wasn't even actually happening in our own community. Ten years ago, we didn't know who we were because we'd lost the knowledge of all the family linkages, so we started trying to bring that back as well. I never thought of that effort as what you would call "leadership." I didn't. It took a number of people, friends and family, to point out that what I was doing was leadership. I was afraid of what leadership meant and the responsibilities that came with it. What motivated me was wanting to get rid of my corrupt uncle! (Laughter.) Seriously, I wanted to change things from where one person was getting rich while everybody else was suffering. That's why I became the chief. Moses would always say that the best way to have an impact is to be consistent in what you're doing and what you're saying. Until he told me I was a leader, I didn't see myself as one. I was afraid of this whole "power going to your head" kind of thing.

TA: *Did it? I can't really tell...*
T: No! (Laughter.) I'm sure if it did, I'd probably still be in there. Well... it was tempting sometimes.

TA: *What were some of the things that the government people threw at you to try to corrupt you and turn you into a regular old corrupt band council chief?*

T: They just tried to get me to cozy up with them, you know? Like, "Stop by and let's go for a coffee sometime …" Seriously. You know, they try to treat you just like you're a regular person and say things to me like, "Wow, you're a woman chief, that says a lot" and all this other stuff. It was just so phoney. It didn't appeal to me at all. It was all political! Their whole thing is that they want you to cooperate. They want to be able to say, "We can rely on her to not block that road." To me, that's what it was all about. I say that because it was only when they were cutting down all our trees that I met the premier of the province, so of course they were trying to "build relationships." And it wasn't very often at these things that I'd actually see other Indians. As the band chief, I was the token president of this logging company that we had partnered with, so I would get invited to all these fancy dinners, and of course, all of these politicians were there—they were very uncomfortable evenings for me.

TA: *Did you have to go home and puke afterwards?*
T: I went home and had a long shower to try to clean myself off! I went to three of these events, and I'll tell you, all of them were pure torture. I don't even know why I went back after the first time when I didn't have to travel anywhere. After that, they were in Vancouver, and it was all such a phoney atmosphere. You had all these politicians around, and you had logging industry representatives… And I could tell there were people in that room who were threatened by Indians, yet they kind of want to be nice to you so they can get your trees.

TA: *What kept you grounded through it all?*
T: Well, what can I say, I'm Indian! I'm not like them, you know what I mean? I have principles and values that they don't have and that they'll probably never have.

TA: *When you say you weren't sucked in because you're "Indian," I know what you're talking about. But don't we have to admit that there are other "Indians" who are at the party and just loving every minute of it?*
T: That's because for them it's about money and prestige. At that one event with the premier, there was a fellow there—he was at every one of them— and you know, I didn't even know the man was Indian. He barely looked Indian; but he didn't act Indian, you know what I mean? Like, I went dressed in whatever I was most comfortable with; I didn't get made up in a shiny dress or any of that other crap. I know I stood out, but I didn't care.

And here's this guy wearing a suit and a tie trying to "network" and all of that. I'll tell you, there were so many other times I was asked to go, but I'd say that I was sick, or my kid was sick, or you know, somebody died.

TA: *Wow...*
T: I know, I know. That's bad, but I just couldn't do it. I couldn't go.

TA: *If it's not about money for you then, what is it about?*
T: It's about trying to save what we have left so that we will survive. Lots of people say these things all the time about what we are, based on tradition and the past and all of that, but it's not true anymore. We're so co-opted and assimilated. It's important to me because of my kids, too. I want them to take this forward. Moses used to say that we need to get beyond surviving, but I don't think that we'll get beyond surviving in my lifetime. I don't know exactly why, but I just don't believe that.

Then again, I think that those of us who are fighting for the survival of our people have the opportunity to influence others to do the right thing and to turn around. There are people who will listen, and I think the numbers are growing now. I'm saying this even though I personally tried to leave everything back there recently, because I was so burnt out. Sometimes you just want to say, "To hell with it." But you can't. I've stayed involved in my community in any way that I can because, just like Moses said, "You have to be consistent." See, people always start out that way, but most of them end up as sell-outs. We have a lot of faith in them, but years go by, and they turn into sell-outs.

TA: *How does that happen, you think?*
T: Money and greed. And, for at least the one sell-out that I know real well, the help of people in government, who would make things easy for him.

TA: *Wasn't it his own personal choices, early on in his life and career, that set him up to be the kind of person who could be a sell-out, though?*
T: Exactly. He hasn't lived in the community since the 1960s. He's married to a white woman. The guy's got quite a lifestyle—he's got condos all over the world—and he's very accustomed to all of that. He can't, or doesn't want to, change what he makes and who he is.

TA: *So uncorrupted people like yourself have a different set of values, heh?*

T: I like material things too. I'm not going to say I don't. But that's not what controls me. I think what makes me different is that I see and I feel what's going on, and I don't like it. What makes me feel good is learning and appreciating our culture and traditions and all that stuff. That makes me feel better than driving around in a new car, or flying to Vegas for a long weekend, or whatever. These other values are what I hope to bring forward, because without them, we're nothing.

TA: *Were you born this way, or what?*
T: I think it's just who I am. I was raised by my grandmothers, not only my mother. With my great-grandmother, nothing made her more happy than her own children and to see them learn and grow and teaching them songs and dances. I was about five years old the last time I ever saw my great-grandmother dance, and she did it with pride. She danced at her son's funeral, making sure that he was sent home properly. It's the teachings she left me that have shaped me. Even my grandmother, who's still here today, and my Mom—because she was very caring and giving and didn't have a selfish bone in her body—it's been those women who have helped me. I would take a day at a potlatch over a day at a casino, that's for sure.

TA: *Are you an optimistic person?*
T: People always used to say I was optimistic, but I'm really frustrated because of the divisions among our people. There are some of us that believe so strongly in the culture and our values, but then there are others that want to sell-out our rights, thinking that it's going to solve all of our problems if we just own land and pay taxes like everybody else. I don't really worry about it a lot though, because I think that if you just do what you can to make things harder for the government, you're really doing something. That's what I like to do: make things difficult for them. We started doing that at home, but then we sort of fell down. So now I'm frustrated. But maybe we'll get going again once we get a real leader in there at the higher levels, instead of the ones we have there now and who are just in it for the money and the status.

The question in my mind centres on what makes Tahesoomca different from her uncle and the other co-opted and corrupted leaders who populate the institutions that purport to govern and represent Onkwehonwe. Tahesoomca was, as always, honest and remarkably candid, yet the place she and I arrived at in our conversation didn't satisfy my attempt to understand why Onkwehonwe can turn their backs on their own people and sign on to help the colonial governments further undermine Onkwehonwe nationhood or become part of the colonial machine itself. I found myself still thinking that it couldn't be just monetary motivation, sheer greed, that turned someone against his or her people. I needed to think more deeply about the nature of co-optation and corruption and delve into the aspects of this process brought to light by Tahesoomca's reflection on her uncle's life. His early experiences and choices had set him up to be a willing intermediary of white power in the Nuu-Chah-Nulth community. This, I believe, was key to understanding how he and others can become collaborators with the colonizer.

The Burmese democratic movement leader, Aung San Suu Kyi, who spent years imprisoned by that country's ruling military dictatorship, has said that, "It is not power that corrupts but fear."[22] To me, she means that the holder of power fears losing it, and the ones subject to power fear the scourge of it.

Five hundred years of physical and psychological warfare have created a colonial culture of fear among both subdued and dominant peoples. We have emerged out of a shameful past, a history of racial and religious hatreds, of extreme violence, and of profound injustice. It is impossible to even acknowledge it truthfully. Colonial culture, for both the victims and the perpetrators, is fundamentally a denial of the past and of its moral implications. It is an aversion to the truth about who we really are and where it is that we come from. More than the moneyed privilege of the newcomers, more than the chaotic disadvantage of the original peoples, this is what we have inherited from our colonial past: relationships founded on hatred and violence and a culture founded on lies to assuage the guilt or shame of it all. We are afraid of our memories, afraid of what we have become, afraid of each other, and afraid for the future. Fear is the foundation of the way we are in the world and the way we think about the future. It is normal, and we have grown used to it.

All of what we know as government and law is founded on these fears. The powerful in our society manage the words we hear and the images we see to ensure that we remain afraid. Although the past and its implications are self-evident, we are complicit in their denial because it is too painful or arduous or costly to imagine an existence unbound from the lies. Emotionally and psychologically, we are attached to this mythology of colonialism because it explains the Euroamerican conquest and normalizes it in our lives. The perpetrators know that it is wrong to steal a country and so deny it is a crime; the victims know that it is shameful to accept defeat lying down.

Yet, complacency rules over both because the thought of what might come out of transcending the lies is too... fearsome.

Lying complacent in a narrow conception of the past and nearly paralyzed by fear in a constrained vision of the future, both the colonized and colonizers have been forced to accept and live with a state of unfreedom. This is the most profound meaning of colonialism's modern turn. Of course, this is made possible because the vast lie has been embedded in every aspect of our lives for so long as memory, as identity, and as political and economic relations of domination and exploitation.

What kind of culture has been produced by this denial of truth and wearing down of authenticity—of rooted, healthy, and meaningful ways of life—in the service of political and economic power? This question must be asked not only of the subdued but of the dominant as well. Colonialism is a total relation of power, and it has shaped the existence not only of those who have lost but also those who have profited.

Delving deeper into the problem of corruption, beyond the simple notion of rule or trust-breaking for material gain, it is apparent that, as Aung San Suu Kyi has explained, fear is the root. Corruption in fact can be understood best as a kind of panicked grasping for control in the face of profound fear of losing what one has or the potential to get what you think you are due. This corruption leads to the bribery and nepotism that have become the normal methods of political relation in First Nations governments and organizations. Corruption can also show itself as spite, the fear of one another translating into hostility. It can also be wilful ignorance—the fear of knowledge. Whatever its form, corruption slowly but surely destroys one's sense of right and wrong. This is the key to understanding how Onkwehonwe who think they can change the system from within instead get changed from within themselves.

This understanding of corruption, and how people are manipulated by governments playing on their fears to set patterns of behaviour and to structure choices, is crucial to understanding how the most fearful and striving of people in our nations, those who make up the intellectual and political elite in the recently emerged "aboriginal" middle classes, have conspired with the state to maintain the status quo and legitimize the colonial system, and more than this, to criminalize radical turns in the Onkwehonwe movement. What I think of as aboriginalists within our communities—politicians, economic elites, and moderate intellectuals who actively conspire with the colonial authorities to prevent the activation of a political or cultural resurgence against the colonial order and who are dependent financially and for their personal status on that order—fear the consequences of change on one level or another (in some cases on multiple levels). The anti-warrior partisans of order, those pacifists, legalists, and reformists among us, set themselves up in a position to support compromise versus action.[23] This is their role and function in the colonial relationship.

Many readers will no doubt have observed this phenomenon of fear and self-loathing play itself out. The best example I can remember from my own experience happened in Geneva, Switzerland, at the meeting of the United Nations Working Group on Indigenous Peoples, when I heard the Inuit politician, John Amagoalik, one of the instrumental figures in arctic politics and in the surrender of Inuit land title to form the Canadian territory of Nunavut, give a talk to a group of indigenous delegates and European attendees. Amagoalik was introduced to the audience by his host, the Canadian ambassador, as "the only living Founding Father of Canada." He then proceeded to deliver a strident speech supporting the government of Canada's policies on self-government and land claims, arguing that cooperation and negotiation are the only ways to solve problems between indigenous peoples and states. He stated bluntly that the Inuit were awarded a territorial government and land rights in Canada because "we are not Indians, who run around on blockades with guns causing trouble." When confronted on this statement by a European woman, who chastised him for his arrogance and disrespectful words toward Onkwehonwe who had fought to defend their lands and lives at Oka and Kahnawake in 1990, Amagoalik backtracked and admitted eventually that, "before 1990 the government wasn't taking us very seriously, and after Oka they gave us everything we wanted." To me, this was a supreme example of ignorance, spite, greed, and fear all rolled into one shameful display of kowtowing to the colonial master. But corruption of the less famous and less costly type, at the community level, is just as rampant and responsible for maintaining the status quo.

The most common form of corruption in indigenous communities is plain and basic material greed. Onkwehonwe are understandably reluctant to expose this unsavoury feature of our political life in public discourse; it is difficult to get people talking about issues of corruption because of the close family ties between people within communities and the persistent Onkwehonwe cultural aversion to direct confrontation, as well as the fact that right-wing politicians and the mainstream media use negative stories about indigenous community life to justify their racist attacks on our existences. Not everyone is afraid to tell the truth (though there is a great aversion to be singled out as someone speaking against one's relatives). I met a woman from another West Coast First Nation on Vancouver Island who agreed to talk with me about the problems in her community and who gave different kinds of answers to the question of just what makes people who stand up for the truth different from those who cooperate with or profit from unjust power.[24]

TA: *If I mention the words "indigenous resistance," what comes to your mind?*
A: Oka 1990. The most important thing about Oka for us was that it made our people aware that you can be militant, that there are other options to being complacent, and that they include standing up for yourself. The thing with a lot of our people, though, is that there is a conflict between taking a political stand and their own personal economic position. A lot of our people are loggers. A lot of our people work in the very industries that are threatening our traditional culture and our environment. So what do you do then? If you shut down logging, you don't have a job! How do you sustain yourself?

TA: *Is there any thought on that question at all, to try to get beyond the obvious stalemate that tends to do nothing or participating in destroying the culture and environment?*
A: I think it's starting to move in that direction. I see discussions around this today, whereas no one even talked about it ten years ago. We were so colonized intellectually that we never even thought beyond what the government told us to think about. The fact that some of our people started to get educated opened up a lot of ideas, and it led us to start speaking out about them. We were just emotionally, physically, intellectually tied up by the government—everybody was complacent. It's only been in recent years that things have started to change, and a lot of that had to do with Oka. That was something that people had never experienced before.

TA: *In the communities, you see lots of people who are very strong in their identity and close to the traditional culture, but yet in politics, especially at the higher levels of politics, the people involved in that are so assimilated and cooperative with the provincial and federal governments.*
T: Oh, there'll be a lot of internal friction in the next few years. It's the young people who are standing up and demanding that our leadership take a different route and turn away from what the government is offering us. Who are the ones in power? Who are the ones sitting at negotiating tables? It's all the old people who don't mind compromising. But then again, look, if you are somebody in your late fifties with a high school education getting

paid $200 a day to sit at conferences and meetings, and if this is your only income, you're not going to change.

TA: *If it's just about someone preserving his job and scamming money like any other politician, that's easy for me to understand. But I wonder if there's something deeper to it. It seems like there might be a cultural difference between the generations. Maybe it'll be a situation where ten years from now there will be a whole generation of assimilated compromisers calling themselves "elders" who will be totally alienated from the younger generation making up 70 per cent of the population? That would be a much more serious problem.*

A: A lot of it is that the older people are only looking for what they can get right now. They're not looking into the future. We always hear how Indian people in other places talk about your actions today affecting future generations. You don't hear that in our community! Let's be honest: those guys at the negotiating table are not sitting there for what their children are going to get, they're there for themselves. It's got nothing to do with the seven generations down the road. You actually hear people talking like, "So what, let the loggers come in and rape the land. Who gives a shit? We're getting millions of dollars." I've heard it! I grew up hearing that.

TA: *Ho-la! It's worse than I thought.*
A: It really is. You're writing about greed and short-sightedness? You want to see greed and short-sightedness? You come to our area when it's fish day, when the salmon are running, and when we sit down with the Fisheries Commission and the federal Department of Fisheries to set the quotas to allow so many fish to go up river so the stock can survive. They're not thinking about the future. A lot of it is greed, for sure. I don't care who complains when there's hardly any fish left and says, "The white man did this..." It's been going on since I was a kid among our own people, and I've seen it. This is the kind of thing that we have to get past. But it's hard to say these things, because we're talking about poor people who've never had anything, and once you get something, it's very hard to go back to not having it anymore.

TA: *Is there any work going on to try to rebuild a solid indigenous cultural foundation in the community so that people have the intellectual and cultural tools to resist this kind of thing?*
A: I think there are a few youth that are taking the leadership in that area. They are the ones who are telling the politicians to stop. They really under-

stand the need to reclaim and to understand the culture and to use our culture as the basis for any kind of movement. The more I understand our leadership, the more afraid I get about the future, about the place we are headed ten years down the road. They're still so damn afraid of the white man. And not only that; they still believe he's smarter than us. Look at our communities; who runs them? Who are the managers of our programs? In my own tribe, our band manager is white! For all of our own people who have gone through law programs and who have a higher education in other areas, who do we hire to sit at negotiation tables with our leaders, and who do we pay $1,000 per day? White lawyers. And the way we treat them, you'd think those white lawyers were the Queen of England when they walk into our territory—people are giving them Salish sweaters and blankets… I say, "Christ, we're paying them a thousand dollars a day, we're the ones who should be getting presents from those friggin' idiots!"

Ah, but then again, look at the age of our leaders. They're all in their fifties and early sixties; they're all from the Old School and believe you have to do Indian politics in a certain way. But the real world is just not like that any more. We really need to get some younger people in there with new ideas, people who are focused on the culture. Culture never comes into play with our current leaders. In my own experience working in the tribal government, we did do some small things, but it was just, how would you say, a display? Like, we had elders opening up meetings, but were they there to negotiate, or advise, or make decisions? Of course not. The elders were just brought in to do their little prayer song, and then they were escorted right back out the door. I was just horrified to see that things like this were still happening.

From fear as the cause of corruption, it is possible, with the insight provided by this woman's brutally frank observations, to conclude that perhaps the fear so common among Onkwehonwe is the effect of the long process of deculturation so central to the colonial process. On the West Coast, residential schools certainly created a generation of people who for the most part were stripped of their language and indigenous cultural identity. Yet these same people were promoted as the leaders and spokesmen of their nations. Without a culture (for they were never accepted and integrated into white society) and lacking real skills or an indigenous ethical framework, these people were given a large voice and the responsibility to lead their people and control the colonial structures that existed in their communities. If you were one of these people, would this not be a fearsome situation to face? How can we expect people who were shaped largely by the experi ence of having the worst of white people (racism, greed, and sexual perversion) forced upon them as children to react when they were handed heavy responsibilities and near-absolute power over their people?

SPACES WE OCCUPY

In many countries, the term "aboriginal" is seen as an inoffensive and innocuous substitute for more caustic words like "Indian," or "Native." Unpacked as a social, political, and intellectual construction, however, it is a highly offensive word. It reflects the prevailing colonial mentality in its redefinition of Onkwehonwe away from our original languages,[25] because it fashions "the people" as a symbol and concept constructed on, and totally amenable to, colonialism. Being aboriginal, once the implications are fully understood, is repugnant to anyone who desires to preserve Onkwehonwe ways of life. The ideas that Onkwehonwe will be inevitably integrated wholly into the Settler society (meaning that their autonomous existences will be terminated actively or voluntarily) and that their governments and lands will be subsumed within the colonial state have become the accepted ideological frame of Settler society, state governments, and many Onkwehonwe themselves. It is the lens through which they view the problem of colonial injustice. Aboriginalism is the new paradigm. But what is it, exactly?

Aboriginalism is assimilation's end-game, the terminological and psychic displacement of authentic indigenous identities, beliefs, and behaviours with one designed by Indian Department bureaucrats, government lawyers, and judges to complete the imperial objective of exterminating Onkwehonwe presences from the social and political landscape. It is the final stage of the annihilation of an independent existence for the original peoples, a cultural and political-economic process of state-sponsored identity invention to dispossess and assimilate the remnants of the Onkwehonwe who are still tied to this land and to indigenous ways of life.

Aboriginalism is the ideology of the Onkwehonwe surrender to the social and mental pathologies that have come to define colonized indigenous existences and the inauthentic, disconnected lives too many of our people find themselves leading. It is the latest version of the many ideologies of conquest that have been used to justify assaults on our peoples' rights and freedoms. The Settlers have been very successful, through education and religion, in turning Onkwehonwe against one another and creating a segment of people in our communities who will collaborate with government to do the work formerly assigned to colonial agents. But beyond this obvious complicity, there is also the widespread descent into defeatism among many of our people. In fact, the real effect of this widespread defeatism—social suffering by Onkwehonwe—is the most visible feature of our communities to the outside world. Aboriginalism obscures everything that is historically true and meaningful about Onkwehonwe—our origins, languages, and names; our land, our heritage, and our rights—and puts in their place views of history and of ourselves and our futures that are nothing more than the self-justifying myths and fantasies of the Settler. Onkwehonwe, Anishnaabe, and Dene are denied their full and rooted meaning, and our people are made to become aboriginal; in the process real and meaningful connections to our pasts, our rights, and our strength are severed. This is the genocidal function of aboriginalism, the prettied-up face of neo-colonialism that is dispassionately integrated into the media, government, and academic discourses as integration, development, and, sometimes more honestly, as assimilation. It is the attempt to destroy authentic existences and replace them with ways of life and self-definitions that best serve Euroamerican wants, needs, and beliefs.

All forms of so-called action within the aboriginalist paradigm and mentality differ from true Onkwehonwe resurgences in a basic way: Onkwehonwe resurgences are eruptions of heritage, tied to the thick roots of indigenous values and modes of relation and ethics. Aboriginalism is a modern false consciousness fixated on fear of the white man, calculations of interest, and the construction of instrumental soft identities in the context of a paradigm and mentality built on the values of material efficiency and social Darwinism, the concept of progress, and the fundamental but rarely stated belief in Euroamerican cultural and racial superiority.

Aboriginalism is a cultural strategy on the part of the state; spiritual defeat and cultural assimilation thus accomplished, political and economic negotiations become a sort of mopping-up operation. Justice in its aboriginal configuration is founded on taken-for-granted assertions, powers, and modes of relation that would force Onkwehonwe to accept and integrate into the liberal democratic institutions of Euroamerican society. This process is founded on the idea that all cultures are mutable and constantly changing and that all cultural boundaries are contested—but with the practical caveat, of course, that it is only Onkwehonwe cultures that change and mutate to accommodate the supposedly natural and just cultural exchange and interaction.[26] With this hypocritical premise exposed, aboriginalist justice appears as nothing more than a post-modern restatement of capitalist rule, and aboriginalist freedom simply means bringing Onkwehonwe from one state of oppression, achieved by previously excluding us and denying our rights, to another form of control predicated instead on integrating us as decultured individuals and defining our rights in conformity with the needs of the liberal capitalist state.

If we contrast this current turn of empire, represented by spiritual and cultural annihilation and the denial of authenticity, with the classic imperial strategy of brutal physical dispersion and dispossession, which often left the spiritual and cultural core of the surviving imperial subjects intact, could we with any certainty say which form of imperialism is more evil or effective in killing off nations in the long term?

Neo-colonialism differs from earlier colonial experiences in Africa and Asia in that its object is not to preserve the racially based subjugation of indigenous peoples. Instead, it promotes their elimination by assimilation, as embodied in the notion of aboriginalism. This is nothing more than the promotion and legitimacy of a politically denuded ethnic form of identity constructed by the state through law and policy and based on a pan-indigenous non-culture stripped of any spiritual meaning or social significance beyond that of the multicultural mainstream of Settler society.

In this spiritual and psychological war of genocide and survival, immersed in colonial cultures, surrounded by Settlers, and falsely labelled as citizens of the states which have forcibly integrated them, Onkwehonwe are offered only two choices on the question of culture and identity within the aboriginal paradigm: accept being excluded—and the alienation, loss, and frustration that that situation implies—or choose to become assimilated. It is difficult to counter, even difficult to imagine, a way to act against such an insidious form of controlling and destructive power. Some theorists of resistance have imagined countering this post-modern imperialism with new and autonomous social constructions of counter-empire, based on the understanding that imperialism is a machine that destroys indigeneity in all its forms and produces identities, like that of the aboriginal, that are compatible with empire's capitalistic purposes. Scholars of the modern globalized empire must surely recognize the aboriginalist identity as what the political theorists Hardt and Negri, in their influential work *Empire*, term a "mimetic euroself" instrumentally constructed to serve the state.[27]

Both of the broad aboriginalist paths, represented by the two choices above, are roads to nowhere for Onkwehonwe. As the Canadian philosopher James Tully has outlined in his recent critiques of modern constitutional democracies,[28] electing to disengage and accept exclusion means that Onkwehonwe face the well-documented deadly consequences of the range of strategies colonial states use to disempower and destroy indigenous nations. Pre-eminent among these are formal denials of land and of the human and political rights of indigenous collectivities. This involves the negotiation of Onkwehonwe land cessions and extinguishment of rights in return for false guarantees of democratic representation as indigenous peoples where the exercise of autonomous authority is severely limited by design and exists only through the toleration of the state and Settler populace. Whether the destabilization of emergent aboriginal "governments" is formal or covert—by denying access to adequate resources or undermining the capacity for effective and locally staffed governance—the effects of this kind of control on people and communities are the same: they are excluded from the essential benefits of connection to their lands and existence within their nation.

Assimilation is simply the direct and non-contentious route to the same place where those who resist within legalized channels and using political processes established by the state find themselves eventually. People who choose assimilation embrace and are allowed the promise of transcendence to the Settler society's consumer culture and civic identity. But there is a large problem with assimilation even for those who choose it over any form of resistance: full assimilation is impossible.

The promise of an easy transcendence of colonialism is another of the white man's lies. However, one can only discover the cruelty of the hoax once he or she is far down the road to nowhere. The colonized can try to love the colonizer. Sure enough, secret self-hatred and demonstrating love for the oppressor through emulation is a common affliction of aboriginals. Ultimately, the aboriginal comes to see that it is impossible for an Onkwehonwe to assimilate and be fully accepted in a colonial society. An attempt to adjust ones skin, habits, food, clothing, living style, and sexual desires to get along in the mainstream results in nothing but frustration, pathos, shame, rage, and, over time, spiritual or physical death (usually at one's own hands).

Aboriginalism is a sickness, an aspiration to assimilation, expanded into a wholesale cultural project and political agenda. It is a false consciousness, a thorough and perpetual embedding of colonial identities. Within this inauthentic consciousness are non-contentious cooperative identities, institutions, and strategies for interacting with the colonizer. The lost people who accept the aboriginal status created for them by the colonizer can assume various postures; lacking an identity rooted in an Onkwehonwe culture, they

129

find it necessary to select identities and cultural choices from the menu presented to them by the Settler society and the machinery of the state. The most pronounced and obvious of these are the "victims of history," who seek only to *recover* from the past and live in peace with the Settlers, and the "aboriginal litigants," who pray with their white brothers and sisters to a Christian god and strive before white judges for *reconciliation* between Settler and Onkwehonwe. Both the victim and litigant reflect the essential colonial process of civilizing the Onkwehonwe, making us into citizens of the conquering states, so that instead of fighting for ourselves and what is right, we seek a *resolution* that is acceptable to and non-disruptive for the state and society we have come to embrace and identify with.

This is the basic vocabulary of aboriginalism as a political ideology: recovery, reconciliation, and resolution. To this I may also add *resistance*, because, even though it is outwardly hostile to the "enemy," constructing one's identity and life strictly in opposition to the colonizer is another form of white-man worship. All of these are false representations of the Onkwehonwe heritage of struggle. All of them, from the soft and passive legalist to the hard-core guerrilla fighter, demand on the part of Onkwehonwe an abandonment of our rooted identities and the adoption of one that is consistent with a submissive culture or a foreign culture. To fight against genocide, we are told to arm ourselves and take vengeance upon the white man. To fight against economic oppression, we are told to become capitalists and to live for money. To fight against unfair laws, we are told to become lawyers and change the system from within. None of these paths is our own! And none of them are capable of liberating us from colonialism with our Onkwehonwe spirits and identities intact. They demand that we surrender our true selves to become what it is we are fighting against, so that we may better it or defeat it.

All of these submissive or foreign ways of facing colonialism are predicated on a dualism of one sort or another, locking us into a perpetual relationship with the force we are opposing. The paths open to us now in the aboriginal paradigm are incapable of removing us from the us-versus-them dialectic which is the fundamental defining feature of colonial relationships. Any success at armed resistance, economic development, or in the law in fact implies a profound defeat in the long run for Onkwehonwe. What is the difference between genocide perpetrated to destroy a people and armed insurrectionary violence to defeat a state? Or the difference between enforcing poverty on indigenous people and destructive exploitation of the land and non-indigenous people to create wealth? Or the difference between discriminatory laws against us and constitutionally entrenched privileges for us? Each of these mean nothing more than changes in degree or a reversal of roles in a relationship that preserves its oppositional essence and in a system that remains the same and annihilates us spiritually and culturally no matter what the strategic outcome of the struggle. Reversing the Conquest, self-destructing on a personal level, and self-terminating on a collective level are all aboriginalist visions of engaging the state, and in each of them, the Settlers are the victors and Onkwehonwe are the losers.

Meaningful change, the transcendence of colonialism, and the restoration of Onkwehonwe strength and freedom can only be achieved through the resurgence of an Onkwehonwe *spirit* and *consciousness* directed into *contention* with the very foundations of colonialism. Onkwehonwe do need to challenge the continuing hateful conquest of our peoples, but not with a misguided rage channelled through the futile delusions of money, institutional power, or vengeful violence. Seriously, what is the best hope these can offer us? Social order and cultural stasis enshrined in law; mass conversion to the white man's religion of consumerism; or killing a few whites. None of these reflect the ideals of peace, respect, harmony, and coexistence that are the heart of Onkwehonwe philosophies. We are taught to confront hate with the force of love and to struggle to live in the face of ever-present death and the bringers of it. But we must do it *our* way, or risk being transformed by the fight into that (and those) which we are struggling against.

This Onkwehonwe spirit and consciousness that I am speaking of is sacred memory. It is our truth. The resurgence of this consciousness among our peoples is explosive in its potential to transform individuals and communities by altering conceptions of the self and of the self in relation to other peoples and the world. Its elements are the regeneration of an identity created out of the stories of this land, standing up for what is right, and restitution for harm that has been done so that we can wipe away the stain of colonialism. Only then can we begin to build better relationships, see the resurgence of our culture, contend courageously with the threats to our existences, and gain universal respect.

In this world, where imperial arrogance, lies, and false consciousness are normal, Onkwehonwe paths are the only ones that lead to freedom.

Aboriginalism, the social and cultural reimagining of genocide, cannot offer life to Onkwehonwe. It is based on the idea that what is integral to our peoples is frozen in the past (which is irrelevant) and that if we are to have a future, it will be one defined by and allowed only at the discretion of the dominant society. It assumes that in negotiating new relationships between Onkwehonwe and Settlers, everything that is important and valuable to

131

Onkwehonwe must be abandoned, or at the very least severely compromised, and everything that is important and valuable to the Settler be preserved and honoured. This is not only unfair, but puts in place a process that will lead to our disintegration. With aboriginalism, all the independent bases of Onkwehonwe existences are abandoned or compromised in the negotiation of our dependency and integration in every way into the Settler society's institutions. Total loss of our nationhood will inevitably follow our cultural assimilation after the loss of our economic and political autonomy. Aboriginalism is the way of death for our peoples.

As a political program and set of cultural assumptions, aboriginalism manages to gently step through the minefield laid by formal definitions of genocide in international law. But this psychological and legal security exists only because Settlers refuse to examine their government's agenda and policies as well as their own attitudes through a self-critical lens, one that is open to a full spectrum of logical conclusions, some of whose truth may burn brightly enough to scar the precious emotional attachments they have to the founding myths of their country and their personalities.

Yet this self-examination, either by Settlers or many Onkwehonwe themselves, simply does not occur in the course of social and political relations in colonial countries. The severe destructive and disintegrating effects of colonization in Onkwehonwe communities and the momentum towards aboriginalism, combined with the active construction of structures to support the elimination of authentic Onkwehonwe existences, make such self-examination nearly unthinkable in most people's minds. Instead, accommodations with colonialism are sought after and celebrated.

Aboriginals, because they are, at base, cultural mirrors of the mainstream society and because they aspire to elite status inside Settler society, are afforded opportunities to usurp the voice and rights of Onkwehonwe to represent what it is to be indigenous culturally and politically. This is a powerful attack on authentic indigenous movements, whether it is organized politically around the question of nationhood and the recognition of collective rights based on indigeneity, or culturally around questions of identity and the responsibilities of being indigenous.

As in Latin American countries, Onkwehonwe demands for nationhood are pitted by the state against ideas of indigenous struggle defined in strictly ethnic terms. Aboriginalism in Anówara can be compared to the Latin American concepts of "indigenism" and "ethnicism." This is an approach that one Latin American scholar has called "integrative indigenism," an "opaque, naïve and mystified" vision of being indigenous that has been raised to a political project and a "cunning exploitation" by the state of organic and indigenous consciousness.[29]

The integrative strategy is, in fact, the main thrust of existing indigenous rights movements. In Latin American countries, institutionalized indigenous movements advocate a notion of "autonomy" that is very similar to the concept of justice and the models developed by the Canadian Royal Commission on Aboriginal Peoples in the mid-1990s and that is advocated in the vast majority of progressive scholarly literature on this issue.[30] Theoretical approaches to resolving the so-called Indian Problem and that are variants of aboriginalism not surprisingly result, on the ground, in very similar policy and legal reform proposals even though they respond to problems in very different cultural, political, and economic environments. The conventional "indigenous rights within the law" approach basically redistributes existing legally constituted authority; it is not transformative in the least. This internalist (to the state) strategy is characterized by a focus on domestic solutions within state law, the legalizing of aboriginalism as an ethnicity within the broader context of state citizenship, according state-created comprador "governments" small measures of autonomy within colonial structures, and demarcating jurisdiction on territory to facilitate further economic exploitation of the natural environment.

In contrast to this internalist approach—which we could summarize as an acceptance of assimilation with demands for mediation of its effects *within* the state—a more rooted indigenous peoples' movement has been emerging globally over the last 30 years as a movement *against* the state and *for* the re-emergence of Onkwehonwe existences as cultural and political entities unto themselves. Onkwehonwe are in relationships with Settlers, but are not subsumed within the state and are not drawn into its modern liberal ideology of selfish individualism and unrestrained consumption. Central to this, and in stark opposition to the reformist internalist aboriginal approaches, has been indigenous peoples' direct contention with capitalism. Especially in Ecuador and Bolivia, and with the Zapatista movement in Mexico,[31] Onkwehonwe have acted on their realization that capitalist economics and liberal delusions of progress are not opportunities for indigenous peoples' gain, but the very engines of colonial aggression and injustice towards their peoples. The goals of this globalized indigenous movement have been developed to reflect the people's sensitive understanding of the political economy of neo-colonialism: the recognition of Onkwehonwe national existences along with collective rights of self-determination; respect for Onkwehonwe connections to their lands and the rights that flow from those connections; and the preservation and revitalization of indigenous cultures, especially languages, religions, and forms of governance.[32]

These indigenous movements are truly movements against what the dominant societies see as modernity. They share the notion of a balanced existence tied in meaningful ways to their heritage and the belief in the necessity of actively defending their existence. For Onkwehonwe, their politics is the carrying-out of the right and responsibility to be different from mainstream society. This is indeed the fight of all Onkwehonwe who remain true to the spirit of their ancestors: it is a fight for independence and for connection to one's heritage.

Aboriginalism has been given primacy to the point of nearly completely excluding authentic Onkwehonwe movements legally in all of the decolonization processes initiated by states in response to activism and contention for indigenous peoples' rights. Whether the integrationist approach has been actively promoted by the state, or whether the state simply selects a negotiating partner from among Onkwehonwe who fits with its need for complementary goals, the result has been the same in all neo-colonial countries. Only indigenous representatives who compromise their existence as Onkwehonwe with the dominant colonial identities, mainstream culture, and state legal authorities are engaged as negotiating partners. Depending on the specific situation and country, authentic Onkwehonwe are ignored, mocked, criminalized, or suppressed with deadly force.

The American legal scholar Deborah Yashar's broad survey of contemporary indigenous-state negotiations on issues of land claims and self-government explains that discussion and negotiation encompass a wide range of topics and offer many creative reform models.[33] But a close reading of her research reveals that all these processes—in Latin America as well as in the United States, Canada, Australia, and New Zealand—fall short and strictly define indigenous peoples in the context of colonial structures and within the framework of Euroamerican values and cultures. At this point, decolonization discourses exclude the discussion of what the colonizers consider to be their exclusive purview: elements of statehood. What's more, Yashar's research points out clearly that all of the so-called decolonization and reconciliation processes that have been implemented so far are premised not on altruism or a sincere desire on the part of Settlers for either justice or peaceful coexistence with Onkwehonwe, but on what she calls the premises of a "neoliberal discourse." This means the promotion of existing political, economic, and social institutions and the integration of

134

Onkwehonwe into colonial society on terms acceptable to the Settlers—the reduction of collective rights, the promotion of individual rights, and decentralization of governance to aboriginal structures designed to mimic colonial forms of authority.

The authentic Onkwehonwe reaction to this has been diverse in terms of defining the ideal relationship of the Onkwehonwe nation and the state (there are varying approaches to the practical implementation of the nation-to-nation concept that underlies all Onkwehonwe ideas of coexistence). But Onkwehonwe are united in their demand of the Settler state a recognition of cultural diversity, political autonomy, collective identities and rights, legal pluralism, and indigenous forms of political representation. Yet they have run head-on into the fundamental reality of state sovereignty and the Euroamerican notion of power: control and monological thinking. Onkwehonwe ideas and complex, pluralistic beliefs are too complicated and difficult, it seems, for simple-minded Settler institutions and the elites who control them, who reduce the world into categories of us-versus-them and right-versus-wrong. Aboriginalism, with its roots in this dichotomizing essentialism, plays the perfect foil to the Euroamerican mentality. Settlers can remain who and what they are, and injustice can be reconciled by the mere allowance of the Other to become one of Us. What higher reward or better future is there than to be finally recognized as achieving the status of a European?

Disentangling the elements of the Settler state from our lives any time soon seems out of the question for many of our people. But I wonder whether Onkwehonwe can even hope to survive without respect for our freedom and rights as nations of people? Think of the European definition of sovereignty, and try to imagine how any people could preserve themselves for long without possessing the elements of such a national existence: the power of and cultural capacity for self-definition; a singular or unitary identity; a shared belief in their independence and rights as a people; the capacity for self-defence; and land and a connection to the land that provides the bases for self-sufficiency and for an independent existence. Without *all* of these things, a people will not be long on this earth.

Yashar has surveyed the current situation facing indigenous peoples; considered the rising tide of dissatisfaction with aboriginalist-integrationist agendas pushed by aboriginalist politicians, as well as the expressed demands for recognition of national existences; and concluded that we need to come up with different and more complex political mappings that are capable of balancing the Euroamerican preoccupation with individual rights with Onkwehonwe's diverse collective identities, forms of representation, and

135

evolving structures of governance. In doing so, she hits on the core obstacle to peaceful coexistence in this post-modern imperial age: the implicit homogeneity of neoliberalism. Seeing nations as political units and as administrative structures, she argues that "institutional pluralism" in a multi-ethnic setting is the only way that Settler states can preserve themselves while honouring the principles of justice, which must recognize that Onkwehonwe prior existences entitles us to cultural, administrative, and political boundaries that "crosscut, transcend and are distinct."[34] Yet, her progressive proposal is still framed within the state. This is its fatal flaw, reflecting the futility of all internalist approaches. The state itself is incapable of relating to other entities in a pluralistic and peaceful way. Acceptance of an Onkwehonwe existence within the colonial state, however creatively imagined, is a death sentence for that indigenous nation. The imperative of the state by design is homogenization and singular control by the monopoly of force and legitimacy. Without a fundamental remaking of the state itself, there is no chance to reform the relationship of the state to indigenous peoples.

Even the state's moderate advocacy of aboriginalism's goals has not been acceptable to the conservative core of colonial society. Beyond the commonplace superficial rhetoric of toleration and reconciliation in contemporary neo-colonial countries, state policy and the law remain solidly *sovereign* in their effective denial of distinctiveness and autonomy for indigenous nations in any way, shape, or form that can be construed as meaningful to the continuing existence of Onkwehonwe.

For example, Beverley McLachlin, shortly after being appointed to her position at the head of the Supreme Court of Canada in 2002, acknowledged that at least one aspect of indigenous peoples' rights was an intellectual and juridical challenge for Settler governments. She admitted that Onkwehonwe land entitlements in the law were a significant issue because, as she stated, "Whether we like it or not, aboriginal rights are an international matter." In other words, the age-old Indian Problem still needed to be resolved, and this time the obstacle to the colonial project presented by Onkwehonwe was the international spotlight on the way Settlers have failed, even in the framework of their own laws, to acquire definite ownership of the territory over which they claimed sovereign title. Chief Justice McLachlin referred to the recognition of indigenous peoples' land rights in international legal instruments, in particular, the International Labour Organization's (ILO, a branch of the United Nations) *Convention on Indigenous and Tribal Peoples in Independent Countries* (ILO Convention 169), which recognizes "the aspirations of these peoples to exercise control over their own institutions, ways of life and economic development and to maintain and develop their identities, languages and religions, within the framework of these states in which they live" and which obliges states to protect indigenous peoples' rights to land, religion, customs, and political participation. She also made note of how the UN's *Universal Draft Declaration on the Rights of Indigenous Peoples* acknowledges the need for states to actively protect indigenous peoples' rights, how it envisions empowering Onkwehonwe to define their status and determine the appropriate means of protecting ancestral rights, and calls upon state governments to transfer the authority to determine the content of rights from the state to indigenous peoples. She also noted—no doubt with some relief!—that her own country, Canada, is not a party to Convention 169, and that the Draft Declaration is still in its preliminary form. However, she did point out that these documents can be seen as reflecting expectations that in due course they may inform debates on indigenous peoples' rights in Canada.[35]

The most noteworthy feature of this, the first and only direct statement of Canada's Chief Justice on indigenous issues, is the total lack of concern for the problems in the indigenous-state relationship as anything other than a legal conundrum. Even with the (very) generous reading I have given her remarks, the only imperative to action implied in her statement is that of the burden of activism and creativity on the part of the Supreme Court itself to eliminate any inconsistencies between domestic and international law. The colonizer's solution, which assumes a total lack of support in Settler society for adhering to decolonized frameworks of relationship with Onkwehonwe among the state and general population, is to negate the potential of international law as a beneficial avenue for advancing indigenous rights. Indeed, Canada, the United States, New Zealand, and Australia have stalled all progress towards a meaningful recognition of indigenous peoples' rights at the United Nations and in other international forums.[36] McLachlin's statement also points to another state strategy used to maintain the illusion of legitimacy: the state will simply refuse to ratify those international conventions that are unacceptable to the colonial enterprise. In Canada and other colonial societies, the current process of negotiated settlements involving land and self-government are purported to be resolutions to the problems of a colonial legacy. There is no denying that they are negotiation and resolution, as such, but they fall far short of being a means to address injustice.

Negotiation and reconciliation as defined and implemented thus far are perversions of justice in that Settler societies end up gaining legal possession of not only land and governing power, but Onkwehonwe histories and identities, integrating the desirable and useful elements into their own social fabric at little or no moral or economic cost. In their efforts to co-opt First Nations politicians and to legitimize their presence in this hemisphere, Settlers attempt to take root the only way that it is possible for them to do so, by seizing the indigenous heritage of the land. Through negotiation and the development of compromise solutions with aboriginal politicians who they themselves employ (through the financing of representative aboriginal organizations as well as through the direct appointment and payment of individual spokespersons), the Settlers are in effect buying the legitimacy of their state, although they are buying it from people who have no right or authority to be selling it in the first place. In the long-term view though, protests by "traditionalist" Onkwehonwe who hold out against validating the colonial project through negotiations mean nothing to the colonizers. The token amounts of money given and the limited minority-group rights granted to indigenous peoples are a very small price to pay for the Settlers to be released from the moral repercussions of conquest and for their legitimacy as nation-states.

Instrumentally reforming indigenous cultures so as to make them more amenable to this endeavour, recognizing them, and then making amends for "historical" injustices against those reimagined and now *aboriginal* artifices is the perfect colonial end-game. It assuages the guilt of colonization while allowing for its continuance. This cleansing is a lie, the creation of a wholly false, romanticized, and palatable aboriginal culture that allows Settlers to delude themselves into believing they have transcended their own brutal, immoral, past and generated a new society free of the sins of empire.

People who decide to play as aboriginal foils of the lie do receive something in the bargain: the chance to survive and prosper as individuals. But there is a heavy psychological cost to cooperating in this process of ethnic and moral cleansing, and there are enormous long-term dangers for those who engage in this negotiation. After all, the negotiation is between unequal partners; the terms of restitution are calculated not according to morality or rationality, but according to what the Settlers themselves determine they can afford or want to pay in return for their new post-colonial identity. The aboriginals who are enabling the decolonial delusion are putting their faith and trust in the honesty, integrity, and generosity of the Settler. Who am I to question their choice of non-contentious accommodation of colonialism in exchange for their individual survival and certain material benefits? We've never been lied to or cheated before, have we?

It is possible for Onkwehonwe to cut through the miseducation and colonial mythologies presented to us as the truth. This perseverance of indigeneity in spite of the lie of aboriginalism was exemplified best for me in the words of a young James Bay Cree student I met at a luncheon after a lecture I gave at John Abbott College in Montréal in March of 2002. After first listening to everyone else in the group that had gathered to talk about the challenges facing First Nations leaders, she quietly offered her own reflections. She told the story of a painting that hung on her grandparents' living room wall in their home up north in James Bay. Picturing a Cree bush camp, it had been painted by a white man from the south. She believed in it. It formed her image of what it was to be Cree.

After reconnecting with her culture and the land, she discovered that the artist who painted that picture knew nothing about the Cree or about the bush. In the painting, there is both a huge flock of geese and heavy snow on the ground—things which are never seen together in the same season. When she looks at that picture now, she said, she knows that "He didn't tell the truth about Cree life." She would have always thought that it was a true picture of Cree life if she hadn't gone to spend more time with her grandparents and hadn't actually lived out on the land.

Her story reminded me that there are many compelling but fantastic lies and illusions that need to be shattered before we come to know the truth of our existence as Onkwehonwe.

It is a big question. What is being Onkwehonwe? From what I've been told, and from what I've seen in all the time I've spent among Onkwehonwe all over the world, "being Onkwehonwe" is living heritage, being part of a tradition—shared stories, beliefs, ways of thinking, ways of moving about in the world, lived experiences—that generates identities which, while ever-changing and diverse, are deeply rooted in the common ground of our heritages as original peoples.

The great Palestinian literary scholar Edward Said understood being part of a culture as participation in an ongoing dynamic process of change that revolves around people's attempts to answer certain crucial questions about themselves in the public life of the community, questions such as how the central traditions of a people are held onto, what is considered as tradition, and how a people's history is read.[37] Like Said was of his own identity as a Palestinian, I am drawn to the idea of indigeneity as practice, a dynamic of reflection and dialogue; I've written in the past about the idea of a "self-conscious traditionalism."[38] My sense is that the notion of peoples' interactions with their history is the foundation, but that a meaningful concept of

Onkwehonwe identity, one that is consistent with Onkwehonwe teachings, must go beyond reflective practices to an actual political and social engagement with the world based on consensus arrived at through broad conversation among people who are part of that culture.

There is an Onkwehonwe identity. It is one layer of identification among the multiplicity of layers that form people's sense of self—from the individual, to the family, to the clan, village, nation, and then on to our participation as Onkwehonwe in a more expansive conversation that links us to other indigenous peoples in other parts of the world who share our thoughts, feelings, and plans of action. This is another part of being Onkwehonwe: the transcendence of national and patriotic identities to a sense of self and relationship based on the commonality of belief that is shared among Onkwehonwe in other nations.

Isabel Altamirano, a political scientist who is completing her doctoral studies at the University of Alberta, is Zapoteca, from Oaxaca, on the Tehuantepec Isthmus in southern Mexico.[39] She is quietly assertive and radiates inner strength, something that impressed me when I first met her in Québec City, at an academic conference, where she was quite comfortable and, it seemed, naturally dressed amid the suited academics in the traditional clothing of her people. It immediately became clear in talking to her that resistance was in her blood and that she knew what it was to live it. She told me in Spanish-inflected English, with her eyes focusing the strength of her carefully selected words—a spare and elegant mode of communication—that her people were one of the few who had resisted Aztec domination even before the arrival of Europeans and that her heritage of struggle was deeply rooted. Isabel's insights into the idea of "being indigenous" as a practice, as a question of identity, and in terms of its implications personally and politically were thought-provoking and enlightening.

TA: *You've had a chance to experience life in both the south and the north. Do you think that there is such a thing as what we might call an "indigenous" identity?*
IA: I feel that we, and this includes myself, should insist on unifying something that is now dispersed and manifested in many separate ways. The idea of "North America" continues to be reduced to just Canada and the United States, and I find that indigenous people have adopted those mainstream ideas as well.

TA: *Is there is any possibility of peoples in the north and south working together, as a movement?*

140

IA: If people do not get beyond these mainstream attitudes, it will be very difficult to even talk about any collective action as indigenous peoples. People in Canada and people in Mexico are too worried about their own lives and their particular situations to care about what is happening beyond the borders. On both sides of that border, there are feelings about indigenous peoples being "different," but what is truly the main difference? The north are the ones who want to say a lot, and the south are the ones who have to follow what is said in the north.

You can extend these feelings and this problem even to internal borders, because indigenous people in Mexico are divided as well. Despite what many people in the north think, there is in fact no one unique or unified indigenous movement in Mexico. We have many different experiences, and people do not feel represented by those who claim to speak for us. The Zapatistas are well known around the world, but that is not the only indigenous movement in Mexico. There are perhaps some even more important organizations there, but you don't hear about them since they can't act all the time. The Zapatistas have become symbolic of the indigenous movement in Mexico, but everybody out there insists that this is *the* movement in Mexico, which is a mistake. It shows the lack of knowledge of what is really going on over there. When something happens anywhere in Mexico, people up here inevitably say, "Chiapas," because that is what they know, or what they think they know, very well. It's the same misunderstanding of the real situation there in Mexico. What people know about the north is this: Indian reservations. And they are sure this is not what they want. If you ask people in Canada and in Mexico who the indigenous peoples are in the other country, they don't know. If there is going to be a coming together for collective action, it will not by any means be in the near future!

TA: *What is it that's driving indigenous peoples to stand up to the Mexican government?*
IA: There are several reasons: human rights violations, exclusion from opportunities in society, racial injustice, and, of course, the plundering of our land. These are historical problems indigenous communities experience every day in their lives; even before the Zapatista uprising, our communities were being mobilized to defend their lands and to stop local "strong men," who were abusing their power and violating the people's most basic human rights. Right now, even if the Zapatistas remain hidden, there are many mobilizations, because indigenous people are struggling to survive in all senses of that word.

TA: *What do you mean by that, "struggling to survive in all senses"?*

141

IA: At the organizational level, there is a discourse of demanding political autonomy. However, this discourse is not the voice of the people or the language of the communities. People in Mexico do not believe in laws. Even if accords are reached and laws passed, there is no guarantee that Mexicans will respect such laws—it's not as simple as coming to an accord or passing some laws. The problems of indigenous people in Mexico are much more complex than they seem to be; it's because a strong Mexican nationalism, different ideas about citizenship, an ever-present racism, and deep ignorance are all affecting the situation at the same time.

TA: *Have you found anything that is common, or shared, culturally, between indigenous peoples?*
IA: Well, there is not a unique indigenous identity, because indigenous peoples are diverse. However, there are many common things in the way we all see our culture and history. I think that there are several elements that are common to indigenous peoples, not only in the north, but anywhere. The most evident element is that indigenous peoples have a strong relationship with their land and territories; they see them as the social space where they recreate themselves, so land and territory are not only commodities. To indigenous peoples, religion and culture are linked to their natural contexts. It is not rare to find animal representations being linked to human beings, as with the raven in cultures from the Pacific or the deer in Northern Mexico. The role of elder is something shared among indigenous peoples too. Elders are seen as those who have accumulated knowledge, who have answers, or who know how to do things according to tradition. In many communities, the idea of keeping balance or equilibrium among the different elements within a community is expressed in the way those who transgress the rules are punished. In non-indigenous people's justice, those who do something wrong must go to jail. For many indigenous communities, punishment has to be implemented more as a way to restore the equilibrium and heal communities than as punishment. These are some of the things I see indigenous peoples here and anywhere share.

TA: *What does it mean to you to be "indigenous"?*
IA: I think that to be indigenous means many ways of life and many languages that are not the mainstream's languages. To be indigenous is to use our dreams, not as a way of thinking about what we are not, but as a way to interpret our reality, our circumstances. To be indigenous is to have a sense of community as whole, a sense of exchanging and talking until we all have

a similar vision of where we are going. To be indigenous is consensus and is reproducing certain ways of doing things. Being indigenous is to have a collective memory of our myths, the ramifications of our concepts, and of what is behind our language.

What the state creates as indigenous identity is based on what indigenous peoples have *not* to be, not in what they are. In my country, we say that the Mexican state recovered the greatness of indigenous cultures as a way of building the *mestizo* identity, but what the state recovered was the history of dead Indians, not living Indians who have a culture that is rooted not in the pyramids but in everyday life. Dead Indians are secure because they do not oppose what the state does. Dead Indian cultures are good for the state because they are reduced to folklore, rather than forming a conception of the world, politics, and otherness.

TA: *How do you stay connected and alive in your culture while living away from your homeland?*
IA: Primarily by remembering who I am, where I come from, and what my personal story is about. All of that makes me feel that I am here because I have jumped over many bushes to get here and that everything is possible if we remember who we are and if we realize that we are strong enough to get where we want to go. I never feel intrinsically at a disadvantage because I am indigenous. Whenever that feeling wants to come up, I recall my people's history and I feel proud of being who I am. Also, every single time I travel to my home town, I confirm where I come from, in case living in another country contributes to me forgetting it!

It's funny, but perhaps because of the way I look, I never can forget who I am. Many, many times when I come across an indigenous person here, that person will always say, "Hello!" That is a way of saying, "You are like me" or "I recognize you as something similar to me." Somehow, that makes me feel that, even here, I have a place; even here there are those who recognize me as an indigenous person, and not in the way white people do when they encapsulate me in the vagueness of the term "Spanish." I do not feel any closeness to whatever they mean by "Spanish" but very close to indigenous peoples from the Big Turtle.

Speaking with Isabel about being indigenous had a sobering influence on my initial thoughts on the concept of a common indigenous identity. Clearly, in her experience, a broader transnational indigenous identity was a powerful potentiality far from being realized. It seems as if the spiritual connection is something that does exist, and is celebrated, but it has not been organized to be an actual unifying force of our existence. As Isabel pointed out, people are dealing with all of the local problems that affect their lives, and the potential power of a unified indigenous identity (one new layer on top of others that already exist) as the foundation for political organization and action lies untapped. The domestication within the state of our formerly independent notion of ourselves—our being distinct peoples—the restriction of our identity and action to arenas built by Settlers, is maintained primarily by the limitation of our self-identification to the Settler state. Breaking out of this would generate enormous collective power in the unity of our voice, and numbers, as well as resources. This expansive identity was woven through traditional teachings, but has been lost as restricted, colonial, narrow conceptions of self and of community were imposed to break the solidarity of Onkwehonwe nations in their homelands and control them by relegation to small bands on limited reserves of land.

We resist the notion of a pan-indigenous identity because our narrow self-definitions are now so deeply embedded in our psyches and in the life of our communities. The mundane conflicts and challenges of survival are manipulated and managed by state governments to ensure that we remain focused on who we are as colonial beings. Funding programs, laws, and policies are built on the localized management of the symptoms of our division. Yet, we continue to accept our status as *Indians* rather than fight to free ourselves from that colonial identity and create a bigger sense of self capable of carrying us out of our colonized situation. To bring the indigenous identity back to life will require a transformation and shift from the politics of pity that defines our present relationship with the Settlers to a politics framed not on a posture of victimhood but on an ethic of courage. It will require an awakening of indigenous intelligence, a reorientation of mentality, and a reconstruction of the Onkwehonwe movement so that it is capable of achieving the objective of freeing indigenous peoples from the grip of imperialism. It will mean moving our politics from a grievance to a cause.

Our basic problem is spiritual defeat and how defeatism is manifested in the conduct of politics by most of our politicians and in the inherent structure of our aboriginal organizations. The Onkwehonwe movement stands defanged, tamed, and no longer able to present an effective resistance, to fight, or even to recognize the extremity of the situation we face. The main source of this situation, and the ongoing problem of spiritual defeatism, is the effect Christian churches have had on our people.[40] The role of *Christianity*, as distinct from the institution of the *church*, among our people has always been and remains complex: indigenized forms of Christianity practised in Onkwehonwe communities have provided moral bearing for many of our people, especially in previous generations. And because of the strong affiliation between alcohol and drug treatment programs and Christian teachings, Christianity has become in effect the foundation for sobriety for many people. Who can argue against these things being on the whole positive for our people?

Nonetheless, we must consider what institutional Christianity—the effort to convert Onkwehonwe into Christians and to have them submit to the authority of the churches—has wrought, overall, for indigenous peoples collectively. The balance of Christianity's effect is very clear: churches provided financial backing for colonial enterprises; churches rationalized racism for their white parishioners; churches caused Onkwehonwe to accept the biblical ethic of suffering and to normalize their oppression by seeking transcendent rather than imminent redemption; and churches were responsible for residential schools, which were the main instruments of the policy of outright assimilation. How do we confront this reality and its ongoing effects?

Granted, missionaries have gone from being the shock troops of imperial conquest to, really, ineffectual do-gooders—the stature of churches in Onkwehonwe communities is no longer what it used to be. For the most part, religious orders and church activists have been officially relegated to the role of quaint humanitarians. But even without active proselytizing (this practice has ended for mainstream churches and, to the extent it does occur, has been taken up by American-based Protestant churches active mainly in the northern and more isolated areas of Anówara), the power of the church and the purveyors of twisted readings of ancient North African and Middle Eastern teachings to create criminal complicity and moral paralysis on the part of our people is still very much there. The effects are self-generating now that the seed has been planted. The Christian Bible has brought fear into the hearts of our people. This is our main weakness. I say it is fear because the combination of an authoritarian reading of the Bible, the lack of experience with contention, and the threat of retribution and violence are terrifying. This fear has paralyzed our communities, preventing any form of effective resistance to the colonial church-state agenda. Unfortunately, this is the cultural foundation upon which our existing indigenous organizations are built. On such a foundation, is it any wonder they have failed to mount an effective challenge against the institutions that control us still, or to lead us in the revitalization and restrengthening of our people?

The approach to making change employed by aboriginal organizations is text-book perfect, if we were reading a primer on losing strategies. But even though we are concerned with turning things around and building a new movement free from the faulty premises and inherent weaknesses of the present system, we should not throw out the book so fast. Think about it: a lot of time and money is spent on promoting the "best practices" type of advice to politicians and technocrats involved with Indian Affairs bureaucracies, but isn't there just as much to be gained by debriefing ourselves on the problems and failures of our organizations and leaders as well? Of course, this is not the ego-boosting feel-goodism most of us crave when we ask for feedback on our efforts! But nonetheless, honest self-criticism is always a good thing in the long run. I didn't have to do any "scientific" research to gain a solid sense of these losing strategies. I've been working with First Nations organizations and band councils for nearly 20 years, and I only had to reflect for five minutes on the experiences I've had to come up with a set of failing principles drawn from political life in the era of aboriginalist accommodation, considering the lessons of our unfortunate record of few successes and many frustrations.

Basically, as an overall movement, indigenous peoples have done everything that someone committed to failure would, could, and should do. Through our own lax organization, bad decisions, and strategic missteps, we have lent immeasurable assistance to our enemies and adversaries in the achievement of their aims. And our politicians have led us down this road with incredible efficacy and, sometimes, unbelievable arrogance.

If I were asked to advise an organization on how *not* to achieve their goals in a political struggle, I would pull a few tools out of the aboriginal organizational pack sack and suggest a few things like:

+ *Do not be strategic at all!* Be totally transparent and tell your enemies exactly what you are going to do. Tell them, directly, everything that you want and need and what you are willing to accept. Hell, just hire ex-Indian Affairs employees to make sure that the government has a direct connection to your organization and community. This will allow the colonizers to plan an effective response to your moves far in advance and to allocate the appropriate resources to undercut your plan even before you have time to implement it.
+ *Work in isolation.* Reject any form of real collaboration with like-minded groups who have the same interests as you do, alienate all

potential allies' participation in your struggle, and work only with people who are related to you or who live in your own region. This will allow the colonizer to play off your group against another group of Onkwehonwe, cutting you off from any strength that may be gained in numbers or in a broader appeal for your cause among other nations or in the non-indigenous population.

+ *Be selfish.* Do not join the issues you are fighting for with other people's concerns or problems and define your problem in a narrow way so that it only applies to you and yours. This way, people will have no reason to care about you (everyone has their own problems to deal with), and the colonizer will have free rein in creating and promoting the perception that your problems are in fact your fault, not his.

+ *Act undignified.* Point fingers at people and be generally rude, shrill, and annoying. Cry in public, get angry and accusatory in conflict situations, and level personal attacks against your colleagues in a gossipy manner. This way, people will think you are stupid or just end up hating you for no particular reason. Then the colonizer will be able to crush you with nary a hand being raised in objection, by anyone other than you.

I know I'm not the only one carrying around a sense of frustration about our political situation. Most Onkwehonwe are dissatisfied with their own government and with their situation, yet are incapable of articulating their anger or of reasoning out of the situation. This sense of frustration was expressed perfectly by someone I know from the Kanien'kehaka community of Akwesasne. Reflecting on the gap between so-called traditionalist rhetoric and our people's nationhood claims and the actual behaviours and life choices of individuals in our own nation, I traded anecdotes with Darren Bonaparte, a keen observer of community life and a former band council politician himself. I asked him about the political and cultural schizophrenia that seems to have descended on our people when it comes to their political identity and activism in recent years. He answered that question with characteristic and provocative irony:

> It is my feeling, based on what I've seen as a council member, that the communities are at a crossroads and aren't sure what to do. They don't know whether to get mad at the white man's government or their own, or both. But they do know they should be mad

about something! It's weird. September 11th has had an impact, especially for us here with our reservation right on the border, and those close to us, like Kahnawake and Kanesatake. The status quo is being set in stone, and the border will soon have a real Berlin Wall to mark it. Our own cops are enforcing the border now. Both band and tribal elected governments are strutting around like sovereign nations, but behind closed doors they're cozying up to the feds and even the provinces to see how they can "mirror" the outside laws. Meanwhile, the cloak of fake "traditionalism" gets spread even thinner. The problem is the people can't make up their mind if they want their local councils to be branch offices of the Department of Indian Affairs, or Banana Republics in their own right, or a combination of both, like they have now.

Tos'ké! He's right! After two generations of struggle to create the political and cultural space for a reassertion of our Kanien'kehaka existence, we are directionless on what to do now that we have succeeded in surviving. Physically, culturally, economically, we are indecisive on what the next step should be. And Kanien'kehaka are in this case representative of a general psychological and social malaise among Onkwehonwe who have by all other criteria achieved what should have guaranteed not only their survival but their fulfilment and happiness.

This recent phenomenon of directionless nations who are unable to formulate an ongoing political and social vision once material needs have been met points to the fact that oppression at its root is not a physical phenomenon so much as it is psychological. Keeping in mind that the freedom of our nations, with the restoration of our people to their land and the preservation of the cultural heritage of our ancestors, is the goal—not the accumulation of material possessions and elevated incomes—we should question why it is that our people have stopped short of this goal and begun to adapt to the existing colonial power relations.[41]

There are of course many reasons for the accommodation, but the fact that our children are educated and socialized in public school—and even in First Nations schools—into the belief that existing power relations are right plays a huge role in creating the conditions for complacency among our people. There is also the popular news and entertainment media's reinforcing of the conservative belief that radical change is not only undesirable but impossible. Add to this the fact that television and the popular music and sports entertainment industries provide convenient distractions and sensory satiation that stifles any potential for community-based action. The prominence of fear in the Judeo-Christian cultural tradition, as discussed above, and the manipulation of that fear by governments and corporations create the general sense that change will lead to something worse than what already exists. Also adding to the inertia is the political manifestation of the Judeo-Christian heritage: the myth of progress or the irrational belief that things can and will inevitably get better over time. In the meantime, the liberal welfare state always ensures that people have the ability to meet their minimal needs to satisfy their basic goals and desires within the existing system. Of course, this all leads to a situation in which our peoples' primary identifications merge with that of the mainstream Settler society on a nationalist patriotic ("I Am Canadian!") or religious ("I Am a Christian") basis. Perhaps one of the most important reasons, among all of these, that people do not act against their "oppressor" is that they implicitly understand that the state will deal with serious challenges to its authority and power by using violence—and people are not prepared for violence.

Seeing through the reasons for complicity and complacency this way causes one to wonder, what are people so afraid of? Colonization is a lie. It is built on flat-out propaganda and the manipulation of innate human fears to force the acceptance of the false claim of Settler authority over our people and the land. We are complicit, to be sure, but recognizing that the power dynamic is essentially one of mind control, using techniques and strategies for generating belief, fear, and legitimacy out of nothing but claims, attitude, and falsehoods, the way to confront colonialism begins to reveal itself. If colonial authority is an artifice built on lies, then the way to confront and defeat it is with truths.

Reconstruction of Onkwehonwe knowledge systems and the ethics that emerged from them is the first step in reorienting ourselves to being Onkwehonwe in the practice of our lives. Learning is itself a struggle. The Onkwehonwe method of learning is really one of transformation, and it is experiential, observational, and practical. The process of gaining knowledge (what we call "education") is a radical action, an act of defiance against conventional reality. Education, in this sense, defines a warrior. Education and transformation through the acquisition of knowledge, power, and vision is a dynamic process of learning and teaching, combined with a core desire to respect the completeness of the circle of transformation: to observe, to experience, to practise, and then to pass on the knowledge by mentoring and teaching the next generation.

As people struggling against our own colonization, we are called on to be this kind of knowledge warrior, to defy fear, and to act in spite of the many frightening forces that keep us caged inside our present reality, our comfort, our job security, our social and family relationships. The truth is more precious to the transforming and change-making warrior than any of these things. The struggle to recognize and target our own ingrained fear is the primary act of a warrior.

We are called on to defy arrogance—we cannot allow false pride or delusional fantasies to detract from the intensity required to increase our realization of deeper truths. We must anticipate the eruptions of pride inside ourselves and understand that the vision-blurring secretions of over-confidence can very easily overwhelm any progress we have made toward self-realization.

And we must defy the attraction of authority itself: deliberately stand against it and resist the temptation to become a part of it or to accept the power to command and rule others. Because of the spiritual power and knowledge warriors do gain on their journey, these opportunities will present themselves often.

Becoming tired of the fight, a kind of battle fatigue or boredom, is another danger, and the warrior must have perseverance as part of his or her character to resist the feelings of self-satisfaction that come from one's achievements over time or to deal with the disillusionment and loss of vision that may descend when we fail. Spiritual and physical fatigue are grave dangers to anyone involved in struggle. It is a common affliction that makes one vulnerable to cynicism or to the machinations of one's enemies and adversaries. Eventually, this kind of fatigue leads the warrior to rationalize leaving his or her original path and turning away to serve the enemy and adversary.

Anyone on the journey can surely relate to this. Elders often speak of the eventual achievement of our goals as fleeting successes. Even when we finally do succeed in fighting through the obstacles in front of us, gaining higher knowledge and an appreciation of what it is to be Onkwehonwe and a human being, the epiphany is short-lived, neither a permanent nor redemptory transcendental experience, but only one step to the next level of struggle. The central teaching here is that we must guard against being satisfied. A warrior holds on to, cherishes, and embraces as his or her life and existence the feeling of unease that is the true sign of being in battle as a warrior; personal strengthening and increasing awareness is the warrior's lifetime struggle.

In this way of seeing the world and our role in it, being Onkwehonwe means being against the concept of *history*,[42] which is rationally constructed by imperial minds as conclusive, terminal, and instrumental to an imperial political order. Being Onkwehonwe is perpetual and continuous living. Building a movement on this sensibility and philosophical outlook means shifting away from the goals we have set for ourselves and our nations based on imperial mentalities and Euroamerican morality. Applied indigenous intelligence will lead to a rethinking of the very basis of Onkwehonwe politics, and the struggle will be recast.

In my mind, *regeneration* is the direct application of the principle of acting against our ingrained and oppressive fears. Imagine if regeneration of ourselves and our nations took the place of the goal of "recovery" (so individualizing and terminal and so much a part of the industry built up around residential school and substance abuse healing among our peoples). Think of the freedom inherent in embracing the struggle to transcend what has been done to us rather than the effort to gain compensation for the crimes or to placate feelings and sensibilities.

Restitution, which is the application of the principles of clarity and honesty to politics, would take the place of the goal of "reconciliation," which is promoted so vehemently by liberal thinkers and church groups, but which is fatally flawed because it depends on the false notion of a moral equivalency between Onkwehonwe and Settlers and on a basic acceptance of colonial institutions and relationships. Reconciliation gives Onkwehonwe a place inside of Settler society with no requirement for Settlers to forego any of their ill-gotten gains personally or collectively. Restitution, as the alternative antidote and perspective, is based on the proven notion that real peace-making requires making amends for harm done before any of the other steps to restore the fabric of a relationship can be taken. Restitution is, in fact, the precondition for any form of true reconciliation to take place.[43]

Resurgence, which applies the principle of courageous action against injustice, could replace the notion of seeking "resolution" to the colonial problem. Certainty and finality of land settlements are the objective in the Settler society's courts and are promoted through state-sponsored negotiation processes to achieve order in the relationship, order which ratifies colonial institutions and facilitates the perpetuation of the original injustice, from which comes their very existence. Resurgence is acting beyond resistance. It is what resistance always hopes to become: from a rooted position of strength, resistance defeats the temptation to stand down, to take what is offered by the state in exchange for being pacified. In rejecting the temptation to join the Settlers and their state, seeking instead to confront Settler society in a struggle to force an end to the imperial reality and to lay down the preconditions for a peaceful coexistence, we would choose to use contention as a means of widespread enlightenment and societal change.

This reframing and recasting of our struggle provides the moral and ethical basis for a truly indigenous movement, one that, unlike any in Anówara since the days of Pontiac and Tecumseh, will be consistent with our heritage and the goals that emerge from within Onkwehonwe cultures.[44] It is a monumental challenge to even conceive of such a shift of thought and energy, given the extent to which our indigenous governments and politics have been compromised by co-optation and corruption. And from where we stand now, the toughest shift will be to dislodge the notion of "reconciliation" from the public mind as the goal of our struggle. Reconciliation as a concept or process is not as compelling, factually or logically speaking, as resurgence because, being so embedded in the supposedly progressive discourses on Onkwehonwe-Settler relations and so weighted with funding and scholarship support, it is almost unassailable from within established legal and political discourses, thus presenting a huge obstacle to justice and real peacemaking. It is non-threatening, requiring of the Settler only a trite statement of regret and ceasing of the practice of the most open forms of racism—such easy things for liberal-minded Settlers to agree to that it has gained huge public and government support as *the* framework for resolving the colonial problem and has become the paradigm of post-colonial colonialism.

Reconciliation itself needs to be intellectually and politically deconstructed as the orienting goal of the Onkwehonwe struggle. How do we break the hold of this emasculating concept? The logic of reconciliation as justice is clear: without massive restitution, including land, financial transfers, and other forms of assistance to compensate for past harms and continuing injustices committed against our peoples, reconciliation would permanently enshrine colonial injustices and is itself a further injustice. This much is clear in our Onkwehonwe frame of understanding. But what about other people's understandings of the nature of the problem we are facing? The nearly complete ignorance of the Settler society about the true facts of their people's relationship with Onkwehonwe and their wilful denial of historical reality detract from any possibility of meaningful discussion on true reconciliation. Limited to a discussion of history that includes only the last five or ten years, the corporate media and general public focus on the billions of dollars handed out to the Onkwehonwe per year from federal treasuries and spent inefficiently. The complex story of what went on in the past and the tangled complexities of the past's impact on the present and future of our relationships are reduced to questions of "entitlements," "rights," and "good governance" within the already established structures of the state. Consider the effect of lengthening our view and extending society's view. Considering 100 or 300 years of interactions, it would become clear even to the Settlers that the real problem facing their country is that two nations are fighting over questions of conquest and survival, of empire or genocide, and moral claims to be just societies. Considering the long view and true facts, the Indian Problem becomes a question of the struggle for right and wrong, for justice in its most basic form. Something was stolen, lies were told, and they've never been made right. That, I believe, is the crux of the problem. We must shift away from the pacifying discourse and reframe people's perception of the problem so that it is not a question of how to reconcile with colonialism that faces us. Instead, we must think of restitution as the first step towards creating justice and a moral society out of the immoral racism that is the foundation and core of all colonial countries. What was stolen must be given back, amends must be made for the crimes that were committed, from which all Settlers, old families and recent immigrants alike, have gained their existences as citizens of these colonial countries.

When we say to the Settlers, "Give it back," are we talking about them giving up the country and moving away? No. Irredentism has never been the vision of our peoples. When we say "Give it back," we're talking about Settlers demonstrating respect for what we share—the land and its resources—and making things right by offering us the dignity and freedom we are due and returning our power and land enough for us to be self-sufficient.

Restitution is not the play on white guilt that reconciliation processes have become—guilt is after all a monotheistic concept foreign to Onkwehonwe cultures—nor is it a brooding, under the threat of punishment, over past misdeeds to the point of moral paralysis. Restitution is purification. It is a ritual of disclosure and confession in which there is acknowledgement and acceptance of one's harmful actions and a genuine demonstration of sorrow and regret, constituted in reality by putting forward a promise to never again do harm and by redirecting one's actions to benefit the one who has been wronged.

Even the act of proposing a shift to this kind of discussion is a radical challenge to the reconciling negotiations that try to fit Onkwehonwe into the colonial legacy rather than to confront and defeat it. When I speak of restitution, I am speaking of restoring ourselves as peoples, our spiritual power, dignity, and the economic bases for our autonomy. Settlers understand implicitly that reconciliation will not force them to question what they've done and will allow them to congratulate themselves for their forbearance and understanding once Onkwehonwe—or, to be precise by using the language of the conciliatory paradigm, aboriginal peoples—are reconciled with imperialism.

Reconciliation may be capable of moving us beyond the unpalatable stench of overt racism in social interactions; this would be an easy solution to the problem of colonialism for white people, and no doubt most would be satisfied with this obfuscation of colonial realities. But logically and morally, there is no escaping that the problems of colonialism experienced by Onkwehonwe are a direct result of the theft of their lands and cannot be addressed in any way other than through its return to them.

There are at least two aspects of this large problem. The first is comprehension of the economic dimension, the continuing effect of Onkwehonwe being illegally dispossessed of their lands, and the second is the social dimension, the political and legal denials of Onkwehonwe collective existences. Recasting the Onkwehonwe struggle as one of seeking restitution as the precondition to reconciliation is not extremist or irrational. Restitution, as a broad goal, involves demanding the return of what was stolen, accepting reparations (either land, material, or monetary recompense) for what cannot be returned, and forging a new socio-political relationship based on the Settler state's admission of wrongdoing and acceptance of the responsibility and obligation to engage Onkwehonwe peoples in a restitution-reconciliation peace-building process.

The other side of the problem is methodological: restitution and reconciliation can only be achieved through contention and the generation of constructive conflict with the state and with the Settler society through the resurgence and demonstration of Onkwehonwe power in the social and political spheres. It is impossible either to transform the colonial society from within colonial institutions or to achieve justice and peaceful coexistence without fundamentally transforming the institutions of the colonial society themselves. Put simply, the imperial enterprises operating in the guise of liberal democratic states are by design and culture incapable of just and peaceful relations with Onkwehonwe. Change will happen only when Settlers are forced into a reckoning with who they are, what they have done, and what they have inherited; then they will be unable to function as colonials and begin instead to engage other peoples as respectful human beings.

Research on the question of the persistence of colonial mentalities has led some Australian scholars to conclude that there are serious constraints to the recognition of indigenous rights in that country, because the imperative to assimilate all difference is in fact an inherent feature of liberal democracy.[45] Their studies also examined the differing political logics of indigenous and liberal democratic systems and demonstrated how attempts to move away from the racist "protection-segregation" relationship so typical of colonial countries are handicapped by the framing of the entire decolonization project in the legal and political context of a liberal democratic state. Detached from the colonial mythology of the Settler society through the application of a disciplined logic of just principles, Onkwehonwe-Settler relations cannot be obviously reconciled without deconstructing the institutions that were built on racism and colonial exploitation. For justice to be achieved out of a colonial situation, a radical rehabilitation of the state is required. Without radical changes to the state itself, all proposed changes are assimilative.

There are fundamental differences between Onkwehonwe and Western models of societal organization and governance. Onkwehonwe cultures and the governing structures that emerged from within them are founded on relationships and obligations of kinship relations, on the economic view that sustainability of relationships and perpetual reproduction of material life are prime objectives, on the belief that organizations should bind family units together with their land, and on a conception of political freedom that balances a person's autonomy with accountability to one's family.

Contrast this to the liberal democratic state in which the primary relationship is among rights-bearing citizens, and the core function of government is to integrate pre-existing social and political diversities into the singularity of a state, assimilating all cultures into a single patriotic identity, and in which political freedom is mediated by distant, supposedly representative structures in an inaccessible system of public accountability that has long been corrupted by the influence of corporations. How can anyone expect that these two totally different political cultures are reconcilable? They are not. Colonial institutions and the dysfunctional subcultures they have spawned within indigenous communities are the *result* of failed attempts to force Onkwehonwe into a liberal democratic mould. Given the essential conflict of form and objectives between indigenous and liberal governance, one or the other must be transformed in order for a reconciliation to occur. As majoritarian tyrannies within colonial situations, liberal democratic societies always operate on the assumption that Onkwehonwe will succumb and submit to the overwhelming cultural and numerical force of the Settler society. Huge costs are involved, monetarily and socially, in the effort to make Onkwehonwe assimilate to liberal democracy and Judeo-Christian cultural values, with no justification other than those weak arguments formed on ideological and cultural prejudices toward the supposed superiority of Europe's cultural and intellectual heritage. This is why reconciliation as it is commonly understood is unjust—any accommodation to liberal democracy is a surrender of the very essence of any kind of an Onkwehonwe existence.

Unprejudiced logics of decolonization point instead to the need to create coexistence among autonomous political communities. Eventual peaceful coexistence demands a decolonization process in which Onkwehonwe will be extricated from, not further entrenched within, the values, cultures, and practices of liberal democracy. If the goals of decolonization are justice and peace, then the process to achieve these goals must reflect a basic covenant on the part of both Onkwehonwe and Settlers to honour each others' existences. This honouring cannot happen when one partner in the relationship is asked to sacrifice their heritage and identity in exchange for peace. This is why the only possibility of a just relationship between Onkwehonwe and the Settler society is the conception of a nation-to-nation partnership between peoples, the kind of relationship reflected in the original treaties of peace and friendship consecrated between indigenous peoples and the newcomers when white people first started arriving in our territories. And the only way to remove ourselves from the injustice of the present relationship is to begin to implement a process of resurgence-apology-restitution and seek to restore the pre-colonial relationship of sharing and cooperation among diverse peoples.

Settlers rebuke attempts to reason logically through the problem in this way. Elazar Barkan, in his study of restitution processes globally, outlines how mainstream arguments about restitution and reconciliation always end up becoming conservative defences of obvious injustices against even the most principled and fair arguments for restitution. It would no doubt be commonly accepted that legitimizing injustice promotes further injustices. Tolerating crimes encourages criminality. But the present Settler state argument presumes that since the injustices are historical and the passage of time has certainly led to changed circumstances for both the alleged perpetrators and for the victims, the crime has been erased and there is no obligation to pay for it. This is the sophisticated version of the common Settler sentiment: "The Indians may have had a rough go of it, but it's not my fault: I wasn't around 100 years ago" or, "I bought my ranch from the government, fair and square!"

The first argument, pro-restitution, is powerful in itself. It is precisely the reluctance of the Settler to investigate and indict his own actions and those of his ancestors that allows the injustice to compound continuously and to entrench itself within the dominant culture. But given the facts and reality that define Onkwehonwe-Settler relations, even the counter-argument, of historicity, points to the necessity of restitution. Placing the counter-argument in an actual social and political context negates any power that it may otherwise have in a theoretical or mythical context. The key to this is in the assertion that the passage of *time* leads to changes in *circumstance*. This is fundamentally untrue, especially when made in relation to Onkwehonwe, Settler societies, and the injustice of a colonial relationship. Between the beginning of this century and the beginning of the last, people's clothes may have changed, their names may be different, but the games they play are the same. Without a substantial change in the circumstances of colonization, there is no basis for considering the injustice *historical*. The crime of colonialism is present today, as are its perpetrators.

Where are we on these questions now, in terms of the way Onkwehonwe demands are put forward to the state, when represented accurately and not co-opted or moderated by aboriginal compradors? Generally speaking, Onkwehonwe have three main demands, which are consistent in many different contexts and countries:

1. exclusive governance over a significant territory;
2. control of resources within that territory, with the expectation of sharing the proceeds of development with the state; and
3. the legal and political recognition of Onkwehonwe cultural norms in the territory.[46]

Just as Onkwehonwe have commonality in our basic demands, responses to those demands have been the same across borders among the (so-called) progressive Settler states, those with significant indigenous populations and that seek an accord with those peoples. These state governments have refused territorial concessions to halt or redress patterns of colonial occupation; they insist that all resource development be jointly administered; they defend the legal and constitutional supremacy of the colonial state and insist on a subordinate governmental status for Onkwehonwe nations; and they insist on rights equivalency among Settler populations and Onkwehonwe, even in those territories recognized as Onkwehonwe homelands and in settlement lands within the indigenous nations' recognized spheres of governmental authority. From Nunavut in the Arctic to Tierra del Fuego and across the Pacific Ocean to Aotearoa, there is consistency in this pattern of demand and response.

The intransigence of Settler states has resulted in further degradations of Onkwehonwe lives and sparked serious violent conflicts in all countries with significant Onkwehonwe presence, ranging from the overt violent racism in Australian society, to the intractable and costly legal disputes over land title in Canada, to the armed insurgencies and violent repression common in Latin American countries. Unfortunately for Onkwehonwe, the intransigence of the Settler has been a profitable strategy, as Onkwehonwe groups have found it extremely difficult to continue to push for their demands in the face of the multiple strategies of delay, distraction, and containment employed by state governments.

Even in purportedly progressive countries like Canada, with the Nunavut settlement of the eastern Arctic land claim and the creation of the Nisga'a Lisims Government in northern British Columbia, we can see how Onkwehonwe demands have been sacrificed through a collusion of manipulative colonial administrators and compliant aboriginal compradors in order to achieve resolutions that accord prominence and legitimacy to the Settler state's intransigence and claimed colonial prerogatives. Settler societies are unable to accept the essential compromise that would be key to developing processes that are truly decolonizing: Settlers must come to accept Onkwehonwe existence as autonomous nations and, with this, recognize the need for a fundamental reshaping of their countries. Onkwehonwe must come to accept and validate Euroamerican settlement and the legitimacy of Settlers' existence in this part of the world and, with this, recognize the need for fundamental reform of the institutions and governing structures of their own nations. Onkwehonwe have demonstrated incredible generosity, flexibility, and patience in accepting this compromise in the interests of advancing toward peaceful coexistence. The Settler society has demonstrated nothing but a selfish obsession with their own material interests. This is why colonialism still exists.

In the face of this intransigence, this generation of Onkwehonwe have some serious choices to make. Depending on whether we confront the challenge before us or not, there are a number of possible scenarios that may play out for our people. Our societies may collapse, and our next generations will die of self-destruction because of our decision to allow things to continue the way they are going. We may choose to retreat from the challenge in front of us, to become stagnant and passive, and to rely upon bureaucracy and technology for solutions to our problems, giving the

Settlers even more control over our lives. Or, we can choose to fight for our existence as Onkwehonwe and our inherent rights and freedoms; we can embrace our challenges and engage our predicament.[47]

Facing these scenarios as very real possibilities, how do we define our predicament in political and strategic terms? As people committed to making change so that unborn generations will have the opportunity to live as Onkwehonwe, we come up against the major obstacle that there is no live culture of resurgence in our communities. One of the main challenges we face is, in fact, just to develop the intellectual support for the *idea* of standing against the tide of government policy and the program of assimilation advanced through government-sponsored organizations and co-opted leaders in our communities. An emergent culture of resurgence that is capable of supporting real social and political movement will depend upon the formulation of an intellectual foundation by Onkwehonwe thinkers. Unfortunately, there are few Onkwehonwe scholars who seriously challenge the co-opted mentality in either a cultural or political way. In the realm of the mind, our people need to be provoked into rethinking what it is to be Onkwehonwe and they need to be provided with ideas on how to reorient the course of governmental and social action in their communities.

To gain some perspective on this question of intellectual defiance against colonialism, I spoke with Audra Simpson, a Kanien'kehaka anthropologist who teaches at Cornell University, who has studied questions about Onkwehonwe political identity formation, and who has perspective on the issue from her own personal struggle as an Onkwehonwe and as an intellectual engaged in challenging colonial mentalities and white power in her world of academia.[48]

TA: *Do you think that resistance, or confrontation, is needed to remake our communities into something different than the colonized places reserves are today?*
AS: Confronting? Possibly. But, you know, I'm very sympathetic to day-to-day forms of resistance. Most of the thinking and writing on indigenous peoples has ignored the day-to-day and in doing so has ignored the bulk of our existence and of our humanity.

TA: *Small forms of resistance are no doubt the first elements in any struggle. But the problem I have with some of those thinkers is that whenever things threaten to get radical, or violent, they stop talking.*
AS: Does resistance always have to be violent?

TA: *I don't think so.*

AS: Okay then. The question you should ask me now is: What are other forms of resistance?

TA: *Just so you know, that was going to be my next question anyway! As someone who thinks about culture a lot, do you think that we can hope to build a movement to regain our land and our rights on the cultural foundations in our communities today?*

AS: As a Mohawk, I think our cultural foundation totally provides for that. In short form—although I'd hate to see it put this way in print—we did not take shit. Respect was a given. If we didn't get respect, that was it, boy! Three warnings, and we went to war. Traditionally for our people, going to war was a perfectly acceptable form of communicating and expressing your political will. And now I try to think about this in terms of my role and my own intellectual industry. It is very much within our culture, even today, to expect respect and failing that, to demand it. A lot of our frustration in politics, and with day-to-day life out here in mainstream society, is that people just don't expect the same things that we do. That's why we get pissed off and angry all the time. That's why we cling tenaciously to certain ideas, like "the reserve" as something that should be preserved and protected. I see myself as part of this: preserving and protecting and producing our intellectual and cultural space, of "going to war" for very good reasons. But compared to a long time ago, the mode of warfare is different in the different spaces we occupy. There are very few people who can appreciate that.

TA: *What do you mean when you say you're comfortable with the idea of going to war?*

AS: War is a form of communication. It's a way of persuading someone, to convince them that they're wrong. In this new context, it might mean imposing my will on them in a way that is not violent. It could even be something like dissecting or deconstructing an argument so that it cannot stand up anymore.

TA: *You're thinking of war not as physical destruction but, it seems, as a kind of intellectual annihilation.*

AS: My notion of war is intellectual or deconstructive. I think there are arguments about indigenous people put out by scholars that really don't stand up well, but that have a lot of pomp and circumstance to them, and that get treated as right only because of the tacit acceptance of white power as "knowledge." I think it's my job as a responsible Iroquois scholar to take those arguments apart. As somebody whose responsibility is to those around me in my community and in the indigenous world beyond it, I have to try to persuade those white scholars that they are wrong.

TA: *Some people might be surprised by such rhetoric coming from you and to find out that you've targeted white scholars and want to annihilate their work. Behind your back, they might say, "There goes another Mohawk with unresolved anger issues." To your face, they might say something like, "Why do you want to disturb the peace, Audra?"*
AS: I am peace loving. That's why I'm doing this. Without respect there is no peace. My mind is not at ease as long as those people are writing about us like that. My mind is not at ease so long as someone else can write The Book on our people and cut the story off at 1794. They have to be made to realize that our people are still going on. I'm for the promotion of good minds, and I think that's a natural calling for any intellectual, white or Indian, Iroquois or Cree.

TA: *What does peace mean to you?*
AS: It's when people's minds are aligned—when your mind or the collective mind is unencumbered by grief or by suffering. Peace is what we strive for. War, as I'm thinking of it, is a way of achieving that peace because sometimes you need to change the other person's mind. My definition comes from our culture.

TA: *The way you've described it, as a state of mind, is exactly how Spinoza, the philosopher, referred to it. He said that peace is more than the absence of war; in his words, it is "a disposition for benevolence, confidence, justice." Can you think of a time in our history when peace has been achieved by our people?*
AS: Aside from the original Great Peace that started it all off, I don't think we've ever achieved it. Personally, I can't think of a time in my life when my mind has been unencumbered by the grief and stresses and worries of the present situation we live. I don't know peace in my life, and I don't think any of us do. We hold it up as an ideal and we strive for it in our lives and in our work. And I know many other people are driven by this principle and are driven to achieve it too. I think that's why our people are so difficult: because we're frustrated that we can't get to this point of peace. People say we're so difficult; you know how we are!

TA: *Oh, I know… It's one thing to have stability, but another thing to have happiness. We see peace as happiness.*

AS: And this can only be achieved when your relations are in order and your mind is at ease. We value respect, we value peace of mind and thinking clearly above all else. Isn't that a beautiful thing? It's so enlightened, such a brilliant and just way of being in the world. And it's what we all want but can't have because of who and where we are right now, living in the seat of unease.

MY GRANDMOTHER, SHE RAISED ME UP AGAIN

There is a always a danger in speaking of colonization in theoretical ways, whether legal, political, or sociological. Those of us in a position to be able to rethink our own identities and our nationhood, and to contribute to the remaking of our relationships and institutions, cannot allow ourselves to distance our minds or our hearts from the present and personal realities that the vast majority of Onkwehonwe are living. The spiritual disconnection that I am claiming here to be the root problem of colonization has affected us all in painful and psychologically debilitating ways. This must be acknowledged and respected.

Disconnection is the precursor to disintegration, and the deculturing of our people is most evident in the violence and self-destruction that are the central realities of a colonized existence and the most visible face of the discord colonialism has wrought in Onkwehonwe lives over the years. Now we will turn to gaining an intimate understanding of what that disconnection means, of the personal effects of colonialism, and of the hopes we have of overcoming those effects by using the strength within ourselves, our families, and our communities.

For those unfamiliar with the quality of life in most indigenous communities, getting a grip on the seriousness and intensity of the effects I am referring to here is difficult. Our communities for the most part are closed to outsiders, and Settler scholars and the corporate media have ignored our living realities in favour of reportage and scholarship on economic and bureaucratic issues; they have not conveyed to the mainstream any sense of the challenges we face. It is even difficult to obtain reliable data or statistics from the colonial government institutions that claim the mandate to manage our affairs. But to give some sense of the problems faced by Onkwehonwe communities, consider the information contained in a 1999 report from the United States Justice Department's Bureau of Justice Statistics,[49] which stated that Onkwehonwe are victimized by violent crimes at more than twice the rate of all American residents. The report, more than a decade old and covering a period before more recent surges in drug abuse and violence in Onkwehonwe communities, covered the years 1992 through 1996 and found that the average annual rate of violent acts among Onkwehonwe (referred to in the study in legal terms as "Indians," which includes "Alaska Natives" and "Aleuts") was 124 per 1,000 people ages 12 years and older; this figure was compared with 61 violent victimizations per 1,000 African-American, 49 per 1,000 Euroamerican, and 29 per 1,000 people of Asian ancestry.

It is important to note as well that the anomie experienced by youth generally is combined, for Onkwehonwe young people, with colonial psychologies of self-hating, repressed rage, drug and alcohol dependency, and an overall social climate of racism which create a situation in which they are more likely than any other group pf people to experience interracial violence. In addition, the study found that alcohol is a major factor in the violent acts committed by and against Onkwehonwe (this was a problem reported across the whole country). Add to this the main legacy of colonial dislocation and physical dispossession that have led to widespread poverty and governmental neglect: health problems. Onkwehonwe suffer health problems at rates exponentially higher than that of Settler populations; epidemic diseases, obesity/diabetes, HIV/AIDS, and the effects of Fetal Alcohol Spectrum Disorder are the primary concerns.[50]

Cycles of oppression are being repeated through generations in Onkwehonwe communities. Colonial economic relations are reflected in the political and legal structures of contemporary Onkwehonwe societies, and they result in Onkwehonwe having to adapt culturally to this reality and to individuals reacting in particularly destructive and unhealthy (but completely comprehensible) ways. These social and health problems seem to be so vexing to governments; large amounts of money have been allocated to implement government-run organizations and policies geared towards alleviating these problems in both the United States and Canada, for example, but they have had only limited positive effect on the health status of our communities. But these problems are not really mysterious nor are they unsolvable. The social and health problems besetting Onkwehonwe are the logical result of a situation wherein people respond or adapt to unresolved colonial injustices. People in indigenous communities develop complexes of behaviour and mental attitudes that reflect their colonial situation and out flow unhealthy and destructive behaviours. It is a very simple problem to

163

understand when we consider the whole context of the situation and all of the factors involved.[51]

If we are truly concerned with social justice—concern for the well-being of individuals as distinct from the larger and explicit rights-based justice claims of indigenous peoples as nations—and want to end the constant recycling of oppressive behaviours of colonialism in Onkwehonwe lives, we must address all of the layers, including the roots, in the cycle. We need to respect the complexity and vastness of the problem. I believe it is absolutely crucial to start decolonizing at the personal level: the self is the primary and absolute manifestation of injustice and recreating ourselves is the only way we will ever break the cycle of domination and self-destruction it breeds in us and in our communities. Individual decolonization means focusing on the mental, spiritual, and physical aspects of being colonized and living the effect of such a condition.

We bring health into our lives and begin to break the power of empire at the foundation when we repel its constant negative pressure on the practical reality of our lives. I see three kinds of imperial forces that are causing our demise: destructive forces, which cause discord and imbalances in our lives that lead to sickness; deceptive forces, which cloud our minds and prevent us from seeing and thinking clearly about our situations; and useless forces, which are simply distractions that use up our time and energy to no good effect with wasteful and self-indulgent behaviours that prevent us from realizing our true potential as Onkwehonwe.

We are bombarded daily with the power of these destructive, useless deceptions in the form of popular culture, mainstream education, and government propaganda. The image of the "Indian" and "aboriginal" are both manifestations of the power of empire to implant destructive delusions and to decoy our rationality with fantasies of assimilation. As weapons of disempowerment, control, and dispossession, they are superbly effective. Yet their full and most immoral purpose remains the spiritual defeat of our people. For too many of us, the psychological landscape is defined by extremes of self-hatred, fear, and co-optation of the mind; the impact has been the creation of a reality and culture in which people are unable to recognize, much less realize, their value as human beings.

Reason is the counter-power that is capable of breaking through the emotional dark cloud of delusion that presses down on us. Enlightenment and awakening is healing. And healing is also the creation of an association with success and strength in people's minds to reconvince them that they have worth, deserve to be happy, and have their rights respected. But in following the path of the government-funded healing industry that has arisen to take advantage of this situation, many of us have fallen prey to a selfish, survival-mode, pragmatic view of recovery from colonialism. Governments and Settlers do not want to get to the root of the problem but hope to contain the situation to a set of individual processes of hurt and healing. The mainstream vision is of coping and, as such, implicitly promotes a continuation of the cycles of loss and abuse that are at the sick core of colonial societies. In following this path in our attempt to alleviate suffering, we have lost our ability to dream our new selves and a new world into existence. We have mistakenly accepted the resolution to our problems that is designed by people who would have us move out of our rusty old colonial cages and right back into a shiny new prison of coping defined by managed fears and deadened emotional capacities. The psychological process involved in transcending colonialism is one of growth: expansion of one's self-conception, of one's view of the world, and of the opportunities for a fulfilling life. Freedom from colonization is the sense of unbounded self and the ability to live fully in a wide open world. It is to feel and live large! Being "Indian" and being "aboriginal" is accepting a small self, imprisonment in the small space created for us by the white man: reserves, aboriginal rights, Indian Act entitlements, etc.

There is little distinction between the mental processes that cause imbalance and negativity at the personal and social or political levels. In practical terms, we transcend colonialism and begin to live again as Onkwehonwe when we start to embody the values of our cultures in our actions and start to shed the main traits of a colonized person: thinking of ourselves before others and projecting our imaginary fears and harmful attitudes onto situations and relationships.

Disconnection from heritage is the real cultural and physical disempowerment of a person. Health and *healing*, truly, is achieved by rejecting the modern toxic lifestyle; physical and mental healing and cultural reconnection are linked. Physical health is the bodily manifestation of recovered dignity. When clear, calm minds and strong bodies are connected, we have whole persons again, and working together we become strong and dignified nations.

The Ditidaht artist Tsaqwuasupp was the spirit of this kind of regeneration. We still mourn his passing to the other side of the sky, but yet, we remember with pride the life he lived in this world. He was a man who made the hero's journey from disconnection, fear, and pain, facing and defeating demons at every step of the way. As we knew him, he stood as the most powerful carrier of his people's heritage and their most sensitive and dignified voice. Meeting Tsaqwuasupp in person was to be drawn into his strength. What was most effecting was the sense he projected of his profound connection to the deepest roots of his people's experience—all of his nation's pains, joys, sufferings and triumphs crystallized in the living existence of one man. This life of dignity was not an inheritance; it was fought for with blood, tears, and sacrifice, recovered out of the ashes of a life fire nearly destroyed by what his people did inherit: loss, abuse, violence, and drugs. If there ever was a person who embodied the spirit of a warrior reborn and who taught us how dignity can be recovered, it was this man.[52]

TA: *What connection did you have before to being Ditidaht?*
T: I didn't have any connection when I was young. None. When I reflect back on that part of my life, it's like I was completely displaced. When I first started at the residential school, I had two languages—my father's, Ditidaht, and my mother's, Coast Salish, *Cowichan*. I didn't fit into white society because I spoke these two languages. And then I was rejected at home because the languages were beaten out of me in the residential school. Those people beat our culture and language out of us. I went home a tortured boy, a fractured, fragmented kid displaced from my people. I was displaced from society. As this displaced person, at 13 years old, I left home and became a logger. I did that for nine years until I injured myself, the whole time working with white people, predominantly. I learned their language. They had no sympathy for my situation, and I knew that.

TA: *It sounds like a tough situation for a teenager.*
T: It was actually pretty scary. What happened with me is… I was abused at school. When I started work, I ended up bunking with this old white man. He spoke a foreign language—Italian, I believe. There was no communication between us, but there was lots of fear. I was a really racist bastard at that time, saying things like, "Fuck you, white man," and "You white cocksuckers," and all that kind of stuff, all the time. That attitude didn't fit with this man, but I didn't care. He noticed that I was a really troubled person. So we got to talking about it, and I told him a little bit about some of the abuses that had happened to me, and he actually got kind of angry about it. One morning, he kind of set me straight as to who he was. He sat me there and said, "Look, I am not the guy that abused you. I'm not the guy who beat you up. I'm just an old man working at this job, and we have to get along. You and I, we bunk together. I don't do those kind of things. I've got a

loving family, a nice wife, I got children. I don't do that stuff!" There was a sense of ease there after that, and I was comfortable with him.

That lasted until my buddies came to the logging camp. I moved in with them right away—they had a bigger bunkhouse. Then time went by, and after nine years of working as a logger, I was really alcoholic, and I had become really drug dependent too. Things were so bad that I ended up spending seven years on the streets in Vancouver. I had a $300-a-day alcohol and heroin addiction. Just a waste. I hid from my family...

TA: *Do you think that was because of what happened to you in the residential school, or were there other reasons, other conflicts that drove you down?*
T: It was a lot of things. During potlatch, when it come time to recognize the family, the ones who went to residential school were treated almost like, "This is the stupid side of my family, and I don't want them to be seen right now, so we'll just talk about them and then get on with our business." We heard the songs, we saw the dances, and we saw all of the beautiful ceremonial things moving around, but we didn't fit in. We didn't fit in with our own people, and we didn't fit in the outside society. We were rejected by both sides. That rejection goes a long way to explaining my being an alcoholic and then being dependent on drugs on the streets of Vancouver.

TA: *Anyone ever try to pick you back up?*
T: Every once or twice a year, my parents would find me. How they did it, I don't know—that's immaterial right now—but they would find me and nurse me back to health to some extent, put some groceries in my fridge, get me some clothes if I needed them, put some furniture in my apartment if I needed that, and try to coax me out of it. I wouldn't go. The last thing that happened to me on the streets was that my grandmother came over. By that time I was already in a hospital. I had institutionalized myself to get rid of my heroin addiction. I knew that I was already close to the end of it. I was 110 pounds, just skin and bones. My grandmother came to see me in the hospital and talked to me. "You have to become somebody else," she said. And she looked into my eyes and told me, "You're a better person than that." She said that I needed to... I guess if you translate it into English, it would be, "You need to put on another face. You need to put on another set of warrior clothes. You need to have those things with you." She told me that her dad, my great-grandfather, was the one that used to rub my hands and talk to me when I was a baby, tell me how *atsic* I was going to be, or "good with my hands." She told me that story, and it made me feel

loved. After that, I knew there was something else to life other than what I was doing to myself.

TA: *It sounds like even though you felt totally disconnected, there were people still holding on to you on the other side.*
T: I knew my grandmother loved me. But with my parents, I felt abandoned: they had brought me to that residential school and just left me there.

TA: *You looked at your grandmother with respect, but saw your parents differently. Was that basically because they had given you up to the residential school, or did they treat you differently too?*
T: I found my grandparents a whole lot more compassionate about what was going on in my life. Actually, not in too much great detail, but they explained to me about the laws at the time I was sent to school. They said, "Your parents were forced to drop you off there, and they were forced to leave you there. They were not in control." That's as far as they could explain it.

The thing about my grandparents, on both sides, was that they had a big cultural background behind them. I noticed it when we'd go to potlatches. I'd notice how people would respect them. I saw all of the dignity that they'd pack around. They would walk into that place with their faces up, not looking at the ground like a lot of us were. I saw people come over and shake their hands and welcome them to that place. It was a very respectful thing. I never saw my parents do that. Up to that point, when I was 22 or 23 years old, I had never seen my parents do those things. It almost seemed like they were ashamed of our culture. But my grandparents were never ashamed of it.

So when my grandmother came to Vancouver to see me in the hospital, she said, "When you get out of the hospital, you come and see me. Phone your dad and I'll come and get you." So I phoned my father when I was ready to come out, and the very next day my grandmother was there. My dad had a car, but she said, "No, I'm going to do this by myself." She came on the bus. She was 83 years old at the time, and she took the bus down from Nitinat Lake. She travelled all night. The first thing we did together was go back over to Vancouver Island, to a place just outside of Victoria they call Goldstream Park. There's a pathway that leads to a waterfall up there. Our people used to go up there to do what we call, *oosums*, traditional bathing. My grandmother's parents used to go bathe up there. That's the first place we went.

There was no highway at the time, there was nothing there. It was a day trek in, a day trek out. When we got to Goldstream, she told me we were going to *oosums*. I already knew what that word meant. She said, "Take off your clothes, we're going to go in and *oosums*." It was like… I'm watching my grandmother undress. But she was naked and she had no shame, nothing. She walked right in the water. She said, "Come on, Son!" And it was cold, for me. But I could see her, and when I looked at her I noticed that she was singing a song, and there was not a quiver in her voice. It was in the month of October, and it was cold out. She bathed me, and she used these special songs, and she said, "We're going to make you a better man." She said, "You shouldn't be killing yourself; you need to be a better person. I know who you are, because I've already seen. I asked about you, and I was told about the things that you're going through, so I need to work with you." She brought me home. She called my dad, and they brought me down to Nitinat. I never went to my dad's place; I went to her place. She'd do what we call, *ahapta*, which is talking all the time. Talk, talk, talk. Talk about how my great-grandfather was a whaler, where he used to *oosums*, the songs that he used to dance.

TA: *She was giving you back your memory.*
T: That's exactly what it was. We had days of that. I don't even know how many days. It seemed like we were there for a month. We never saw anybody else. I think that was probably her instruction, that nobody come over and bother us. We'd get up in the morning at daybreak, we'd have breakfast, we'd go out, and we'd go *oosums*, do some bathing in the ceremonial places. We'd come back home, we'd eat. We'd never go by car, only by boat. We'd row across the lake and then go into the river. And we'd come back home, and we'd eat. And then some more *ahapta*: talking, talking, talking, about who we are. "Who am I?" "What's your destiny?" she would ask me. She'd say, "My daddy gave you your destiny years ago by rubbing your hands and singing songs to you when you were a little baby. He placed medicine in your hands and put them together. *Atsic* means good with your hands, anything you touch. My daddy gave that to you. What are you going to do with that?" It seemed that I knew it was empowering, because it was like a real physical thing. I could feel something coming back.

After a while, we started going to all of the ceremonies that were happening in our area. I used to go to all of the ceremonies on the Salish side with my other grandparents too. Watching my grandmother, I could see that she understood this side of the Island and the Salish side as well; she was able to communicate in both languages. Listening to her speak in our language was fascinating to me. She said, "You know something? You used to do the same thing when you were a little boy. When you first started talking, you talked to me in Salish and you talked to me in Ditidaht. It's like you were two different people." My grandfather was a big chief on the Ditidaht side, and my grandfather on my mother's side was the number one chief of the Cowichans. His wife's father was the number one chief of the flats down at Nanaimo. On my father's side, Baquilla was a big chief. My grandmother, her father was a big chief, Watsuquatah. So we have blood running through my body that tells me I'm a bigger person than they said I was in residential school. In there, I was led to believe I was a nobody. But I am somebody.

TA: *You only came to know this only after she raised you back up?*
T: Yep. I didn't have any other skills. I wasn't a carpenter, or a plumber, or a mechanic, or anything like that. All I knew was logging. When I was in my twenties, I came to Victoria for physical therapy after an accident where I hurt my back. I was getting bored, and a friend encouraged me to go back to finish high school, but I wanted to go to art school instead. After about six months of therapy here in town, I finally made up my mind to go back to school. So here I was, this grown man 23 years old, going back to try to finish school, with a grade six education. What a shameful thing. That's the way I felt at the time. But when I got into school and looked around the room, I saw that everyone in there was a product of the same thing as me.

Marie Cooper was our instructor—a beautiful lady from Tsartlip, someone that had real inner strength. She was educated, she knew her language, and she knew her culture. She helped us get through that process. She said, "You all know that you're much better people than what you've been told in the past." Being empowered by her, I went from grade six to grade 12 in six months. That told me something: I was pretty smart. From there I went into art school. My grandmother had told me that being an artist is being the best warrior that you could ever be. She said, "If you don't want to do anything else with your hands, do your arts, because that's what is going to tell people that we haven't died, and prove that they're not going to be able to kill us." She said, "As long as you're alive and doing your arts, people will know that we're not going away."

TA: *Holding onto culture is an act of resistance?*
T: She trained me that way. She knew about my past in the residential school—I told her everything. She knew of all the troubles I had. She knew I was a resistor of some kind: resistance to the education process, resistance to the school, the supervisors, to anybody with authority. Now I know what she did to me: she humbled me to be a better person, to look at things in a different way, through Native eyes again. I'll always remem-

ber her saying, "You've been given white eyes; you look at things through white eyes. You need Indian eyes again. You need to see something better in all of the people; never mind who damaged you, those people will be taken care of somewhere down the road. Don't worry about them."

Through all of that, my inner self was really calming down, but at the same time, the artistic side was coming up. Even at that time, I had the smarts to go down to the museum and look through all the catalogues and find pieces that belonged to different people and then to reconstruct them in my own mind. When I started doing my art, it really meant a lot to me at potlatch time, when somebody would say, "Can you make me a headdress?" I'd ask him, "Where's yours?" And he'd tell me, "It's in a museum in New York." It's really unbelievable how, as an artist, you can contribute back to the people and give them strength. You can see the pride that they get from getting something back that belonged to their fathers. In the songs that they used those things for, it seemed like they danced better. One of their old treasures had come back, and the women danced with smiles on their faces.

TA: *When you were talking about your grandmother, I was thinking about how different her attitude was from what so many other people carry around with them. She seems so real. To me, it's not like who we truly are as indigenous people to withdraw within ourselves and give up the fight. What we're doing today, it doesn't seem like something our ancestors would have done.*
T: It's hard to be active in the culture and to try actively to give somebody back their own strength. It's easier to lay down and say that you're beat. But it takes courage to do both of these things, actually. It takes a certain kind of courage to take it as a victim when your heart is still beating inside.

TA: *Maybe they both take courage, but I have to believe that resistance has more value.*
T: I have a lot of friends who are still on the street. When I see them now, I give it right to them straight. I tell them that they were actually beat up when we were in school. They were and they still are beat. I tell them that they have never got out of the submissiveness that came with being beaten. That's what controls them.

TA: *One of my cousins lived on the streets in New York City for years and years. His sons went back and got him, picked him up, and brought him back home. There are very few people who come back from the streets and do what you and he have done: lived to tell about it.*

T: I know that a lot of the friends I had in the residential school are still out on the street. I feel bad about that, but it's not my stuff to own. Whoever has the guts to step out of all that and come back to life with our people … those kind of people are rare.

TA: *I've often thought about it, and it's like they put on the mask of defeat and shame, and then they forget how to take it off.*
T: I remember, really well, being in Vancouver and being stuck in that place. But I could still feel the heartbeat inside of me, heh? I could feel the heartbeat, and I was still alive, and I survived another day. Ever since I came back, my heart always went out to those guys who were on the street. I used to go back there, time and time again—but never go down to stay— and I'd say, "Come on you guys, come on back to my village." And they'd be like, "Ah Christ … it's easy for you to say, but it's hard for me to do." They'd always say those words, just like that.

TA: *Maybe they can't imagine that there is a place they can go back to where they can exist as a whole person, as who they really are. Whether that place is a cultural, political, or physical space, it's crucial to have. Without safe space, human beings seem to suffer fragmentation and disintegration. Being part of a community is just so important.*
T: I've had individual forgiveness, but as a community member, I've never had that forgiveness. I've never been told by other people at home, like in the way my grandparents talked to me, "We forgive you for who you are, because that's not really you."

TA: *Even now?*
T: Yeah. When I go home, they say, "Oh, that fucking high and mighty Art Thompson is back here again." And I say, "No, it's Art Thompson, Tsaqwuasupp. I'm Tsaqwuasupp, so I'm just like one of you people. The only thing that I've done is created good things with my hands. And it was all for the name of Ditidaht. It was all for the name of my family and for my mother's family: my father, my grandmother, all of you that are supposed to be related to me. Every time I sign a piece of artwork, I don't just sign it 'Art Thompson,' I sign it 'Art Thompson, Tsaqwuasupp, Ditidaht.' That's all of us. And when I come home, you browbeat me! What I've done as an artist is hold you up. Yet when I come home, you beat me down again."

TA: *People haven't come to understand…*

T: They can't see the good that I've done. They can't see the recognition that I've given them as the Ditidaht Nation.

TA: *Maybe the community as a whole needs to go through the same kind of recovery that your grandmother led you through?*
T: The people in the village need to forgive themselves for who they are. That has not happened, and I don't think it'll happen for a long time. My grandmother told me that it's going to take at least three generations for us to get over this. I know we can't go back to the way it was before. We'll never go back and live in longhouses. But we can create a Longhouse, and we can go back in there and sing the songs that our grandparents sang. We can live in these white man homes, but as long as we have that symbol, we can still go back to the way the old people were thinking. We can always do that, because every time we sing our songs, we visit our grandparents anyway. But what kind of people is it going to take to get there?

These are the kinds of things I have say to people back home: "We're still weak people; we're still very, very weak. I can talk to you for one minute and have you in tears. And you! I can talk for two minutes and have you in tears. About what? About your family history and the history of this place, and where you sit in this tribe." I'm not going to do that, even though I have the power to do it. I say to them, "What I do as an artist is hold you up, and it's up to you to come back and say that you're going to stay up there and that you're not going to be beaten down any more." My grandmother always said, "You guys are big people, because it flows through your blood. Look at your bloodlines, and where they come from: you're huge!" It's taken such a long time; I'm 52 years old now, and it took up until two years ago to get it back from my brothers that, "You know, what you've done for the past 38 years is pretty good, because you've held us up, you've always used your name, you've always used Ditidaht." It's taken that long for my own brothers to see that. That's sad, in a way, because it shows the weakness in the village. I can see it still.

TA: *It also shows the wisdom of your grandmother, who knew what a long and hard road it is for our people.*
T: You're right when you say that the whole village needs to recover. We saw that a long time ago, which is why with my own family, we've almost disenfranchised ourselves by living here in the city instead of in the village. We choose to be here because we don't like what goes on there. We know that we can have a better place for ourselves here, but we have to create it for our-

selves and for our children. My grandmother said, "You don't have to live here to be Ditidaht." She said, "Look at your family; your family's dispersed all over the whole west coast of the Island, and all throughout the states, and the east coast of the Island. You don't have to live in Nitinat Lake to be Ditidaht. You can live anywhere and be Ditidaht, and you can be a strong one out there too."

TA: *Thinking about the experiences of so many of our people living in the city, it brings up the question of what it really is to be Onkwehonwe, an indigenous person. How do you and your family manage to hold on to such a strong identity living away from the village?*
T: I think being indigenous is within oneself. You have to have self-identity. You have to be reassured as a Native person in order to expand as a person and give back to the culture. If somebody has pride and projects that pride, it makes your people stand up a whole lot better. I'm at a point in my life where I know who I am, and I'm able to give lots back—it may seem really big to other people, what I give back, but in actuality it's not even a thimbleful of stuff. This year, I'm going to be giving back to two potlatches, and they think it's one of the biggest things. When I'm on the art market, I charge thousands of dollars for these things, but when I go back to the village I want 20 halibut and some dried fish, or I say, "Gimme two five-gallon pails of herring eggs." It makes me feel like a king. That's what I always tell my family, "We're like kings, we're eating salmon all the time!" That's the way I was taught: when there was an *atsic* person who could create anything, his goods would be distributed amongst the village first to make them feel big about themselves, to make them stand up in a potlatch and dance, to make these women smile with sparkling jewellery, to give them a sense of self-pride.

TA: *You talk about how it is within oneself, but then right after that, you start talking about the connection to community. There's creativity, flexibility, and freedom in what you're saying about being Onkwehonwe, but there's also the need to have a connection with the past, with the culture, and with the community as well.*
T: I think it's necessary for everybody to interact with the history. We do that anyway: we speak a language, we go to potlatches, we sing songs. That's all touching our grandfathers. That's like breathing the same air as all of your ancestors, and all of your descendents, and all of the people that you're related to. You know, my auntie passed away last year, and when it came time for her burial, my cousins asked me, "What are we going to do?" I said, "Well, you remember what we did when Granny passed away. What did we do then?

Are we going to do the same thing with my auntie, your mother, where we argued about all her stuff?" No. Everything got gathered up. They opened up her box and put in all of her silver jewellery, all of her ceremonial rattles, all of her basket-weaving stuff that she needed. The way the old people talked, she was going to need that wherever she was going. So we buried her, and in death, we gave her dignity back to her. The thing I'm getting at is this: we give pride back to our people when we do these things, when we insist on honour and respect. It's being a different kind of warrior. You stand up for old values, forgotten values.

Tsaqwuasupp has shown us the way to recover dignity and regenerate ourselves. Anger and hatred need to be overcome and replaced as the motivating focus of our resistance to injustice with courage and determination. Dignity is truly what has been lost in the colonization of our peoples. Dignity is what must be recovered. Law and government policy and money do not impact on Onkwehonwe lives nearly as much as any effort of *self-determination* to recover dignity and personal strength. On an individual basis, as the self-told story Tsaqwuasupp's return to his true being illustrates, strong family support, traditional teachings and culture, and caring mentorship is the indigenous method of re-rooting a person so that they can stand up again, rededicated to understanding the sources of our pain and of our potential strengths as a way of being authentically indigenous. Another friend of mine, the Acoma poet Simon Ortiz, has written of the crucial connection between ourselves and our traditional culture, our communities, and our homelands: "We insist that we as human cultural beings must always have this connection because it is the way we maintain a Native sense of Existence."[53] Tsaqwuasupp's grandmother showed him that we need to find a way to once again see the world through Onkwehonwe eyes, to hear what people are telling us with Onkwehonwe ears, and to use our Onkwehonwe voice to speak the truth. Learning, doing ... reawakening to who we can be. This is the positive sense of self-determination that we need to carry us forward.

NOTES

1 *Basic Call to Consciousness*, rev. ed. (Hogansburg, NY: Akwesasne Notes, 1981) 18-22.

2 Jack Forbes, "Nature and Culture: Problematic Concepts for Native Americans," *Ayaangwaamizin* 2,2 (1997): 203–29. See also Forbes' essay, "Intellectual Self-Determination

and Sovereignty: Implications for Native Studies and for Native Intellectuals," *Wicazo Sa Review* 13/1 (Spring 1998): 15; and, Glen T. Morris, "Vine Deloria, Jr. and the Development of a Decolonizing Critique of Indigenous Peoples and International Relations," *Native Voices: American Indian identity and Resistance*, ed. Richard Grounds, George Tinker, and David Wilkins (Lawrence, KS: University of Kansas Press, 2003) 97–154. Bhiku Parekh has also written compellingly and critically on the patterns of Western thought in relation to imperialism, specifically on how justifications of colonialism and rationalizing inequality are at the core of liberal thinking. See his essay, "Liberalism and Colonialism," *The Decolonization of the Imagination*, ed. J.N. Pieterse and B. Parekh (London, UK: Zed Books, 1995).

3   See Robert D. Kaplan, "Looking the World in the Eye," *The Atlantic* (December 2001) 68–82.

4   Héctor Díaz, *Indigenous Peoples in Latin America* (Boulder, CO: Westview Press, 1997) x.

5   See Albert Memmi, *The Colonizer and the Colonized* (Boston, MA: Beacon Press, 1991) 43. A notable and honourable exception from Memmi's own time is Jean-Paul Sartre.

6   Audre Lorde, "The Uses of Anger," *Sister Outsider* (Freedom, CA: Crossing Press, 1984).

7   *Globe and Mail* 17 September 2003: B13.

8   *Globe and Mail* 17 September 2003: A17.

9   The most powerful indictment of monotheism as a source of vindictive violence is Barrington Moore's, *Moral Purity and Persecution in History* (Princeton, NJ: Princeton University Press, 2000), and one of the most perceptive critiques of the Western religious and philosophical tradition is John Mohawk's, *Utopian Legacies* (Santa Fe, NM: Clear Light Publishers, 2000). For expanding my understanding of the concept of the "One Right Way," I am indebted to John's scholarship and to his animated oral presentations on this subject over the years.

10 I will note here the exceptional Latin American movement called Liberation Theology and its brief challenge to the orthodox role of Christianity in colonial societies. On this movement, see Christopher Rowland, ed., *The Cambridge Companion to Liberation Theology* (Cambridge, UK: Cambridge University Press, 1999). There are other exceptions as well, such as the spiritual Christian anarchism of Leo Tolstoy and the utopian socialist Judaism of Martin Buber.

11 See Lewis Lapham, "Res Publica," *Harper's Magazine* (December 2001): 8–10.

12 See Thomas Flanagan, *First Nations, Second Thoughts* (Montréal, QC: McGill-Queen's University Press, 2000) and Alan Cairns, *Citizens Plus: Aboriginal Peoples and the Canadian State* (Vancouver, BC: University of British Columbia Press, 2000).

13 From Jerry Mander, *In the Absence of the Sacred* (San Francisco, CA: Sierra Club Books, 1991) 128.

14 See Diaz, *Indigenous Peoples in Latin America* 140–43.

15 See Bruce Clark, *Native Liberty, Crown Sovereignty: The Existing Aboriginal Right of Self-Government in Canada* (Montréal, QC: McGill-Queen's University Press, 1990); Claude Denis, *We Are Not You: First Nations and Canadian Modernity* (Peterborough ON: Broadview Press, 1997); and Paul Havemann, ed., *Indigenous Peoples' Rights in Australia, Canada and New Zealand* (Auckland, NZ: Oxford University Press, 1999).

16 See Elizabeth Furniss, *The Burden of History: Colonialism and the Frontier Myth in a Rural Community* (Vancouver, BC: University of British Columbia Press, 1999); and Hugh Brody, *The Other Side of Eden: Hunters, Farmers and the Shaping of the World* (Vancouver, BC: Douglas and McIntyre, 2000).

17 For a critique of the discourse of sovereignty, see Alfred, *Peace, Power, Righteousness*; and Taiaiake Alfred, "From Sovereignty to Freedom: Towards an Indigenous Political Discourse," *Indigenous Affairs* 3/01 (2001): 22–34.

18 See Patricia Seed, *Ceremonies of Possession in Europe's Conquest of the New World* (Cambridge, UK: Cambridge University Press, 1995).

19 For more on the urgency of redefining the colonial reality, see Memmi, *The Colonizer and the Colonized*, 103.

20 For more on this point see Day, "Who is This We That Gives the Gift?"

21 Tahehsoomca was interviewed at the University of Victoria in August 2001.

22 Aung San Suu Kyi, *Freedom From Fear*, rev. ed. (New York, NY: Penguin, 1995) 180.

23 The phrase "partisans of order" is from Frantz Fanon, *The Wretched of the Earth*, 59. His seminal work contains a full discussion of the notion of co-optation and complicity among colonized indigenous elites.

24 She was interviewed at the Vietnam Garden restaurant, in Victoria, BC, in August 2001.

25 I will remind the reader here that I am using the word "Onkwehonwe" because I am Kanien'kehaka, and that in rejecting the white man's word, in this act of linguistic resurgence, I am not meaning to obscure or discourage the use of *Anishnaabe, Dene, Dakelh*, or any of the other authentic words for the people in indigenous languages.

26 I am indebted to James Tully for this critical insight into the flawed concept of liberal justice and to the notion of exclusionary and inclusionary injustice. I draw on a lecture he delivered at Wesleyan University's Center for Humanities on November 4, 2002, and his article, "The Unfreedom of the Moderns in Comparison to their Ideals of Constitutional Democracy," *The Modern Law Review* 65,2 (2002): 204–28.

27 Michael Hardt and Antonio Negri, *Empire* (Cambridge, MA: Harvard University Press, 2000).

28 See James Tully, *Strange Multiplicity* (Cambridge University Press, 1995).

29 See Diaz, *Indigenous Peoples in Latin America* 73–74.

30 Diaz, *Indigenous Peoples in Latin America* 87–105; *Gathering Strength*, the final report of the Royal Commission on Aboriginal Peoples (Ottawa, ON: Government of Canada, 1996).

31 See Melina Selverston-Scher, *Ethnopolitics in Ecuador: Indigenous Rights and the Strengthening of Democracy* (Miami, FL: North-South Center Press, 2001); John Holloway and Eloina Peláez, *Zapatista!* (London, UK: Pluto Press, 1998); and Allison Brysk, *From Tribal Village to Global Village: Indian Rights and International Relations in Latin America* (Stanford, CA: Stanford University Press, 2000).

32 For further discussion of the globalized indigenous movements' structure and goals, see Brysk, *From Tribal Village to Global Village*, 59.

33 Deborah Yashar, "Democracy, Indigenous Movements and the Postliberal Challenge in Latin America," *World Politics* 52,1 (The Johns Hopkins University Press, 1999): 76–104.

34 From Yashar, "Democracy, Indigenous Movements and the Postliberal Challenge in Latin America" 5–9.

35 Beverley McLachlin, Chief Justice of Canada, "Aboriginal Rights: International Perspectives," Remarks at the Order of Canada luncheon, Canadian Club of Vancouver, Vancouver, British Columbia, 8 February 2002.

36 For a full description of international law as it relates to indigenous peoples, see James Anaya, *Indigenous Peoples in International Law* (Oxford, UK: Oxford University Press, 1996); for the current status of the politics surrounding the development of international legal instruments affecting indigenous peoples see John B. Henrikson, "Implementation of the Right of Self-Determination of Indigenous Peoples," *Indigenous Affairs* 3/01 (2001): 6–21 and Taiaiake Alfred and Jeff Corntassel, "A Decade of Rhetoric for Indigenous Peoples," *Indian Country Today* (11 May 2004).

37 See Said's classic, *Culture and Imperialism* (New York, NY: Vintage, 1993); and for a concise and accessible summary of his views on this subject, see Edward Said, "Impossible Histories: Why the Many Islams Cannot be Simplified," *Harper's Magazine* (July 2002): 69–74.

38 See Taiaiake Alfred, *Heeding the Voices of Our Ancestors* (Don Mills, ON: Oxford University Press, 1995) 75–79; and Alfred, *Peace, Power, Righteousness* 80–89.

39 Isabel Altamirano was interviewed in Edmonton, Alberta, and via email in the fall of 2001 and spring of 2002.

40 On the function of Christian churches in the colonial enterprise, see Memmi, *The Colonizer and the Colonized* 71; and Fanon, *The Wretched of the Earth* 67. For a more developed exploration of the relationship between institutional Christianity and the evolution of European empires, see Tom Harpur, *The Pagan Christ: Recovering the Lost Light* (Toronto, ON: Thomas Allen Publishers, 2004).

41 On why people accommodate unjust power relations, see Jeremy Brecher, Tim Costello, and Brendan Smith, *Globalization from Below: The Power of Solidarity* (Cambridge, MA: South End Press, 2000) 19–20.

42 I was influenced here by Russel Barsh and Sakej Henderson's notion of "general" and "borderline" histories, in their book, *The Road: Indian Tribes and Political Liberty* (Berkeley, CA: University of California Press, 1980) x.

43 See Vern Redekop, *From Violence to Blessing: How an Understanding of Deep-Rooted Conflicts Can Open Paths to Reconciliation* (Montréal, QC: Novalis, 2003).

44 See John Sugden *Tecumseh* (New York, NY: Henry Holt, 1997).

45 For the comparison between indigenous and liberal models of governance, I draw in particular on Geoffrey Stokes, "Australian Democracy and Indigenous Self-Determination, 1901-2001," *Australia Reshaped: Essays on Two Hundred Years of Institutional Transformation*, ed. G. Brennan and F. Castles (Cambridge, UK: Cambridge University Press, 2002) 181–219.

46 Hale, *Resistance and Contradiction* 192.

47 These scenarios for the future draw on Duane Elgin, *Voluntary Simplicity*, rev. ed. (New York, NY: William Morrow, 1993) 179–91.

48 Audra Simpson was interviewed at Restaurant Porto Fino in Montréal in September 2001.

49 The American Justice Department report was outlined and discussed in "The New Violence Can Be Checked," *Indian Country Today* (11 February 2002). For more detailed information on these issues and for an influential discussion, see Duran and Duran, *Native American Post-Colonial Psychology*.

50 See T. Kue Young, *The Health of Native Americans: Toward a Biocultural Epidemiology* (New York, NY: Oxford University Press, 1994) and the numerous up-to-date research papers published on the Internet by the Canadian National Aboriginal Health Organization <http://www.naho.ca>.

51 See Michael J. Chandler and Christopher Lalonde, "Cultural Continuity as a Hedge against Suicide in Canada's First Nations," *Transcultural Psychiatry* 35 (1998): 191–219.

52 Tsaqwuasupp was interviewed at his home in Victoria, BC, in August 2001.

53 Simon J. Ortiz, *Out There Somewhere* (Tucson, AZ: University of Arizona Press, 2002) 1.

indigenous resurgence

Today we say: We are here. We are rebel dignity, the forgotten of the homeland.[1]

—Emeliano Zapata, Nahual

We have considered strength and clarity, two of the elements needed both for the regeneration of ourselves as individuals and of our peoples collectively and for the resurrection of a truly indigenous and effective movement for justice. Now we turn to the other essential part of the overall picture: commitment. What is this quality? Internal strength, perseverance, tenacity, and indomitable will are all traits that characterize people and groups who have been successful in transforming themselves, their environments, and their adversaries. These traits reflect an unbreakable commitment to the struggle for truth that is the backbone of any movement for change on a personal or societal level. Onkwehonwe have already demonstrated incredible commitment and courage simply in surviving the constant and vicious assaults from colonial forces on their dignity and on the very idea of their existences over the past 500 years. The challenge for those of us seeking to move beyond mere survival, to engender social and political movements taking us to a place beyond colonialism, is to convince Onkwehonwe to draw on our inherent and internal resources of strength and to channel them into forms of energy that are capable of engaging the forces that keep us tied to colonial mentality and reality.

LIBERATORY FANTASIES

There is great danger in attempting to negotiate structural changes to our relationships before our minds and hearts are cleansed of the stains of colonialism. In the absence of mental and spiritual decolonization, any effort to theorize or to implement a model of a "new" Onkwehonwe-Settler relationship is counter-productive to the objectives of justice and the achievement of a long-term relationship of peaceful coexistence between our peoples. As is becoming evident in the (supposed) decolonization processes already underway in colonial countries—which are fantasies of liberation obscuring the hard realities of persistent colonialism—structural change negotiated in a colonized cultural context will only achieve the further entrenchment of the social and political foundations of injustice, leading to reforms that are mere modifications to the pre-existing structures of domination. A real commitment to justice points us towards both a deeper challenge to the very foundations of the colonial state and culture and the need for an effort to deconstruct and then reimagine the surface and symbolic reflections of the heritage of empire.

In most of our communities, there are people dedicated to this kind of deep decolonization, people whose credibility as Onkwehonwe, as leaders, and as warriors is well-established. They are trying to build organizations based on indigenous values and principles and from that organizational base launch contentious engagements with state authorities. Whether the particular issue is protection of the land, fishing and hunting rights, treaty rights, or border-crossing (to name a few of the causes that our people continue to fight for), there are Onkwehonwe who are organized and who are working to bring about meaningful change in their communities through direct political action. These people are in the minority, always, it seems, because the principled causes that are so important to our survival are not the ones funded by colonial government programs. Nor are the principled causes legalized and set up as acceptable forms of political engagement by the state— they require pushing the limits of the law by acting contentiously at the edge of acceptability or, as is more often the case, acting in spite of unjust colonial laws. In other words, working for a cause that has indigenous integrity means sacrifice. Such a principled existence means turning away from the huge amounts of government money offered to aboriginalists, instead accepting the burden of being persecuted by state authorities and facing efforts by politicians established within the colonial system to bring contentious movement leaders into disrepute and to discredit their cause. This is the reality of an authentic indigenous existence in political terms. And, evidently in our communities today, there are only a few people who are convinced that taking on the psychological and financial burden of being really indigenous is worth the fight.

What drives a warrior to keep up the good principled fight when most of our people have slunk into dull complacency? To explore this question at the source I sat down with two people whom I know to be truly Onkwehonwe culturally and spiritually, who are committed to the regeneration of our nations through struggle, and who have shown great persistence in maintaining indigenous principles in their work strengthening First Nations political organizations at the local, regional, and cross-national level. There are many of our people working for change (so to speak) "within the system," but very few who do so can maintain themselves as Onkwehonwe after entering the milieu of a governmental organization, with all of the bureaucratic politics and the expectation of ethical compromise it entails. Joan and Stewart Phillip, the Okanagan Nation couple who are the current leaders of the Union of British Columbia Indian Chiefs (UBCIC) are exceptions to the rule.[2]

Joan and Stewart lead the organization that was founded by and which still carries the legacy and vision of the great Secwepemc leader, George Manuel.[3] I asked them to reflect on the heritage of struggle they carry and on the ways Onkwehonwe have attempted to confront the state. On a more personal level, I spoke with them to find out what drove them, as leaders, to move from working in what was a cooperative manner within the band council system to become prominent voices of contention and the rejection of negotiated accommodations of colonial power in the western part of Anówara.

TA: *You are well-known as standing for what you call indigenous "sovereignty." What does it mean for you to be a "sovereigntist"?*
JOAN: Okanagan! There's a meaning to that, in terms of a language and a culture and, besides, a certain "scrapper" mentality and a willingness to defend your rights. There's a real intelligence, a broad vision, and an ability to see forwards and backwards, a way of analyzing the world to figure out where to go from here.

TA: *Is being a leader the same thing as being a warrior?*
JOAN: There are four sacred trusts: looking after that land, looking after the people, looking after the spirituality, and looking after the culture, which includes language. For us, being a warrior and being a leader means

181

being a protector of the four sacred trusts. That's something the elders have told us is everybody's responsibility. It's not just a particular group of people.

STEWART: It's a great responsibility. I'm dressed up in a suit sitting here with you today, but when the need arises, Joan and I both wear camouflage. I've never seen any other leaders do that except us. The other thing is that you have to have a clear mind and a good heart. And you can't be carrying a lot of issues around with you.

TA: *So you have to be a clean person to be a leader and a warrior.*
STEWART: Joan and I went through terrible times in the beginning of our relationship. I was a total alcoholic since I was 15 years old, and our relationship was abusive, with me running around and whatnot all the time. It wasn't until I went into treatment in 1987, shortly after Joan went in, that we started to deal with a lot of our issues. I think that if you're going to dedicate your life to this kind of work, you have to be clean and sober. You can't...
JOAN: You can't be a slave to drugs and alcohol.
STEWART: It's critical, it's essential, it's vital. You have to be of high moral character. You can't be running around. I admit that I did more than my share of running around when I was younger. I remember being involved in the American Indian Movement back in the 1970s, and one of the fundamental activities was just that: running around. You know, you had this kind of uniform—one of those big, black, broad-brimmed hats with a red headband and the bongles hanging off the back of it, and the feather, and the shades... (Laughing.)

TA: *"The Full Minneapolis" ... right on!*
STEWART: And you'd actually walk around like that! But a lot of it was posturing for women rather than carrying on with the struggle. The other thing, besides having good moral character, is that you have to be prepared. And we are prepared. There are very few people who are prepared like we are.

TA: *Prepared?*
STEWART: For anything.
JOAN: To protect yourself.

TA: *Is that what wearing camouflage symbolizes?*
JOAN: It's not just a symbol. What really upsets me about people's thinking here in this country is that nobody questions the fact that indigenous

people in Chiapas had to take up arms to protect themselves, yet, on the other hand, they question what happened in Mohawk territory and the need to take up arms there in 1990. To me, there are two kinds of war: wars of offence and wars of defence. We have every right to defend ourselves against an aggressor. This country has always been our oppressor—it's always stolen from us—and it has oppressed even its own people. When we talk about being prepared, it's being prepared to fight against that kind of oppression, because it happens right here, in Mohawk territory, in Gustafsen Lake, and at Ipperwash.[4]

TA: *Are we prepared as a people though?*
JOAN: No we're not, not collectively.
STEWART: When I think back to 1990, we weren't prepared in our community. We had our reserve sealed off, and had we been assaulted, we'd have been in big trouble. Things are different now for our community.

TA: *So for you, Oka 1990, your involvement in supporting that action, really shaped you as leaders and as indigenous people.*
STEWART: Yes. And not only that. What I gained out of it was a true understanding of leadership. Leadership is not casting a vote once every four years and putting in a band council. Although I do believe that the participation of those people who are involved in negotiations is an action as well. Whether you're sitting around a table trying to hammer out a deal, or whether you're on the barricades, that's all action. It's just a different kind of action.

TA: *But you foresaw the failure of the negotiations, of making deals in regards to land claims and conflicts with the government of British Columbia.*
JOAN: That's right.

TA: *How come?*
JOAN: A lot of it had to do with history, and a lot of it had to do with our participation in 1990, and a lot of it was also just our spiritual understanding of what our responsibilities are, and everything that goes along with that. One thing I've realized is that our struggle is part of a global struggle that all revolves around money and control and land and resources. Political power is meaningless unless you control the purse strings. It's the same all over the world. You have Third World countries with so-called political power, but who gives a hoot when they don't control the resources within their own

country? They have the same uneven trade relationship as always—everything comes here, to North America. That's why there's no revolution going on here: we're too fat and happy. That's the long and the short of it, basically. Only when those Third World countries liberate themselves will things really change.

TA: *The resolution to our problems here depends on a globalized struggle for economic justice?*
JOAN: Absolutely. That's why, as indigenous peoples, we have to develop relationships with people in the Third World. When I was in Chiapas, I realized that the legislation passed in Mexico to take away indigenous peoples' communal ownership of lands, so they could be opened up for sale and resale and redistribution, is the same legislation that they're trying to feed to us here. How well they learn...

TA: *Is confrontation part of your own political vision?*
STEWART: It's incumbent upon us to exhaust, absolutely, all legal avenues and options and attempt with every fibre of our being to achieve peaceful reconciliation. But in the event that we are faced with a hostile government that attacks us, we have to be prepared to defend ourselves. There is something starting these days, a new kind of movement among the youth, something that people may not think is very positive or healthy, but which has to be seen as a good thing in the long run, and that is the take-over and occupation of band council offices. We need more of this kind of activism; we need a real grassroots revolution in this country. If that means that every band council office in this country is occupied, then that's a good thing, because it's the beginnings of growth and the beginnings of people waking up, as strange as this may seem. When I was chief of the band, our band office was taken over and occupied, and it was very difficult for me to come to terms with that, and it took me some time to agree to meet with and to try to work with the group that had taken over our office. But we did work it out, and we worked together over a period of three months to come to an agreement and to make changes in our community, because that group represented the voice of our people. We needed, and every band council in this country needs as well, to get back to being a truly representative government. The band council system as it is only divides us and creates factions within the community.

TA: *But there hasn't been much of any kind of action to speak of since 1990, compared to the amount of talking that's been going on.*

STEWART: The government exploited the situation after Oka. We were all energized and mobilized, particularly here in British Columbia, and the federal and provincial governments collaborated and sprung out this "BC Treaty Process" overnight. What that did was buy them ten years. It subverted the movement, and it provided them a way out. Then the more conservative communities chose to get involved in that negotiation process, saying, "We're doing something too, we're negotiating."

TA: *We all know that there are people in our communities who are conservative in their views and who don't look with much favour on the kind of things that you are saying and on the kind of associations that you have. Lots of our people, if they would walk into this room right now, wouldn't be inspired, but turned off instead to see that framed photo of the Westcoast Warrior Society and that poster of the Mohawk Warrior hanging on the wall.*

STEWART: I think we need to realize that oppression creates certain psychological conditions in the group of people that are oppressed. What oppression does is disempower people. Certainly the residential school experience and the reservation system and our whole history of colonization have greatly disempowered our people. Simply put, we lost the ability to believe in ourselves. Joan and I believe and have faith in the power of the people. There are others who don't believe in that power. And there are others who don't believe. Period. They don't really believe in our rights, our right to self-determination, and a just resolution of the land question. Many people pay lip service to all that, but when it comes right down to it, they don't believe in it strongly.

JOAN: It seems that with us indigenous people, we always bring ourselves to the brink before we get motivated to do the right thing! But we'll develop as the struggle develops, and we will be prepared. Up until 1990, not being from the community originally, I didn't say much and always just looked after the kids and took care of the garden, you know?

STEWART: She behaved herself.

JOAN: Yes I did! (Laughter.) Stewart always says, "We were a peaceful, agrarian people, until you showed up…" But anyway what really did disturb me was that people didn't believe in themselves—they didn't think that they had a right and that they were capable of defending it. They didn't realize that a people united can accomplish absolutely anything. I ended up getting politically involved in this community for the first time after that.

185

STEWART: The most highly respected elder in our community, Louise, told us not to be afraid and to get out there because we were doing the right thing.

TA: *Do you see more confrontations happening in the future?*
JOAN: There's no doubt about it. As long as white people continue, as one of our elders, Napoleon, put it, "to be like pigs, always wanting to take, take, take everything," there won't ever be a time when we won't be protecting what we have and what we own. So long as this country will continue to oppress, things like the Mohawk Crisis will come up.

TA: *We'll always have to be warriors, no matter what happens.*
STEWART: There is no question about that. I was at an environmental meeting once, out on one of the mountains that are sacred to the Navajo and Hopi. There were all kinds of people from all over the place. They brought this Hopi elder out. He was just this real thin person with spindly little legs and long wispy white hair. Two heavy-set guys helped him up onto the stage, and he told this old prophecy. He said that there was going to be a war to end all wars, and that it was going to happen at a point in time when on one side there will be four colours—the four races of man—and it will be the same on the other side. One side will be those who seek to exploit Mother Earth for profit, and the other side will be those who understand the need to defend Mother Earth. I believe that's where we're going. This struggle is not ours alone.

Joan and Stewart's sobering reflections highlight the immense challenge of deconstructing colonialism within ourselves and rebuilding the foundations for a movement that has indigenous integrity. Their notions of "four sacred trusts," the importance of warrior-leaders, and the necessity of contention are what struck me as the resounding lessons of decolonizing action over the last 30 years. There is no *model* or set of Instructions for Building a Movement to draw on, only such principles. The true, indigenous, and effective vehicles for channelling decolonizing forces have yet to be developed and put into practice. There is much more work to do at the community level and on personal decolonization before we are capable of doing much more than defending ourselves from attack. Organizing to protect ourselves and to defend our rights is absolutely necessary and something which we must do immediately and be prepared to sacrifice for. But after speaking with Joan and Stewart, and reflecting back on the results of the various assertions and conflicts Onkwehonwe have been involved in in the modern era, it became clear to me that effectively confronting colonialism implied, in the first instance, an internal struggle to deconstruct the structures of colonial power as they manifest through patterns of behaviour and institutions of power in our own minds and in our communities.

Deconstructing colonial power is not just a matter of having the courage and the right intention and setting off toward the right goal. It means having the right form of organization, a strong social bond, and effective ways of communicating and coordinating our actions. Given the nearly complete absence of these indigenous forms of social and political organization in our communities today, the situation we face is indeed daunting. The one thing that is certain is that people who believe that we are going to be led out of our colonial reality by the colonial surrogate organizations we have running our communities today are not looking at our situation honestly. Rather than thinking through the necessities of struggle and committing to the work of de-organizing colonialism and reorganizing our people and resources to meet the challenges of resurgence, they are satisfied to harbour liberatory fantasies while the harsh reality of imperialism continues on the ground and on pace to destroy the possibility of an Onkwehonwe existence for future generations of our people.

How many times have we heard a frustrated Settler facing the possibility of justice impinging on the exercise of his colonial privileges, ask "What do you people want from us?" There was a time when I angered (more) easily and tended to answer such veiled hostility in kind with statements like, "It's simple, man; I want you out of my face and off my land!" But the question, when asked sincerely and with respect, is a good one. What *are* we fighting for? Land, money, payback…? I say we are fighting for freedom. We want freedom in the form of an existence for our people where we can, for the first time in generations, know the liberatory effects of experiencing whole health, personal fulfillment, and the ability to express ourselves and flourish as human beings. All action, politics, and economics are instruments to the end of freedom and of happiness through freedom.

The sources of freedom are attitudes and actions. Here I mean actions of a certain type, actions that restore the selflessness and unity of being that are at the heart of indigenous cultural life, that reject individualistic and materialist definitions of freedom and happiness, and that create community by embedding individual lives in the shared identities and experiences of collective existences.

One of the best examples of people who exemplify this approach to freedom is the many Filipino worker communities that have sprung up all over the globe. Decades of research on the subject of Filipino culture has shown how they, as a people, consider themselves to be the happiest people of all Asian cultures (followed by Malays, with, interestingly, the wealthiest societies, Japan and Hong Kong, at the bottom of the list).[5] Research into the psychological and cultural sources of Filipinos' mental states point to their very inclusive and open culture, the opposite of both individualistic Western cultures emphasizing privacy and personal fulfillment and hierarchical and status-based Chinese-rooted cultures in other parts of Asia. Filipino identity is based on *kapwa*, a Tagalog word meaning "shared being," meaning that there is no concept of a separate existence from others, and everything is shared. Thus, loneliness and alienation is much less of a problem among Filipinos, even in their many expatriate communities.

Another secret of the Filipino workers is their spirituality. In an environment of material poverty and sometimes severe hardship, they maintain their sense of well-being by maximizing what freedom they do have to liberate their spirit (there is virtually no drug abuse, suicide, or depression among overseas Filipino workers). Ninety-seven per cent of Filipinos declare a religious faith, and 67 per cent say they are "extremely close" to God—that is more than double the number of the next two highest groups who do so, Americans and Israelis.

All of this points to the immaterial root of happiness. The base for human happiness is a positive self-conception and outlook on the world. These positive views are always rooted in a spirituality that serves to counter the disturbing and destructive negativities that otherwise emerge when a person lives a culturally poor and spiritually barren existence in an environment of material poverty and hardship. Inner peace is undermined by negativity, not by deprivation. It is negativity that leads to imbalances and the social expressions of deeper anomie and alienation.

The post-modern empire mobilizes strong forces (hatred, anger, pride, lust, greed, and envy) for its political and commercial purposes, and these forces are normalized and even glorified in contemporary society in contrast to peaceful cultures, such as those of the Filipino and other indigenous societies.

It is these imperial consumerist forces that are the deep sources not only of unethical conduct in our lives, but also of the anxiety, stress, and depression for colonized and colonizer alike. They are rooted in the Euroamerican cultural heritage to which Onkwehonwe have been forcefully exposed and to a large extent assimilated. Indigenous resurgences embody the commitment to free people from the grip of these forces and seek to restore the connections that colonialism has severed and that globalization and materialism are erasing forever. We must replace ourselves in the circle of cultured communities that offer the freedom and opportunity for us to foster inner peace and happiness through our shared existences.

Many Onkwehonwe embody the culture of "shared being." Drawing on unseen stores of strength to make the effort to bring people together and to recreate community out of conflict, these Onkwehonwe heroines (for they are nearly all women) keep hope alive through their very being. They are heroines for their willingness to risk scorn, insult, and sometimes even physical harm by going between the fighting factions in their colonized villages to talk of how it would be a better life for the people if they came together as one and worked for their common good.

Sximina is one of those Onkwehonwe women whose love shines brightly through the circumstances of her life.[6] She embodies the theme of commitment I am advancing in this chapter of the book. Her life is an example of the different ways that the concept of commitment manifests as persistence in one's personal struggle to decolonize, dedication to the unity of one's community, and an unstoppable assertiveness in defending the principles and rights of one's people. She is untiring and unbeatable in her struggle to awaken and unify her Nuxalk people, even when faced with daunting pressure to conform to the culture of cynical politics of co-optation. She is a living example of the strong spirit of women who are courageous in staying true to their beliefs in themselves and the potential of their people, although they receive little reward for their hard work and the love they manifest in their dedication to their nations. I talked with Sximina in the building used by the Nuxalk Nation's indigenous government. We began by discussing how and why she became involved in the resurgence of the "traditional" Nuxalk movement.

TA: *What's the story of how this place and this movement came to be?*
S: This is the House of Smayusta, "the house of stories." Our history comes through stories, and this is where a lot of the stories are told when we come together as a people. This is the traditional government of the Nuxalk Nation. I was the one who asked for this place. Our head hereditary chief, Laurence Pootlas, was the one who actually set it up, about 14 years ago. I had come back here from going to school down south, and I started working for the band council. At the band office, I heard a lot of negativity about Laurence and what he was doing. So I went home and told my mother what was going on over there. She told me that I had better go and learn what truth and honesty really is by talking to Laurence. She told me,

"He's our hereditary chief, and we need to respect him." She told me to go volunteer with him so I could find out what the Nuxalk people were really about. So, not very willingly, I went to see him.

This was at a point where nobody was really helping him; the fight in him was gone; he and his wife were doing a lot of crying. They were praying and crying, because there was no movement among our people at all. Every time he would try to do something for the nation, non-traditional people were fighting against him. Nothing was happening. The elders kept pushing him to carry on, but he had no support. So I went to him and simply asked him if he needed help. When I came to them and said that, they believed it was a blessing.

TA: *So what kind of things did you do to help?*
S: I would write letters and things like that. Laurence would tell me to write a letter to all the chiefs and elders and to go deliver those letters. I would write up the letter and then go deliver it to every family and every house that had a chief or an elder. You know, when I go around to people's houses, the people say, "This is what the head hereditary chief used to do before." That chief, he would go to every house and stop in to tell the news—there was no writing back then. The only thing is that back then there were only 40 or 50 houses on the reserve, but it's even more difficult now with over 350 houses!

TA: *Could you tell me how you hold onto your role here in the House of Smayusta while you're also elected to the band council?*
S: I asked the people, in a meeting here in this House, if I should run for the band council. Some people actually came and told me that I have no right to run for the band council, because my position here is stronger and that it would be weakened by being on the band council. But the reason I decided to go there is because I want to be a leader for my people. I stand traditionally until the day I die. But I really believe 100 per cent that I need to be over there right now too, working with the ones who don't understand tradition and who don't have the feeling for the land that I have. I had this dream, and in it, all of my people were "possessed"—they were like little baby children all sitting there blinking at the same time, sitting around a table. I realized that the people around the table in my vision were the ones who are in the band council. They don't understand. The idea behind me running for elected councillor is so that I can get in there and learn what they're teaching them in that office that makes them that way and then help to educate them to see things the way they really are instead.

TA: *You have a lot of confidence in your ability to change people.*
S: I do have faith in my people. Even with the ones who are the most angry, I realize that their anger is coming from somewhere.

TA: *There are about 800 Nuxalk people living here in Bella Coola. How many of them support the traditional government? And what do non-traditional people who don't support it think of the House of Smayusta?*
S: There are a lot of people who support us but who are not open about it or who are not active. But if it came down to supporting a struggle or a fight, they would donate food, quietly. I would say more than half of our people are like that. But here in this community, the House of Smayusta is a name that is used negatively. People doing it don't even know why! I've been labelled, "House of Smayusta," but I tell people that it's not a bad name. People don't know why they have to hate the House of Smayusta, they just do because the bandwagon is going that way.

TA: *With most people, there's still fear of the traditional ways. We could be talking about any Native community. In my experience, the people decide to work in the band council system for practical reasons, because that is where the action is—the money and the power. But when it comes to their opposing the traditional government, I think too that the word "fear" is appropriate to describe people's feelings. We don't truly understand those ways, and we get the sense that we ourselves are not really Native because of that. I believe that's where the anger, jealousy, and resentment comes from towards people who are involved in rebuilding the traditional systems.*
S: We have to think of ourselves as nations and act as nations. We really need to develop our own governments. When the churches came in and the potlatching had to stop, it took a long time to recover from that. It was 1974 when Laurence had his first potlatch, and the next one was about ten years later; now there are two or three potlatches every year. It's a slow process to rebuild our nation's traditional culture, but being traditional is living it, and making it part of your life.

The churches say that what we do is wrong because they think that we worship totem poles and masks. But this is totally not the case. The Nuxalk have a name for God, the Creator, and that is *Tatao*. We have a name for the Almighty, which is the female part of the deity, called *Atlaxtang*, "the ruler of all." We have a name for the Holy Ghost, *Sminyax*. I read the Bible all the time, and I try to learn from it. What I've come to realize is that we Nuxalk people are no different than anyone else who has ever been put on this earth. But, we have been put on earth in this place, and this place is our Holy

Land. We even had a Garden of Eden. It was called *Ista*. That's the place we were fighting to protect from the loggers a few years ago. People may say that our Nuxalk stories are more mystical than the ones in the Bible, yet in the Bible there was a man who lived for 591 years. So compared to our stories about this place and our ancestors, what's more believable to you?

Part of what I am trying to teach people about being Nuxalk is this: Do you like fish? Do you like to smoke fish and eat it? What about the oolichans and the oolichan grease? What about the deer and the moose? Do you like all that? If you do, you're Nuxalk. That's part of you, and it's part of living here. It doesn't matter what else you believe in—the Bible, other stories, or whatever. If you believe that you have to live off of those things and this earth, and if those things are part of your life, then you're Nuxalk.

TA: *I guess instead of that, most people would say that you're Nuxalk if you have a status card, a band number, and a land allotment on a reserve.*
S: The true sense of what it is to be Nuxalk came to me from the elders. And not only that. Ever since I was a young kid, I grew up on the land, always involved in fishing and planting. We live in seasons. Right now, it's mushroom season. We just finished with fishing season. Before that it was planting season. And in the winter months, it's the season for making things. That's part of living Nuxalk. We survive on our own. I put away everything for food. We preserve and can most of our own food.

TA: *If you were left out here on your own with no electricity, gasoline, or supplies from the white man, could your people survive?*
S: I know my family would! (Laughter.) But I do know lots of people who just live day to day. They don't have food stored up. I don't believe that most people have those skills. This year, I was talking with a young woman who has four kids, and I asked her, "Did you put away any fish?" She said, "No, my grandmother never taught me how to." Her mother had had an illness... That young woman came over here and learned how to do it this year. I believe that's part of my responsibility, to teach. When I was out getting the fish to can, the Canadian government told us that we couldn't take any Coho salmon—they wanted us to throw them overboard, dead or alive. I won't stand for that, so I was taking in all the cohoes anyway and canning them with this young woman, and saving them to use for food at our feasts.

TA: *You didn't care about what the police might do to you?*

S: I was telling the other fishermen out there that I didn't care if they were going to take me to jail. I wasn't throwing my fish back in the water, not when there're people starving in our village and we need this to eat. No way. I carried my fish right up there out in the open.

TA: *They didn't bother you?*
S: Nope.

TA: *Maybe your attitude scared them off. What about the Nuxalk fishermen who obeyed the government order, what do you think of that?*
S: It's pathetic, really. I was talking to some of our other fishermen, and they were throwing back 100 fish every night. Throwing 100 cohoes in the water, dead! It upset them to do it, but they didn't want to get charged by the government. They haven't paid their fishing boats off yet; they still need that licence to fish, so they didn't want to get in trouble and have those fish confiscated.

TA: *So what makes the difference between you and them?*
S: Money!

TA: *What, you don't depend on money and they do?*
S: I think some of them were really high fishermen: rich. Me and my family, we just make a bare living off fishing. But we have our freedom.

TA: *People always divide this way, between the ones who live for money and those who live for something else.*
S: I think we have so much division related to long-standing personality or family conflicts too. I've tried to make a point of overcoming that myself. I figure that if Jesus can love everybody, then I can too. I work with medicines a lot—I make medicine. And when I make the medicine, I do it for everyone. I go around and give it to all the elders. Sometimes it's hard because I know a lady used to say, "Oh, she's so spoiled," and this and that about me and my family. I remember those words and how things like that hurt me. But then I say to myself, "Well, those people just don't know who I am, so I'm going to teach them differently." I've been doing this for a while, and it's been quite difficult, actually, with some of my own family, because of politics—my Mom's brothers and sisters pulled away from me. But because of the work I've been doing, things have opened up, and right now I believe I have a relationship with just about everyone in this village.

That's a start: breaking down my own prejudices against other people and learning not to go on about past grievances and wars amongst families. Here in Bella Coola, it's hard because we are different nations all put into one. There are the *Kimsquit* people, the *Talliomeh* people, the Bella Coola people here, it's called *Kumquoltz*, and our area is *Chimolx*. And also the *Kwatnah* people too. Our traditions are all just a little bit different. I was very young and didn't really understand, but when our elders came together, there was a lot of pressure. Some of the elders would be saying, "Oh those people don't know how to do that ceremony properly." But we had to realize after a while, although to this day some people still don't, that we are different nations brought into one: the Nuxalk Nation.

TA: *What is it that binds the Nuxalk people together today? After all this, and following the work that's been done, what are people here willing to stand up and fight for, together, as one?*
S: I think that if the government, or anyone else, tried to encroach or do anything on our reserve lands, there would be a fight. But there are lots of people who don't fully believe that we also have rights in all of our traditional territory. They call the land in our traditional territory, "Crown lands."

TA: *Even the Nuxalk people, they call Nuxalk territory by that name?*
S: Some of them do. Whereas to us traditional people, the Crown has made a claim on our territory, and it's obvious that they're selling it off as fast as they can before land claims are settled. They're logging it, trying to mine it, all of that. They've taken so much already...

TA: *So everybody would defend the "reserve," but not everybody would defend their "traditional territory"?*
S: Yep. It's a breakdown of tradition, a loss of knowledge. It's also a lack of confidence and security in being Nuxalk. There's insecurity here in the village. I mean, we have to live with the non-native people. You grow up here in Bella Coola knowing that over there is the "White Side" and over here is the "Indian Side" of the village. You don't realize, unless you've been educated in some way, that we have rights and that we have rights in all of our traditional territory!

TA: *Tell me what happened when the traditional people decided to act on those rights and to try to save Ista, your Garden of Eden, back a few years ago. What was the reaction from your own people, and also from the white people here in Bella Coola?*

S: There was a lot of deep, deep anger. They were angry that they couldn't do anything. And there was a willingness to hurt. No willingness to listen. There was pain everywhere. I've always been friends with everybody, but when I came here then, I would see people and their faces would just turn away. They knew that my Mom and Dad supported the House of Smayusta, and they knew where I stood. With our own people, I think a lot of them were really confused. There was strong pressure on the situation from the band councillors. They were saying that we were wrong. The chief councillor at the time was quoted in the newspaper as saying that we only had 30 per cent of the village behind us—you know, he only had 30 per cent of the vote to get in to be the chief councillor himself! (Laughing.) He was confusing the people. A lot of our people sat in the middle, because they are not willing to confront. They do believe that it is our land, and they do believe in our rights, but there was a threat made by the chief councillor that if they acted on those beliefs and supported us, they would not be issued any more welfare cheques. A lot of them chose to not even speak about what they believed in because of this threat. And another threat went out to every employee of the band council administration: they would lose their jobs if they supported us—two of them were laid off for a week.

TA: *Why were the band councillors so strongly against what you were doing?*
S: There were about seven Nuxalk loggers who were supposed to be working in that area. During this occupation, the logging company, Interfor, had moved all the white loggers away and told all the Nuxalk loggers to go out there. Interfor told the Nuxalk loggers, "If we don't log this area, you're not going to get any more work." This is what happened.

TA: *So they were threatened too?*
S: Their jobs were threatened, yes. A lot of this happened because the former chief councillor had his own ideas about putting a pulp mill in here. I know this for a fact because I worked on that plan as my first job out of school, until I just couldn't do it anymore.

TA: *Did the situation ever get resolved?*
S: It didn't. It got logged. They threw our hereditary chiefs in jail, and the stress was so much for the head chief's wife that she died. Then the government made Laurence sign a piece of paper he would never have signed otherwise: a court document saying that he wouldn't be involved in any more

protests. They made him sign this paper so that he could get out of jail to go to his wife's funeral.

TA: *It must be hard to see this as anything but a defeat for your people?*
S: I believe there was some positive in it because it did bring a lot of us closer together. There was a lot of strength among the people that were involved.

TA: *Do you think the reaction would be the same if you decided to make another stand against logging or development?*
S: Yes.

TA: *What are you going to do to make sure that the same thing doesn't happen all over again?*
S: My plan is to go door to door, like that old head chief used to do, and find out where our people stand. I've been to one home already to talk about a proposal to build a mine, and it's just been… anger. Anger at me for being House of Smayusta. They said, "You're going to try to stop this!" Before I left I gave them all a hug anyway. The next time I saw them, they still just turned their faces away from me. But I have been to other people's homes, and found that there are lots of people who believe what we believe in, but they just don't speak out.

TA: *That's a big question. How do you get people to stand up for themselves after being beaten down for so long?*
S: To me, it's a spiritual war. It's a war between good and evil within ourselves.

It was Gandhi who wrote, "Those who say that religion has nothing to do with politics do not know what religion means."[7] The link between spirituality and meaningful political action is all but ignored in contemporary indigenous politics. The political game is essentially a material contest for power defined in terms of money and influence within the colonial system. There is little difference in values or goals between indigenous politicians advocating Onkwehonwe interests and colonial administrators defending the myths and prerogatives of empire—the one difference that does matter in this framework is the minuscule minority status and lack of resources at the disposal of indigenous politicians relative to their colonizer counterparts. Is it any wonder that First Nation and Inuit politics—a contest for power in which indigenous politicians try to get the better of larger, smarter, more numerous, and more dedicated adversaries—is a loser's game?

I asked my friend from Six Nations, Thohahoken, who has spent many years learning from Rotinoshonni elders about our culture and traditions, to talk to me about spiritual power and about one of the most divisive and powerful traditions of thought and belief among people of our nation: the *Kariwiio*, the Code of Handsome Lake. I wondered what he thought of the suggestion that Handsome Lake's prophetic visions and the message of spiritual rebirth he brought to our people in the early 1800s were not just the foundations of what had become a conservative moralistic and insular religious tradition, like most revivalist legacies among Onkwehonwe peoples. Did he believe that Handsome Lake's teachings would be understood more deeply as conveying and containing a revolutionary message that was the continuation of an everlasting tradition of spiritual and cultural regeneration among the Rotinoshonni?[8] His answer illustrates the kind of shift in perspective that needs to happen if we are to revitalize the wisdom and teachings within our cultures, use them to remake ourselves, and transform them into weapons of resurgence. As we stand, we are preserving and protecting, but we are not capable, with the understandings we have, of launching a resurgence on the basis of "traditional" teachings; the element of action is missing from the teachings as we have directly inherited them.

The teachings are radical wisdom, and they must be seen that way if we are to break out from under the weight of colonial oppression. The old understandings have served our people well as shields and, indeed, have allowed us to survive. But today simply protecting our wisdom and knowledge is not enough. These are the days of warriors and of radical action. *Hatskwi!*

Thohahoken explained to me that two words are the roots of Kariwiio: *Kariwehs* and *Karihonni*. Kariwehs refers to the aspect of "being" at some point in time and is usually translated as "a long time." Karihonni means "the reason for..." When these two suffixes are placed at the beginning of a word, like Kariwiio, a philosophical state is implied. This is a very different understanding of Handsome Lake's teachings than is commonly held by most Rotinoshonni. Thohahoken believes that, being colonized and Christianized, we interpret our traditional teachings, like the Kariwiio and the concepts of "peace, power, and righteousness" not as true Onkwehonwe would, but as contrite penitent believers in a religion. We think more like our Christian-influenced conservative colonizers than like the free-thinking philosophical warriors our ancestors were. By solidifying the moralistic aspects of the Kariwiio into a formal code to judge and control social behaviours within our communities, our way of being Rotinoshonni (what used to be called *Kanonsehsneha*, or The Longhouse Way) has turned Handsome Lake's teachings into an actual religion akin to and supplementing the controlling Christianity brought to our people by missionaries. *Kanikonriio*, reasonableness, has been replaced with *kanikonraksa*, unreasonableness, in our minds and in our culture because of the controlling power of superstition and the pattern of moral sanctions that are so much a part of what the Handsome Lake code has become to our people. Thohahoken believes that this kind of "doctrinal mind-controlling assertion" contradicts Handsome Lake's central message: to be aware of and to avoid all mind-controlling agencies (in practical terms expressed as prohibition against alcohol, nostalgia, dancing and partying, gossiping, and promiscuity).

Viewed through a political rather than moral lens, Kariwiio points not to internal witch hunts, but to resurgence and survival. Handsome Lake's concept of resurgence, explained Thohahoken, is expressed in the language through the idea that *kariwiio ne skennen*, a "reasonable, balanced state," is achieved through *kanikonriio tanon ne kashastensera*, "powerful reasoning." In a deep understanding of Kanienkeha, the Mohawk language, the true meaning of "powerful reasoning" is not at all the contrite state conveyed by the English word that is usually used to translate the term, "righteousness." And "reasonable, balanced state" has less to do with what is normally referred to as "the good message of peace" than it does with putting yourself in "a good place." Thohahoken said that Handsome Lake "was telling people to use their heads and think for themselves in order to resist extinction, what he called The Destroyer. He said, 'stay in the Longhouse and beware of those forces around you, *konerhonion—henskariwatentiete*, who will try to tear down what you are trying to build up.' That sounds like resistance to me."

Thohahoken's indigenous re-reading of one of our people's central traditions forced me to think deeper about what it means to be Onkwehonwe. His challenging perspective on the teachings of my own culture shows that there is divergence on ways of thinking about being indigenous among those in the traditionalist circles of our nations and among those who operate in our indigenous languages. It may be that our languages and the philosophies that contain our teachings are so layered and rooted in a precolonial cultural context that our present level of technical knowledge of our own languages is insufficient to recover the true warrior teachings that are embedded in our peoples' stories, ceremonies, and rituals. For most of us, it is truly necessary to regenerate not only the words but the kinds of experiences that shaped and built our ancestors' understanding of those words.

The long process of strengthening ourselves begins with regenerating our indigenous intelligence so that we can begin to use our own conceptual framework to make choices as we move through the world. It means reconnecting to what in my people's language would be called *Onkwehonweneha*, the indigenous way of being. The first steps are relearning who we are, reconnecting with the teachings from our cultures, and remembering the lessons from the experiences of our people. But how do we do this, especially when we are living physically distant from our culturally rooted communities? It is not a simple question, because the *way* we approach the challenge of learning will shape us as much as *what* we seek to learn.

Thohahoken addressed and expounded on this fundamental question in his doctoral dissertation with the concept of Indigenology.[9] In his writing, he described the Western way of teaching, one of passing knowledge from learned people, who are confident in their position of authority, to ignorant people—a model he calls "knowledge fiduciary" (in less academic language, this may be thought of as a form of arrogance and self-centredness). In contrast to the knowledge fiduciary model, he described the Onkwehonwe model as the "aural tradition," meaning that *listening* is the true indigenous way, as opposed to the more common understanding of it as "oral tradition," which of course is all about speaking and *not listening*.

His research into the way Onkwehonwe traditionally conveyed knowledge and understanding down through generations has led Thohahoken to offer his own conclusion on the elements of the indigenous learning process: learning is transformative and involves critical reflection and a positive view of change; it is participatory and involves working with others in the learning process; and knowledge comes from learning traditions within a society of thoughtful people. He wrote:

> A network of communities, like branches on a tree, decides they need each other in order to survive. So they work diligently to maintain relationships... These persons learn how to live in their place. Thus, they are learning individuals, in learning societies that form a learning civilization... Knowledge is transmitted from generation to generation and comprises a shared history of experiences, innovations, and inventions.

I believe Thohahoken has brought an important concept to bear not only on education, but on political change as well. The regeneration of Onkwehonwe cultures must not only focus on restoring Onkwehonwe teachings to primacy in the minds of our people. If we are to have any success in transforming our people through that knowledge, we must do so in an indigenous way as well. And it must be an all-encompassing transformative process that leads to change in action. What is clearly needed, then, is regeneration of a culture of indigenous knowledge among our peoples. Educational institutions and processes, both formal and informal, need to undergo a serious de/reorganization and be made to reflect both indigenous knowledge and Onkwehonweneha, the indigenous way of learning and being. It is this consciousness, thinking like Onkwehonwe, seeing the world through indigenous eyes, taking hold of our responsibilities and living them, that is the character of a transformed and decolonized person.

To be sure, most of our people are in a state of disbelief or misapprehension, not yet convinced of the need for change. How do we convince them of the need for struggle as the way out of the alienation, pain, and discord that defines so many lives? Some are aware of the force and dynamics of imperial power, conscious of their oppression under the weight of lies, but they remain uncommitted and can't get started. How do we get people to act on their knowledge and beliefs, to move? There are a few people in every community who are planning and thinking about resurgence and who are intent on taking action. How do we think through the movements that have begun so that we are oriented around a solid set of ideas and a compelling and achievable set of goals? There are warriors who are actively engaged in struggle, who are doing things to challenge the preconceived and prejudicial notions of an aboriginal vision that defines the status quo and the moderate activist approach. There are people who are working at making change and even some who are directly confronting state authorities. How do we get them all to work together and work with all our people?

These four questions must be addressed in order to move people to change. What is most crucial and immediate is to focus on redefining identity and reorienting world views, on how we achieve the reformation of our personal and collective identities, the generation of new ideas about self (questions on what we do and should believe), and the preservation of our new identities against the inevitable setbacks and counterattacks that will come from the state (questions on how and when to fight).

The first two stages, given the present strong state of the colonial mentality and widespread defeatism among us, is in convincing our people of the need for change and getting them moving on the first steps of organizing and challenging the existing realities and order of power in their communities. This is where most of the energy of those seeking to bring about change no doubt would be most effective

If this is, in the broadest conception, the indigenous struggle, then the revolutionary objective must be recast as self-transformation,[10] not only for strategic reasons of balance of force and numbers, but also because we cannot hope to make the changes we must make through acts of violent revolt directed against the state. A concept of revolution founded on acting against the state has only ever resulted in the replacement of one oppressive order or orthodoxy with another. We need a proactive, not reactive, agenda for change. The French political scientist Gérard Chaliand, who lived through and wrote masterfully about all of the world's major post-war revolutionary movements, summarized beautifully the real revolutionary goal: "to challenge the mythologies of the nation-state, the cult of work, the submission to authority, the imposture of groups and parties who claim to possess the truth—in short, to sift carefully through all established assumptions (for they lie at the root of many consented servitudes)."[11] The true spirit of revolt is not the motivation to crush or overthrow colonial structures and bring in replacement structures but an invocation to the spirit of freedom, a drive to move mentally and physically away from the reactive state of being compelled by danger and fear and to begin to act on intelligence and vision to generate a new identity and set of relations that transcend the cultural assumptions and political imperatives of empire. And therefore to *be free*.

It would be too depressing to think of revolution otherwise: that the essence of all politics is domination in one form or another. What would be worth fighting for? It certainly would not inspire people to ask them to give up their comforts, security, and lives for a slightly less bad system.

The answer to the question of how to motivate people to make change in their own lives and that of our collective existences is this: people will be motivated to make change when they come to realize that they will be freed from the sources of their pain and discontent only through anti-colonial struggle. The key is recasting revolution as a constant challenge to arrogant imperial condescension and specific abuses, to force imperialism to withdraw and break its hold on one's life, and in doing so prove that empire can be defeated as a whole system. We must remove imperialism from the spaces we inhabit and transform those spaces into something other than what they were designed and forced to be within empire. In essence, rebellion in these terms is recreating freedom and aiming to end the humiliation of living identities that were created to serve others.

It is impossible to reverse militarily or politically the patterns of power that exist in society without a spiritual transformation that will break the cycle of violence that inevitably results from violent challenges to state power. If the goal is to obliterate the oppressor's power altogether, any challenge will fail; if we seek instead to initiate a different kind of challenge, in the form of regenerating our own existences in the face of the oppressor's false claims to authority, legitimacy, and sovereignty, we cannot but succeed and, thus, force the state to transform itself.

This spiritually rooted notion of revolution differentiates between opponents as *adversary* or *enemy*. Ascribing the term *enemy* means that we seek his annihilation or obliteration through the application of forces driven by hatred, a relationship which throughout history has generated countless and endless cycles of violence. Considering him as an *adversary*, on the other hand, implies that we have the objective of transformation driven by compassion achieved through teaching generating relations of love.

Many philosophies have delved into this distinction. Aung San Suu Kyi, the heroine of the Burmese people's resistance against totalitarian military rule, has written of revolution in her people's experience:

> The quintessential revolution is that of the spirit, born of an intellectual conviction of the need for change in those mental attitudes and values which shape the course of a nation's development. A revolution which aims merely at changing official policies and institutions with a view to an improvement in material conditions has little chance of genuine success. Without a revolution of the spirit, the forces which produced the inequities of the old order would continue to be operative, posing a constant threat to the process of reform and regeneration. It is not enough merely to call for freedom, democracy and human rights. There has to be a united determination to persevere in the struggle, to make sacrifices in the name of enduring truths, to resist the corrupting influences of desire, ill will, ignorance and fear.[12]

Revolutionary movement and opposition to state power, action in the defence of truth, is at the very heart of anti-imperial struggle. Frantz Fanon wrote, "you do not show proof of your nation from its culture... you substantiate its existence in the fight which the people wage against the forces of occupation. No colonial system draws its justification from the fact that the territories it dominates are culturally non-extant."[13] Struggle, then, is the signal of an oppressed people's still beating heart in a colonial situation. Action is the life sign of peoples whose existence is officially denied. The lack of resurgent indigenous existence in contention to the state is an indicator of submission to the colonial assumption of our demise. In a colonial situation conceived and regulated by forces of obliteration and consumption, we must fight for what is precious to us, or it will be stolen away and used for someone else's benefit and enjoyment. Fight, not talk. Talking back to power is useless if it is divorced from political, economic, and spiritual sources of strength organized and coordinated to affect colonial power. Culture is a powerful weapon when it is framed in the context of struggle and organized as a force within a politics of contention.

So what are the goals of such a struggle and the politics of contention? Hannah Arendt's classic reflections on revolution clearly laid out the broad spectrum—"peace is the continuation of war by other means"—and differentiated between a number of key concepts that most often are conflated, but which are in fact important to understand as distinct ideas. *Power* is the ability of human beings to act together, which she saw as inherent in the simple existence of a group. *Strength* is the property or character of an individual person. *Force* is the energy released by physical or social movement (she distinguished this form from violent force). And *authority* is the unquestioning recognition of an order, by people who are asked to obey, where neither coercion nor persuasion are required. Arendt also wrote, "To remain in authority requires respect for the person or the office. The greatest enemy of authority, therefore, is contempt, and the surest way to undermine it is laughter."[14]

Frantz Fanon's harsher attitude belies his understanding of the same truth described by Arendt: "In the colonial context the settler only ends his work of breaking in the native when the latter admits loudly and intelligibly the supremacy of the white man's values. In the period of decolonisation, the colonized masses mock at these very values, insult them and vomit them up."[15] From the philosophical investigation to the practical consideration of a tactical formula, the line is clear: authority flows from legitimacy founded on respect expressed in deference. To destabilize authority, the counter-formula is to delegitimize by disrespecting, showing contempt, and mockery. The keystone to a regime's survival is legitimacy and the ensuing deference it promotes among those people who are subject to the regime's orders. Delegitimizing the regime is the most fundamentally radical act one can perform.

THE GREAT LAW OF CHANGE

Can we envision a politics of resurgence that is authentically cultured, spiritually rooted, and committed to non-violence in its strategy and that leads to the creation of a credible threat to the colonial order? For guidance in thinking through this question, we must travel from Anówara to the site of the only mass movement that was founded on the premises we are advocating: India, the site of the *Satyagraha* (a Sanskrit word meaning "holding to the truth") campaign against British imperial rule inspired and led by Mohandas K. Gandhi. The Satyagraha campaign was built on the concept of progressive steps toward freedom. It was a movement that grew out of real grievances against the established political order in British-controlled India. It took into account the actual present state of the people, as well as the changing dynamics of power and imperial reactionary politics as the struggle progressed towards evermore intense states of contention and conflict.[16]

From its basic position of non-cooperation with injustice, the movement elaborated and put into effect other strategic and tactical ideas, but the personal and collective refusal to legitimize British and comprador power and authority was the solid foundation of freedom from imperial domination for the countries that became India and Pakistan. After exhausting all legal means of change and building up the capacity for direct action, non-cooperation meant negotiation, issuing of ultimatums, economic boycotts, and strikes. For Gandhi, agitation within the context of imperial law was the first step necessary to demonstrate the ineffectiveness of legal strategies for oppressed people and to undercut any accusation of unreasonableness that might be levelled against the movement by reactionary forces within and outside of the movement. Only then could more intense and severe forms of contention be justified.

The next stage of the movement was civil disobedience, a mass surge of indigenous power against the divisive and controlling state structures. These forms of resurgence took on life when people gave up their allegiances to the state and began to withdraw from the colonial bureaucracies and local colonial offices that were used to control the indigenous population. They started to boycott government structures and developed alternative structures of government in their communities. Following civil disobedience, the functions of the imperial government were usurped by parallel indigenous governments in order to challenge the authority of the empire.

These stages, of course, did not happen in regular succession, or in a neat order, or all at once as a single movement across the country. The British were defeated by a mass movement that took place in many localized settings and that was directed against institutional targets that emerged in the context of people's life situations. In each of these myriad sites of contention, it was when people believed that they were strong and when community leadership and the collective capacity for struggle were realized that anti-colonial contention was justified and became both achievable and necessary in their minds and hearts.

Fifty years after the defeat of the British and the partition of their former colony into the countries of India and Pakistan, we can consider the real lesson of the Gandhian movement: the path to freedom for colonized peoples begins with personal strengthening and then the development of a capacity for collective action. We learn as well that an anti-colonial movement is not total systemic resistance. Instead, its actions are designed to be specific to the evil or injustices being targeted by the movement at whatever time and in whatever place the struggle is taking place. This implies an approach of strategic (though ironic) cooperation with those parts of the imperial system which are in fact good or which simply are not involved with the specific injustices being targeted for action by the movement in that situation. The kind of mass resistance Indians practised against British rule required respected leadership, disciplined and trained warriors, spiritually and culturally confident populations, and an overall dedication to a specific fundamental objective. In our situation, as Onkwehonwe, such a shared inclusive goal would unify the multiplicity of local struggles and help them cohere into a focused force. The movement could then develop an alternative vision of an Onkwehonwe-state relationship, especially once the colonizers' power and will to defend the unjust order has been broken. To even conceive of this kind of struggle's success (and I do believe this approach is the only one capable of bringing about the defeat of colonialism as a power relation and as a mentality), our people must embody the warrior ethic on a mass scale, meaning that there needs to be wide and deeply ingrained belief in the struggle as a just cause. Dignity must be highly valued, sacrifice ennobled, and the methods of contention must be well known and thoroughly practised.

The leaders of the Indian struggle accepted all who would join their campaigns. They developed tactics and rules to meet well-advanced situations of conflict in those local struggles that were successful in moving beyond non-cooperation and civil disobedience to attack the core of imperial authority. Had they been able to select their crusaders and train them for their respective roles in the Satyagraha operation, the movement's effects might well have been even more dramatic.

The ultimate question for us then is how to put this experience and knowledge into practice on a personal and collective level as Onkwehonwe. Politically, we need to think of it as a challenge to build a coordinated movement of Onkwehonwe peoples. This is basically an organizational question, one of leadership. The Indian Satyagraha and Wasáse, the Onkwehonwe movement inspired by it that I am proposing here, are both spiritual at their root and are fundamentally similar in their quest to confront an empire made of lies and to restore truth as the reality of people's lives. Gandhi himself referred to someone who was active in his campaign as a "soldier of peace."[17] I was struck when I read this of the similarity of Gandhi's idea to the Kanienkeha word, *Rotiskenhrakete*, "they carry the burden of peace" and to what the late Tuscarora medicine man Mad Bear described as his concept of an authentic Onkwehonwe existence: the notion of a "friendly warrior."[18]

There are differences between the Indian and Onkwehonwe philosophies, of course. Onkwehonwe philosophies are more rooted in nature, and, whereas the relations among all the elements of creation are honoured, there is a general philosophical acceptance of the imperative for all creatures, including humans, to strive to preserve their existence. This speaks against the mystical influences of Hinduism and the Christianity-rooted redemption in Gandhian notions honouring self-sacrifice and submission to cosmic and other forces. The Gandhian movement was also based on an approach to revolution that was more fully developed as a theory of anti-imperial social action and contention. Gandhi, his collaborators, and their followers, had the experience of decades of resistance against British oppression in South Africa and three separate campaigns against the British rule in India.

So what is the synthesis? I think it will be in an anti-state movement that is oriented towards the reconnection of people to their lands, the reunification of their communities, and the restoration of cultural security in individuals and collectives. It will recreate in people a belief in themselves and their heritage and give them something to fight for as Onkwehonwe. But one thing, somewhat ironically given the long-term objective of restoring Onkwehonwe connections to *land*, is that the movement will not be tied to *territory*. It will transcend Euroamerican notions of time and place that constrain the recognition of Onkwehonwe identities and rights to those who act in ways and live in places sanctioned by the state. Land is not territory, except in a colonial way of looking at the landscape. Onkwehonwe resurgences will act against the boundaries white society has placed on being indigenous and will move freely in our homelands; for Onkwehonwe in Anówara, home is everywhere and we are all related. Territorial boundaries are an assault on this indigenous sense of place and being. So, most likely, given the present trend of large numbers of Onkwehonwe leaving the colonial spaces reserved for us and moving to urban centres, the youthful energy of the Wasáse will cause a movement among refugee exmatriates from the reservations who will make their presence known and felt all over the place, transforming their negative reality into a positive strategy, confronting the privileges and legacies of empire with their heritage of courage, justice, and peace. Wasáse will be a struggle to get rid of our status and identity as this continent's colonized Indians and to make real the wisdom coming from the land and from the experience of our peoples. When I hear the Kanienkeha word, *Kahwatsire*, "all of our fires are connected," I feel it captures the spiritual connections and sense of the relationship I am describing here.

The state is an artifice of Euroamerican rationality—it is mechanistic, bureaucratic, and, actually, quite simple. The indigenous way is to respect relationships and forms of organization and communication that are natural and organic to a people's experience—natural, complex, and somewhat chaotic from a Euroamerican perspective that values regularity and control above all else. Empire is founded on obsessive proceduralism and law; Kahwatsire implies trust. Empire seeks defined solutions accomplishing justice as its ultimate purpose; Onkwehonwe are guided by universal compassion and seek to accomplish connections. Empire leads to alienation; indigenous ways generate human happiness.

Let us turn now to questions of technique. Conducting resurgence action is an exercise in manipulating resources.[19] If we were to appraise the resources available to us as leaders of Onkwehonwe movements, we would see that conducting struggle effectively in the twenty-first century requires a degree of technological sophistication and access to technology resources that were previously the exclusive privilege of those people who held power over us. Mass media technical capacity, money, and institutional support from foundations and foreign sources are absolutely essential. A movement simply cannot hope seriously to challenge power in this technology-based political and economic environment without the financial capacity to effect changes in perception and to convey critical messages on the Internet, radio, and television. This capacity can be achieved to a certain extent by political skill and alliances with journalists and friendly media outlets, but there is no substitute for the financial resources which make it possible to influence people through the projection of voices, images, and ideas in a sustained way using indigenous media capacities. We should also consider the importance of developing a high-tech communications capacity to take advantage of the media resources we access or develop, building alliances with other movements and gaining high-profile support and participation.

Professionalization of our organizations is also a crucial innovation that must happen. We need to jettison the highly structured, specialized, and over-staffed make-work colonial organizations we have today in favour of an organizational model based on the formation of highly educated small bureaucracies where flexibility is built-in and skills are diffused throughout the organization. As distinguished from organizational centres that coordinate action, social and political movements that are successful in making change have certain characteristics: the number of people involved at the core is small, but led effectively by highly skilled and qualified leaders; the movement has a large number of supporters, but their participation is mainly indirect; the relationship among people in the movement is not so much a personal working relationship but an impersonal network of connective structures that relies mainly on electronic forms of communication; the movement asserts its image in the public mind through large, but rare, demonstrations of power; and the movement invites the proxy participation of and promotes its most intense forms of action through militants who are committed to taking on the challenges of direct confrontation and contention.

Yet, even with a clear sense of what physical, technological, and human resources are needed, if the tactical objective is transformation and if we are concerned with engendering substantial social change, there are real difficulties in conceptualizing a tactical plan. Competing for cultural supremacy with other movements which possess and effectively use powerful cultural resources (I mean colonial government-sponsored organizations and programs in Onkwehonwe communities) is exceedingly difficult. The main challenge found in attacking perceptions and mentalities is that adapting to the target audience too well alienates the movement's more committed supporters; a watered-down message plays well for subtly convincing moderates or complacent people, but angers militants. Also, the mainstream consumer-culture habits of thought are ingrained in most people, and this causes them unthinkingly to follow advertising and media signals and to normalize the views and values of white society.

The challenge here is one of consensus mobilization. Spreading a new understanding of the causes of, and solutions to, the major problems facing Onkwehonwe is key to generating resurgences. This is a truly difficult thing to achieve. Take the example of the idea of "Native Sovereignty" and how hard it is to use this concept against the state to promote autonomous indigenous identities that are not rooted in colonial legal structures or citizenship in the colonial country. The inherent meaning and symbolic power of the existing consensus on the "sovereignty" of the state (the United States, Canada, etc.) is embedded in people's minds through media saturation and government propaganda. People know there is a problem with this idea, but it is difficult to mobilize them to move away from it, even with knowledge firmly established in their minds. In this context, the Onkwehonwe challenge to the state's authority seems to everyone but an enlightened minority to be pretentious. Think of people's reactions to First Nations' flags, foreign embassies, sending representation to and participating in United Nations processes, and the like.

There are other problems, too. In any movement for change, established political leaders may not be fully committed to the people's more radical vision and may want to stay within the secure bounds of established political consensus. This can lead to a conscious misrepresentation of Onkwehonwe demands by politicians charged with articulating the people's views. This highlights the other problem of changing perception: with its massive resources, the state can co-opt leadership and movement successes. Think here of the Onkwehonwe warriors' actions in defence of inherent fishing rights at the east coast Mi'kmaq community of Burnt Church.[20] The community's conservative political leaders were co-opted by the Canadian government, and rather than supporting the radical objectives of the Mi'kmaq warrior society and the people who were fighting for recognition of their nation's inherent and treaty rights, the band council politicians used the crisis caused by the militant action taken by their own youth as a lever and negotiated a more advantageous deal for themselves within the established colonial "resource management" system. Think also of my own community of Kahnawake, which after the 1990 "Oka Crisis" became symbolic among Onkwehonwe of the spirit of defiance against assimilation and land surrenders. Since 1990, our band council system has seen huge increases in its federal program funding along with the creation of a bloated bureaucratic infrastructure supporting the negotiation of cooperative service delivery and jurisdictional power-sharing arrangements with federal and provincial governments that fly in the face of principles and objectives held by both the militants and even the more moderate band council in the years leading up to the 1990 crisis. There has been no movement at all to address the issues of our nation's inherent rights and self-determination nor to resolve any of the land issues that were the cause of the conflicts.[21]

With all of these challenges, potential movement leaders must keep focused on true empowerment and the design of new strategies of mobilization to confront the controlling power of the state. In this, the economic dimension is always crucially important. It is the framework of true empowerment, as opposed to strategies that just play politics within the colonial system. Individual and collective self-sufficiency must be thought of as an absolute necessity. This is a situation where our economic dependency is the main weapon used by the oppressor to control our people.

The Zapatista movement in Mexico, for example, refers to its own success in building and maintaining the integrity of their people, and especially in developing the capacity to confront the state, as a function of resisting co-optation:

> They offered us many things—money, projects, aid—and when we rejected them, they became angry and threatened us. This is how we came to understand that, by refusing to accept government aid, by resisting, we made the powerful angry; and there is nothing a Zapatista fighter likes more than making those in power angry. So with singular joy we dedicated ourselves to resisting, to saying no, to transforming our poverty into a weapon—the weapon of resistance.[22]

There are practical realities of being able to feed, shelter, and support the people involved in the movement independently or at least without government or corporate financing. Until we have the ability to put food in our mouth, to have adequate shelter, and to obtain medicine and other basic necessities of life without relying on our adversary to give us these things, we will not have a real movement for freedom. Instead, we will continue to be mired in ideological, rhetorical defiance against pretensions of colonialism, with no real hope of transforming ourselves or the situation for the next generation. This is because strictly ideological liberation movements have always failed to produce meaningful change in the lives of oppressed people.

Economic control and self-sufficiency are hugely important, yet there are very few people who can, like the Zapatistas, say that they have the ability to act independently of the state's control over the resources that ensure their very survival as physical beings and as communities. Most of us Onkwehonwe who were raised in the midst of colonial society have been, so to speak, corrupted by the wealth that surrounds us and cannot even imagine rejecting the comforts of the modern world for the sake of our freedom of action as Onkwehonwe. The Mayans who make up the Zapatista army are incredibly poor in material terms and live surrounded by Settlers who are themselves only marginally wealthier. The Zapatistas are willing to live that way and capable of doing it. Our people are not. This is a reality.

Self-sufficiency must be imagined and realized in the context of our people's actual lives. While gaining independence through a return to "traditional" lives out on the land or in the bush is certainly a possibility and an attractive option for some, this path will not generate a large following among Onkwehonwe. The bulk of our people have been disconnected from their natural environment on reserves or raised in the city and lack the knowledge and fortitude to live the kinds of lives their ancestors did; going "back to the land" is simply not a compelling call for our people any more.

Those Onkwehonwe who have made strides toward self-sufficiency, achieved degrees of independence for themselves, and garnered the support of their people have done so not by withdrawing but by actively engaging the mainstream economic system. They have conceptualized colonialism as dependency and attacked the dependency problem head-on by seeking to create the means to feed, shelter, and otherwise provide for their people on their own terms. In recent years, the Onkwehonwe movement for self-sufficiency and economic control has become virtually synonymous with gaming enterprises and the establishment of casinos and business associated with casinos on Indian reservations.

Onkwehonwe leaders who see economic dependency as the main obstacle to their people's freedom and happiness have sought to take their people out of the cage of colonialism by using a strategy of economic development that is predicated on the ideas that increased wealth will lead to an increased ability to live indigenous lives and that secure control by their nations over large land bases is the guarantor of their peoples' continuing collective existences.

This theory is logically sound. And it has brought results: the nations that have embarked on the path of gaming-based economic development have seen enormous monetary profits generated through their efforts, and many have increased their holdings of land and acquired political influence and institutional representation in the wider governmental system. Without a doubt, they have been successful in their own terms in gaining control over significant financial resources and land bases.[23] Yet, it must be remembered that nothing is free in this world. Is there a spiritual and cultural cost of doing business this way? What have the so-called "gaming tribes" had to sacrifice of their authentic selves in order to gain the political and economic power they now possess? Have they remained true to basic indigenous values and principles in their quest for freedom and power?

Ray Halbritter is perhaps the best person to give us a perspective on these questions. Halbritter is the founder and head of one of the richest and most successful of all the gaming enterprises in Onkwehonwe communities. He holds the official title of Nation Representative of the Oneida Indian Nation, located in what is now central New York State, and is a graduate of Syracuse University and Harvard Law School. Halbritter is also the Chief Executive Officer of the Oneida Nation's various business enterprises. He is a fascinating person to listen to on the questions of neo-colonialism, economic and psychological dependency, self-determination, and indigenous rights. His views are those of a person who has lived through different identities and phases of the indigenous movement and who has put serious thought into what decolonization means for himself and for Onkwehonwe peoples. He is also unique in having had the rare opportunity to see his theory and plan for decolonizing his nation realized!

Halbritter's perspective is also seasoned. He is clearly a leader who has had not only to formulate but also to justify his actions and who has been toughened by having had his credibility, motivations, and strategies questioned and challenged from within by members of his own community and, of course, by his political adversaries in colonial society. He has enormous influence in the political life of his own community and in the region his nation lives, owing to his control over the financial resources of the Oneida Nation's enterprises and his position at the head of the Nation's governing council. His particularly forceful leadership style, his combative personality, and the decisions he has made, both financial and political, have alienated many people in his own community and among other indigenous nations. His bold and unapologetic break with the moral and political authority of the Grand Council of the Iroquois Confederacy (the traditional governing body of the Rotinoshonni peoples), his drive to modernize the social and political institutions of his nation, the way he relishes doing battle, and his dogged determination to build the wealth, land holdings, and political power of the Oneida Nation of New York, even to the point of confronting his own people with other more "traditional" visions, has made him a lightning rod of controversy and contention.[24]

I must admit that I am not generally a supporter of gaming enterprises, and I have personally opposed the establishment of a casino in my own community. Yet, when I think through the questions of the effects of dependency and the importance of economics to the achievement of indigenous freedom, there is something compelling about the example Halbritter and the Oneida Nation have given us. In our Rotinoshonni communities, we like to say that our people have a "just do it" attitude, but Halbritter is a person that has actually just done it and seemingly without regard for the consequences of potential failure or of what people think of him or his leadership.

RH: Somehow, with all the cards and the deck stacked up against us, we've survived. And not just survived as brown-skinned people, but survived with a belief in something about ourselves. Some might say that's by design, some may say it's the Creator's will. But whatever it is, we're here today, and we believe certain things about ourselves, in spite of the circumstances that surround us suggesting that we have no good reason to exist, almost, and that if we do exist, it's not as a powerful proud people.

TA: *A philosophy professor at Cambridge University in England put it this way once: "Native Americans are the residue of history."*
RH: Some people may see us that way. But to me, the essence of our people is belief itself. It's the ability to hold on to that belief. It's the fire of our people. It goes back to a spiritual aspect, and our beliefs that the Creator made us and put us here, and it is his will that we live. There's a reason for us to be here. I don't know what that all is, but I believe that that belief itself is important. It's like that philosopher said: "I think, therefore I am." We believe, therefore we exist. I think it's the nature of men to look out for themselves. The nature of power and of people existing includes a number of things; one is to become more powerful, as powerful as one can be. Just like the accumulation of wealth in a capitalist society, like we have here: you can have all the wealth to take care of any material need you may have, but you keep trying to make money! It's almost like a game; but it's not a game, it's real serious when it comes to nation-building. I think the nature of power is to accumulate more power, just like the nature of wealth. After awhile, it's not even about wealth any more, it's just the game that you know and maybe the nature of the beast itself.

TA: *Are you critical of that at all? Or is that the kind of mode you operate in yourself?*

RH: I wouldn't say that I necessarily endorse or oppose it. But I do recognize it as a reality of existence. Whether people believe that I'm doing right or wrong, we're in a struggle for survival here. We're on a battleground. We're being attacked in a way that really threatens our existence. We've existed since the white men came, over 300 years, but that doesn't mean the war's over. That's why I talk about the nature of power, because the nature of power is to crowd out or destroy competitors. We're still here, but we're an aggravation, an anachronism. Sort of like this "residue" you mentioned: we don't fit in. We're a "domestic dependent nation," as their law says. What does that mean to anybody? I don't know what that means!

TA: *It's interesting that you used the metaphor of war.*
RH: I think that in wartime conditions, a certain leadership is called for, and it's different than leadership in peacetime. Some people think that we're in peacetime right now. I don't think we're at peace at all. I think we're in a struggle for our lives. I think we're in a war. Does that mean that we go and shoot people? No, no, no. It's a different kind of war. It's just like the battle to take this land from us: it wasn't done so much on an actual battlefield, it was done in the courts and in the philosophy of both the government and the church.

When the conquerors first came here, despite appearing to us as nothing but bloodthirsty murdering barbarians, they actually did have a philosophy, and that had to be reconciled with their own conscience and their own views about God and religion. They had to figure out how they were going to come in here and murder all these Indians and take their land and then look God in the eye. They had to make their laws and their history make sense to themselves. Where did the white man get the idea that he could come over here and just claim it? Indians were considered to be less than human. So they figured it all out on that basis, and to this day, they still struggle with that in their courts. All of these court decisions have to go through the same exercise of justifying. First comes the philosophy, then comes the physical result. Indians are so far down now that they don't have to waste their time fighting with us. All they have to do is figure it out on paper, and not even worry about exercising power because they're so powerful. Yes, Indians have resisted and risked their lives in confrontations; we've all done it. Did that work?

I think about this every day. I've been thinking about this for years now. I used to sit there in political meetings and listen to everyone's philosophy. But I've always considered myself a practical person. I work hard, you know. I was an ironworker, I went to law school, I had six kids, all of that. At one point in time, I just started thinking that the real power in this world is knowledge, education, and then economic power. Economic power is what made this country. Everything the United States is today comes from Indian wealth. It all belonged to us, and they all took it! So I used to sit there and listen to this person go on about, "Oh, we're sovereign." And I'm thinking to myself, "What good is it to be making these same speeches? I've been listening to them for 15 years, and we're still right where we were then! We're still just talking."

I'm not trying to offend anybody here, because those were people I respect. But we were going to the United Nations, and people were thinking, "Oh wow, we got to meet with the president of so-and-so, we're tickled, we're falling down all over ourselves 'cause we got to eat teacakes on the White House lawn." And I'm thinking, "Did we feed another elder, did somebody get a job, did we get any land back, did we get any of our rights recognized?" Oh no, but we as leaders got treated on a red carpet, so now we're all paid off. Now we go back home, and we're high as a kite because, "I don't know about anybody else here, but I got to meet the president." I've met Clinton, I've met Ford, I met those guys. We flew down there and spent time with them, but when we came back, our place looked the same. The houses were just as poor, we still didn't have jobs, we still had elders living in places... you have dogs living in better places than that!

One day, we had a fire. My aunt and uncle burned to death, and the City refused to send the fire department. So I said, "I don't know if this is going to be right with sovereignty or what somebody's idea of what tradition is, but we gotta find a way to change something around here."

TA: *Unity, does it mean anything to you?*
RH: Look, I believe it's possible to get to a place of consensus. It doesn't mean everyone agrees, but it means that they're at least willing to go along enough to not object. I think you can get there. You can call it "one mind." What I did—and there were others involved, of course, but I'm talking just about me personally—was because I believed that we just had to do something. I didn't care what it was, even if it didn't work, because at least then we would have given it a shot instead of just having more meetings and more speeches. I don't know how many times I have to hear someone say, "We're sovereign." Okay, I got it already. I got it! We're sovereign, now what are we going to do about it?

The first thing we looked at was the fire department not answering our calls. We needed to figure out how to get fire protection for our families.

So we started a bingo hall in 1975. That's where gaming in the United States for Indian people first started, through that little bingo hall, actually. After that it went to Florida with the Seminoles. In *Seminole v. Butterworth*, the US Supreme Court said that Indians have the right to do bingo without being licensed by the state! I never knew we were going to get there; I didn't have a law degree, I was an ironworker. We just tried to do something for our people. Before *Butterworth*, we started a bingo. Anyway, they then issued warrants for our arrest, that bingo went down, it's a long story. And we were fighting amongst ourselves… same old story.

So, anyway, everybody was fighting each other and I wanted a break, so I went back to school. I obtained an undergraduate degree because I wanted to go to law school. I wanted to go to law school to understand how it is that this country and its people could exist, making the decisions that they did against our people. How could they destroy our people with a clear conscience? What I know now isn't what I knew then, of course. I just wanted to go to the highest levels of education that they had, to find out what it is that they teach you in that building that makes you come out able to do this to us.

Education became for me a way of using all of their own rules against them. It's like Jack and the Beanstalk: here's the stalk, and you're the little guy, but you're figuring out to use the fact that he's so big against him. He can't move as fast. You can hide, he can't. Wait 'till he's asleep. Whatever. You have to strategize for one purpose, and that is to help your people. And what is it to help your people? At first, it meant getting income, money. I saw economic power as the basis for political power. You can't do anything without money—you can't travel, you can't even make phone calls. The United States is so powerful in the world because of its economy. Economic power can't be denied, in my view. You can see it; look around. So we're very successful economically, but the real value to me is the way it's changed the self-concept of our people: how they see themselves.

TA: *Some of your critics might say that you're selling your soul when you're doing this kind of thing. But what you're saying seems like the opposite of that: economic success generates a kind of spiritual renewal among the people?*
RH: Well, it's spiritual in the sense that we were able to build a council house and a cookhouse when we never had the money to do those things before. We were able to do our ceremonies for the first time in anyone's memory because we paid the expenses of people to come down here to do our ceremonies with us. We never had those ceremonies in recent memory, and then we were able to reinstitute them. I think that it is possible, certainly, that

wealth and success can have their own problems. But we were experienced in the problems of poverty, and I wasn't experienced in the problems of wealth and success, so it was good to experience those kinds of problems, as far as I was concerned!

I think we identify wealth as bad because the people who oppress us have wealth, and they're bad in some ways. I wasn't too worried about that. We pushed ahead: we got a health clinic, we got children's health, and we got land back—14,000 acres. We're the first Indian nation in the country to give money back to the Bureau of Indian Affairs. We're the first nation in the history of the Iroquois Confederacy to give land back to our people. We won our court cases because we have the money to hire the best lawyers in the country. I can go on and on and on about these things. I'm not putting down making speeches about sovereignty; you need to hear those words because they help shape you. We're a people with a foundation in this country that nobody else has. This is our land! This is the land the Creator gave us. He didn't give it to them, they stole it from us in the name of *their* creator! Our people's destiny, blood, everything is here. We have the right to live and exist here, and now we can proclaim it ourselves; we don't have to wait for somebody to agree with us. I don't care if they agree or not. It's the intangible value of changing our self-esteem. Almost everything we're doing is to try to get our people to believe in themselves again.

TA: *Nothing like picking a fight and winning it to boost your self-esteem.*
RH: Ha! And you know what? Especially if you're in the right! Especially if you are right.

TA: *What is your passion: justice, helping the people? Or is it the fight itself?*
RH: All I want to do is make sure that our people are taken care of to the seventh generation. I believe in that. It's really important. I just want our people to live in peace and to have a good life. They're entitled to that. They are entitled to be comfortable and secure on the land that belongs to us. I don't think you can feel happy if you're paranoid and insecure or if you feel that you're not as good as other people. Like, I belong to a couple of country clubs, and it's not because I'm arrogant. We are entitled! We're entitled to be whatever we can be, and we shouldn't be afraid of that. When people say that's not being Indian, they're doing exactly what these white people do to us! We're starting to judge and to discriminate and to attack our own people over what we think they ought to be. We should be free enough as a people, and I believe we were at one time, to let every person be whatever they want to be.

TA: *What do you think are some of the obstacles to our people's prosperity and freedom?*

RH: The biggest problem is around the question of unity. Our people are so not used to success, so not used to being in a position where their voice counts, that they don't have a concept of how to work together. People might get upset to hear me say this, but sometimes when you have a meeting, you see how people's pride gets hurt so easy. They're sensitive, they're mistrustful. We're very paranoid. All of these things make it very difficult to get to a comfortable level of consensus on any issue. It's almost like going into a dysfunctional family; they're probably going to fight each other for the rest of their lives. Part of what we have to do is just get people to believe in each other and help and support each other.

That's where tradition comes in for me. The whole essence of our traditional teachings in the Great Law is one thing: unity. That's all it is. We are told a story that has come through time, that we are to be unified and forgive one another and work with one another. How much more of a lesson do we need?

It would be great to be an all-powerful ruler and get anything you want, but that isn't true in anybody's case. I don't get a lot of things I'd like to get. That's why I think education is so important, in giving confidence and self-esteem so that you have the ability to cooperate and work together. Some people are not educated, and they don't want anybody to know that. They become defensive with me because I have an education, or with someone like yourself, Taiaiake, you'll be in a room and people will be intimidated sometimes. But from the way you act, if I didn't ask you, I wouldn't even think that you have a doctorate degree. But yet it does make a difference in the way I talk to you. I'm not trying to say that other people are lesser, or anything like that, it's just a reality. It's something that keeps us from coming together. We can kid ourselves, but we should know what the real issues are, and one of the toughest ones is getting over this and getting our people together.

If anyone asked me, I would say that we are very traditional here. In order to pick our leaders to sit on our Council, we had clan meetings. Out of those clan meetings, they selected people. We got our clans, we chose leaders by consensus, those people come from our three clans—the wolf, bear, and turtle—and they make decisions. We're all represented. We have Nation meetings every year. Me, I was chosen as Nation Representative through that process. All our three clans agreed that I'd be the leader. And the next step, if I were to be a chief, would be to be condoled and recognized in the Iroquois Confederacy. But I know they won't do it, and I'm not even going to bother asking. I already know the answer, so why waste my time? Besides, it's not necessary. I don't need to be a chief. As a matter of fact, I told our Council when they were all talking about chiefs, and how there was a chief at Onondaga, and a chief over there... I said, "Let me tell you something: make believe we're all chiefs, and then make believe nobody's a chief: the job's the same. We still have the same work to do whether you call yourself a chief or not, you still can achieve the same work for your people—get them jobs, get our land back, get our legal rights recognized, protect our people—so stop worrying about what our titles are, all you have to do is worry about the welfare of our people. You don't have to worry about anything more than that." I think that's really what happens: we get fighting about who's who. Why don't we worry about how we get from here to there, and how we do it in a way that's consistent with what we say we believe in?

TA: *What's causing this division? What do people expect that you are not giving them?*
RH: Some people view this wealth as something they should benefit from personally. To me, that is the problem. Their complaint isn't that we're not financially accountable. What's the complaint? To me, it all comes back to the fact that what they were expecting financially did not happen. People have said to me, "I'm sick of working, I don't want to work anymore. I want some more money, and you better start giving it up." And I gave them an answer they weren't real happy with. I said to them, "I think you should start thinking that you are always going to have to work, because as far as I'm concerned, this Nation is never going to give out money so that everybody can just lay flat on their back. We're not going to just mail checks out to people." That answer didn't make that person happy.

TA: *I wonder if there's no ego involved at all on your part. Doesn't it make you feel good to be seen to be the one leading the charge? You must enjoy it.*
RH: Look, I don't like to lose. But I ask people around me, and I ask my family to tell me if they think it's all going to my head, if they think I have too much power or wealth. Whether they're just telling me what I want to hear, I don't know. I want to be sure, but what can I tell you?

TA: *What I'm saying is that they might be responding to a kind of attitude they're not familiar with, the kind it takes to be a successful business leader in the outside world. Our people are not really used to it.*

RH: I get along real good with our Council and everybody else. I don't think it's so much me personally—could be wrong—but I think their animosity derives from not having had their expectations fulfilled financially.

TA: *What about coming from the state, or the feds, or with the local population, are there obstacles there?*
RH: That's different. I'll give you an example. The people that I meet with from the locals and the New York State government, they think I'm arrogant. I've never viewed myself that way. When they first came over here 300 years ago and saw our people standing all proud and strong, they mistook that for arrogance. That's not arrogant. That's just a free man. That's just a man who's not afraid of you! We all have belief in our sovereignty. Our people probably fight harder than anyone else for it. For Iroquois people, it's not even a "fight" so much as just a belief. Of all the people that ought to have been beaten down by now, it ought to be our people! They came to our shores just about first. We've been struggling with them since the 1600s. We're still hanging in there. It's one thing to be sovereign, but it's a lot of responsibility. It's self-sufficiency; that's where the money comes in.

TA: *But isn't that just the "Made in the USA" definition of sovereignty?*
RH: Power wants all the power. Now, we're two cooks in the same kitchen. We have two sovereigns occupying the same place. The United States, because of public opinion, can't just come in and wipe us out. They just can't do it that way. We're not high enough on the radar screen to really get going at, but they keep nipping and chipping at us, and pretty soon it's all going to go. They try to get you all screwed up.

TA: *Or they get us to do it to ourselves.*
RH: To be able to say, "We didn't do anything, they killed themselves," for them, that's the best possible situation. I'm trying to take their rules and use them against them—to beat them at their own game.

TA: *Well, looking around this place, it seems to be working for you.*
RH: We have 14,000 acres back; we've marched that clock back to the early 1800s. We got that much land back, and we're still going. We got a federal court ruling which says that all the land we possess comes under our jurisdiction, our sovereignty, and is not taxable.

TA: *So if this casino ever goes broke, the land is still yours?*

RH: Yes. What we want to do is take the money we're making and create an endowment fund. We want to make that fund so big that if they shut down our businesses, the interest from that fund would pay for our basic needs—our education, our health services—and take care of our people. We create it so big and we have so much money that eventually we're spending less than the interest and keep reinvesting in the capital. We've got it figured out where we can do it in my lifetime. Then they can come in here and take it all away, but we'd still have that money coming in to take care of our people. We could tell them to go ahead and take our businesses away; we'd still have our education and our health care and all of that. We could tell them, "You want to tax us? Forget it then, we're not even going to do business." That's an endowment. That's where I want to be.

TA: *You've come a long way from your radical days, being in the Warrior Society and raising hell.*
RH: Well, yeah, that's true. Everybody's a radical, if you don't agree, if you don't wave the flag… I felt that you had to sometimes take matters into your own hands.

TA: *So is all this a natural trajectory from there? Warriorism updated for the times?*
RH: I think we're still, in a sense, "radicals." We are patriots. Because we're opposing the ethnic majority that we have around us doesn't mean that we are radical. We're a remnant of true patriotism here. Other people look out for their people, and we're just trying to look out for ours. We're pleased with our success, we're comfortable in our lives, and our people have a more stable community. Another way to put it would be to say that you can have sovereignty, but it means taking care of your people and all of their needs. It means a lot of things besides fighting and telling people to mind their own business.

The fire of our people was lit, as Halbritter points out, by a belief in themselves. The real question is whether defining the indigenous struggle in terms of pursuing wealth and political power *vis-à-vis* white people is a struggle that is capable of sustaining this belief. Have the Oneidas of New York and other gaming tribes come up with a successful strategy of decolonization and a viable alternative to dependency on the Indian Act system? Halbritter makes a compelling argument that his approach, while making some compromises of long-standing (and, I sense in his view, obsolete) political principles and moving away from commonly accepted ideas of

221

what an indigenous governance model should look like, capitalizes on a significant wealth opportunity.

The idea I have been developing in this book is that people need not only to be conscious of what they do and what they experience, but also to be realistic about it and themselves. Is the vision represented by Halbritter consistent with this notion of an authentic indigenous existence? Is Halbritter a visionary who is reinterpreting indigenous teachings courageously and differently from other leaders according to a consciousness of changed circumstances and needs? Or, as he is often accused by those who do not agree with the wisdom of trying to rebuild a nation and a people's dignity on the foundation of gambling enterprises, is he leading his people astray in a vainglorious quest defined not in indigenous terms but instead reflecting a high degree of assimilation to the values and perspectives of Settler society? Have Halbritter and the other casino chiefs fallen victim to the old adage, "choose your enemy carefully, for you will become him"?

Many people of the most respected elders in our Onkwehonwe communities tell us that there are essential values and characteristics to being Onkwehonwe that cannot be compromised, ignored, or altered, even in the midst of a life-and-death struggle with a fearsome and powerful enemy. There are people for whom "commitment" means not developing a new vision that is an alteration of traditional principles adapted to the modern realities of power but holding on to the old ways and defending the principles that have been at the core of the Onkwehonwe philosophical and political life since time immemorial. For elders rooted in Onkwehonwe philosophies, the lesson of the traditional teachings is that we must be cautious and guard against the error of going beyond being *practical* to being *pragmatic*, which happens when we separate the principles by which we govern our lives and our communities from their Onkwehonwe philosophical roots and begin to move toward an ethic of efficacy based on calculations of interest and power.

In bringing this point forward, I do not mean to make a definitive pronouncement of judgement against gaming as a strategy or against the particular approach taken by Ray Halbritter. In fact, after speaking with him, I was more convinced than ever that economic power is the foundation of independence. But I was also more keenly aware that maintaining our connection to our cultural roots is the only thing that ensures we remain Onkwehonwe. We need to possess both economic power and cultural authenticity. The question that remains in my mind after speaking with Halbritter and trying to balance what he had to say with other more consciously "traditional" Onkwehonwe leaders' perspectives, is not as simplistic as one that would distinguish between authentic Onkwehonwe and "sell-outs." I suggest a more nuanced question: How do we learn from our teachings and experiences and, without compromising who we are as Onkwehonwe, do what we need to do to gain self-sufficiency and the freedom of action to set ourselves up as a credible political threat to the colonial regime and the Settlers' domination of our people and lands?

To be sure, there are serious unanswered questions about the economic development path's ability to guarantee that we remain culturally and spiritually Onkwehonwe in the pursuit of money and power. Yet, other more principled or ideological phases of the indigenous movement have failed to offer coherent, workable, and lasting paths to freedom as well. Where money-minded leaders neglect the importance of cultural and spiritual rootedness in creating meaningful, healthy existences, the generations of indigenous leaders committed to indigenist or "traditional" principles have all failed to make the connection between an independent economic base and the achievement of freedom. It is easier to critique those on the economic development path because of their obvious neglect of spirituality and culture and their self-conscious emulation of mainstream methods and values. Their separation from an authentic indigenous existence is readily apparent. But I would argue that, because of their neglect of the basic principle of self-sufficiency, the self-consciously "nationalistic" or "traditional" options we have been presented with by our leaders are similarly inauthentic and that we have been misguided in placing our faith in one or another of these ideological movements over the years. This, I believe, is a point worth pursuing beyond the obvious (and conclusive) statement that political approaches to making change that do not include a solid plan for economic self-sufficiency on either a personal or collective level are doomed to fail. Aside from the obvious, what is wrong with ideology?

The frustration of all ideological movements is that "ideology" is the theoretical conception of a problem and its solution from inside one person's head. Ideologies are theoretical formulations flowing from the mind, the feelings, and perhaps the life experience of the theorist. This kind of intellectualism is opposed to what I would call an organic concept of revolution, one that is distilled in a process of reflecting on actual interactions and is mediated through and reflects the collective voice of the people. Just as we can sense something lacking in the pragmatic approaches to empower-

223

ment, as Onkwehonwe, we should be able to recall our failures and frustrations with ideology.

The ideology of Native Nationalism for example, formulated by Onkwehonwe political leaders and thinkers to confront the obstinate denial of our peoples' collective existences by colonial authorities, has led us toward a contest with the state that rather than liberating us from colonial authority has (to this point in our history) resulted in the transformation of our local governments into bureaucracy-mimicking shadows of true Onkwehonwe governance. My first book, in essence, documented the progression of a community's struggle to adapt and survive by using a nationalistic movement, only to see themselves controlled, albeit indirectly, by the awesome force of government money needed to finance an institutionalized and highly bureaucratized "nation" conceptualized in legalistic terms and in accordance with ideologies of nationalism that were influential patterns of thought at the time.[25]

Traditionalism, too, has imposed unrealistic and unproductive ideas onto the political landscape. The second book I wrote reflected the perspective of a political approach that held faith in what was, in effect, a "traditionalist" ideology, which ignored the practical realities of quite extreme dependency and complacency regrettably rooted in the fabric of contemporary indigenous community life. It must be admitted by those of us who held the faith that we were wrong in the noble but futile hope that people can be made to change by simply exposing them to ceremonies, teachings, and truths.[26]

Now we are surrounded by the advocates of another ideological paradigm. Following in the wake of an ill-conceived nationalism and a naïve traditionalism, we are in the political grip of a legalist and non-contentious ideology I am calling aboriginalism, which purports that the solution to our people's problems consists in the delusional notion that legal argumentation in colonial courts can dislodge centuries of entrenched racism and imperial privilege and thus transform colonial societies into human ones. Even more so than with the other two ideological turns, there is simply no experiential basis to support the premise that this ideology rests upon.

All of these paths to change are conceived in ideological terms, imported from texts into Onkwehonwe lives, and are thought of as panacea. Yet, they have proven to contain unfulfilled (and unfulfillable) dreams that have led to frustration, discouragement, and alienation among our people and made them turn away from Onkwehonwe cultures and communities even more and in increasing numbers as well. Life in our communities has come to be framed in ideological and political terms, ignoring the sustaining, the cultural, and the communal aspects that are the roots of our actual existences.

Native Nationalism took a solid core of undeniable truth—our collective existences as nations of peoples—and grafted onto it an ill-suited political analysis and program. Thirty years later, our nations have been co-opted into movements of "self-government" and "land claims settlements," which are goals defined by the colonial state and which are in stark opposition to our original objectives. Our concept of nationhood has been corrupted by placing it in an ideological framework, and, rather than reflecting an authentic sense of Onkwehonwe collective being, the ideological framework itself has become the hijacked vehicle by which bureaucratization and corruption have been brought into our lives. Our people were promised that they would be recognized as nations and that their lands would be returned, but instead of realizing these goals we are left with a nasty case of metastasizing governmentalism.

Traditionalism, the movement to restore the social, cultural, and political integrity of our communities by restoring ancient models of governance and social interaction, has degraded into a laughable form of self-centred New Ageism, a ceremonial show or smokescreen behind which the dark abuses of the colonial master on a personal and collective level continue.

The frustrating and divisive effects of pursuing goals defined in ideological terms, whether Native Nationalism or Traditionalism, have folded into each other and come to form the cultural and intellectual foundation for our present aboriginalist paradigm. I can understand people honestly questioning whether or not what I am proposing in this book is just another ideological turn, a theoretical concept of liberation divorced from experience that is doomed to frustration or failure in the face of the overwhelming power of the state and its cultural assimilation process. Is this "warriorism" the next post-nationalism, post-traditionalism, anti-aboriginalism Onkwehonwe ideology?

I asked Raronhianonha, a man who was at the centre of the warrior society movement in Kahnawake through the 1980s and 1990s, to reflect back on that ideological era in our people's history and to talk about his experience with Native Nationalism and the traditionalist outgrowth that defined our community during those days.[27] In particular, I wondered what the movement was about, what people believed they were doing. In response, he explained the movement that energized a generation of not only Kanien'kehaka but Onkwehonwe activists all over Anówara in this concise statement:

It was a struggle to capture the hearts and minds of our own people, to bring them to the realization that the federal and provincial governments are not their friends, and that the only way to create the freedom that we should be enjoying is by bringing back the traditional system. The struggle that was going on prior to 1985, or thereabouts, was one of education. People were becoming more aware of their culture and learning more about it all the time. The goal is to prevent assimilation. It's resistance against assimilation. That's one end. The other goal is the ability of our people to realize self-determination. That involves the ability of our people to be self-supporting, without having to kowtow to the provincial government. That includes the expansion of our land base so that we're able to provide for ourselves. And also, to be able to deal with other people in an independent manner. We shouldn't be constrained by Canadian laws as far as our trade with other people goes, or in the recognition of our own nationality. This means the recognition of our own citizenship… all of these things are attributes of a nation. I'm not naïve to believe that we can be totally independent as a nation without agreements with the surrounding nations. Every government has to do that, including the United States and Canada. What it amounts to is the repolishing of our treaties and bringing our present-day agreements into that traditional context, rather than accepting the supremacy of the Canadian or provincial government.

I remarked to Raronhianonha that it seemed to me that people in our community then were very committed to taking action and seriously motivated to make change, and that today all of that energy seems to have been used up. I asked him why it was that people were not so radically charged for the fight in Kahnawake any more. He told me:

It is a really different situation now. At the time, the Warrior Society was more active because we were under a siege mentality. Police actions against Native communities caused the militancy to flourish at that time. It was necessary. There were a series of events that caused people, both young and old, to militarize and become active in defending the territory. That was the situation at the time.

In my own study of Kahnawake politics and the rise of a militant movement among our people, I too had come to the conclusion that the Mohawk Warrior Society and the strong assertion of rights by our people in the 1970s and 1980s were spurred on by, as Raronhianonha said, "a series of events."[28] A major factor in the rise of militancy was that people became radicalized by outside forces acting on them and shaping their lives over time; patterns of negative interaction with the state and with Settler society forged a political culture of resurgence in Kahnawake.

The American political scientist Sidney Tarrow has studied the pattern of interactions that lead people to break from cooperating with or tolerating an authority to acting against that authority. He calls it a "cascade of contention." It is worthwhile to consider his full summation of the theory, his explanation of the vocabulary, and his concept of contentious politics:

> Contentious politics is produced when political opportunities broaden, when they demonstrate the potential for alliances, and when they reveal the opponents' vulnerability. Contention crystallizes into a social movement when it taps embedded social networks and connective structures and produces collective action frames and supportive identities able to sustain contention with powerful opponents. By mounting familiar forms of contention, movements become focal points that transform external opportunities into resources. Repertoires of contention, social networks, and cultural frames lower the costs of bringing people into collective action, induce confidence that they are not alone, and give broader meaning to their claims.[29]

This statement outlines the architecture of the kind of political situation that would (or can) result when Onkwehonwe—like the people in Kahnawake in the 1970s, 1980s, and 1990s—create opportunities to "just do it" and actually make changes in their situations, as opposed to merely protesting against or grovelling to the colonial authorities.

Tarrow's phrase, "expanded opportunities," is the key to generating movement from a situation of complacency and stasis. In a frame of contentious politics, a real *movement* seeks to change understandings and identities so that there is support among the people for contention as the appropriate form of political activity. The goal is to achieve a situation in which opportunities (potentialities) are changed to resources (realities), thus lowering the individual costs of fighting against the system. This makes resurgent actions and militant contentious politics a plausible option for people and a real, viable alternative position to that of continuing to cooperate with injustice.

Most important in the context of our political situation is the need and importance of what Tarrow calls "framing contention," meaning the need to justify, dignify, and animate collective contentious dissent, action by our people against the authority of the colonial state and all of its institutions and its representatives. This means that the main task of leadership is to find a cause that people can rally behind instead of what we have now, a set of grievances that people complain about all the time without doing anything to change the situation. Grievances must be named, they must be connected to their real causes, enlarged in the public mind to connect with what people value and see as important within their cultures, and communicated in the form of a uniform message and united power.

This is a constant frustration shared by Onkwehonwe involved in forms of struggle, especially in organizational settings: How do we confront the power of the state and its ability to defeat (in every way) our protests of injustice? Contention has the advantage of attacking the root cause of the injustice, which is the belief system that underlies both the arrogant assumption of the colonizer and the defeatist complacency of the aboriginal. Defeating the big lie of colonial mythologies is possible. The imperial capitalist state is a huge machine, impossible to defeat, or even to confront head-on with force. It must be confronted obliquely and have its most powerful forces turned against itself.

The way to defeat the colonial state is to struggle in creative contention to delegitimize it and to weaken belief and commitment in the colonizers' minds, not by confronting the state on its own terms and playing to its strength, violence. Onkwehonwe need to stop protesting injustice. Conventional protest must be dismissed out of hand as irrelevant to anyone with a serious commitment to political change. Protest strengthens authority; to undo colonial authority, defeat colonial injustices, and create the conditions of peaceful coexistence, it is necessary for Onkwehonwe to embark on a direct attack on the very foundation of state power and authority, which is achieved by the strategies and tactics of creative contention, the middle path between armed rebellion and conventional protest.

There are apparently two ways to attack the legitimacy of governing institutions. The first is to actively confront them, as Jayaprakash Narayan did in India in the 1970s when he launched a "total revolution" against widespread corruption that had come to define public life in that country.[30] The second is a strategy of withdrawing consent and not cooperating with institutions, like the Gandhian and Zapatista defences against imperialism. This was developed as a strategy and put into practice by Vaclav Havel, the leader of the Czech resistance against Soviet occupation and domination of his country, who became president of a free Czechoslovakia. Havel, reflecting on the non-violent contention, commented on how the non-cooperation approach

> showed how helpless military power is when confronted by an opponent unlike any that it has been trained to confront; it showed how hard it is to govern a country in which, though it may not defend itself militarily, all the civil structures simply turn their backs on the aggressors. And this is not to mention things like the principal and as yet unrecognized significance of the modern media as a political power in their own right, capable of directing and coordinating all social life.[31]

Czech defiance of Soviet authority by withdrawal of participation and refusal to cooperate actively in their own subjugation was a powerful movement of creative contention that led to the defeat of that empire and whose example of freedom contributed to the delegitimizing of Soviet authority in the centre of the empire itself.

The very definition of "power" is questioned here. Where the state possesses overwhelming military force, the opponents of the state must use their resources and capacities to prevent the state from carrying out its activities and agenda and so disrupt the system. Our bodies, our minds, and our cooperation are all essential to the functioning of the colonial system. Although military force can create the fear needed to force compliance, it must be recognized that it is a *destructive* force. It can only be used to generate psychological states needed to coerce people. It is incapable of compelling the *positive* operation of the political and economic relationships that form the colonial system once it is employed for alienating and destructive purposes. Military power can force people off the land, disconnect them from their families, and harm their bodies. But it cannot generate anything positive; it is therefore incapable of being the force that colonialism uses to run the empire and induce compliance and cooperation: that force is the psychological effect of the threat of violence. So if a people can withstand the physical assault of military force and maintain their courage and freedom of mind, they remain essentially un-colonized, subject to usurpations of their rights and unjust occupations of their lands, but still spiritually

229

free. The potential to resist the mind-altering effects of colonization and the possibility of freedom remain strong.

The un-colonized possess power which is beyond the grasp and out of the reach of colonial authorities. They remain rooted in their authentic selves despite the objectives of physical assaults and other colonizing activities, which cannot be sustained over the long term without the explicit cooperation and consent of the people.

The politics of contention arise when people recognize the chance to assert their authentic existences when cracks and weaknesses in the colonial system present themselves as opportunities. Recognizing that the colonial system feeds on a collaboration of lies and fear induced by the implicit threat of violence and encouraged by monetary and psychological enticements, Onkwehonwe warriors of the truth, immune from fear-inducing threats and enlightened to the realities of power, call the state's bluff. They force state authorities to demonstrate to the rest of the population what warriors already know: there is no morality, no legal base, no fairness, no truth or justice in any form in the state's power, and its only undeniable power is that of overwhelming violence. Once the spell of law, morality, and cultural fiction is broken, and people come to see that the only thing underlying the Settlers' controlling relationship with Onkwehonwe is brute force, there will be no more legitimacy to the whole colonial enterprise. From this point, it is not much further to a total transformation of the relationship.

So, this politics is basically a mind-game. The battlefield for the struggle is the public's consciousness, shaped and manipulated through the media and through publicized contentious actions. In this environment, it is the way resources, education, and training are directed that is more important than that they exist in communities. This is something overlooked by aboriginalists who imagine that our communities will survive simply by having access to generic public education and capitalist job training. The *kind* of knowledge we have will determine our lives and the prospects for our next generations as much as the question of whether we have any knowledge at all. Our lives as Onkwehonwe will depend on the way we use our resources and educational efforts and whether or not we develop a capacity for resurgent action and a culture to support it. This is a different direction than the assimilationist pathways that have been laid out in the aboriginalist agenda. Creative and non-violent contention, withdrawing from participating in the state's political institutions, and enhancing our presence in and effective use of mass media are the practical pillars that we need to construct to support the decolonization of this hemisphere.

The power of this strategic vision exists in its concrete determination of our being Onkwehonwe. As opposed to the politics of accommodation where Onkwehonwe are divided and face the state in weak, atomized formations, this vision is one of a unified identity and reinforced solidarity. It forces non-indigenous people to pay attention and attend to our demands by obstructing the routine of normal Settler society; people will be unable to ignore the pain of Onkwehonwe communities; they will be, in effect, drawn into the pain and discord and made to appreciate the fact that there are ongoing colonial conflicts. The circle of conflict will broaden beyond the legal arena. The resulting inconvenience and illegality will draw state authorities into public conflicts rather than the current private conflicts between and among Onkwehonwe and their families. These private conflicts are exploited for profit by officials whose job it is to keep the public misinformed and distant from the source of the symptomatic violence and suffering that is endemic to indigenous community life.

I have tried to think of a drawback to this contentious approach, and the only one that has any potential to ruin the vision is that these tactics are difficult to maintain over long periods of time, as a movement tends to divide when state authorities respond with force and less committed people lose heart. This, in the experience of previous struggles, has led to desperate situations for more hard-core members, almost always leading to fatal violence or severe repression by the state.

This question of why movements go wrong is important to face, because as soon as there is an achievement of decolonization at any level or in any situation, state resources will be directed at that site to ensure that the movement is halted. Based on our own failures to sustain struggle and to decolonize through institutional change, and that of countless others as well, we can create a specific and comprehensive list for why movements go wrong: schism, repression, fading out, leadership domination, isolation, co-optation, leadership sell-out, and sectarian disruption.[32]

Before a meaningful decolonization can occur, the vehicle of struggle must be reconceptualized and reformulated from an organizational approach in which all of the problems listed above naturally result, to a truly Onkwehonwe movement in both form and objectives. If we are ever to break the cycle of unfocused assertions leading to corruption and co-optation, we need to work together to reformulate not only our identity but our politics to support coordinated action against the colonial system. We need to make an integrated set of changes in how the Onkwehonwe movement is conceptualized, how it engages Onkwehonwe communities, and how it channels Onkwehonwe energy toward the state.

From where we stand today, saddled with corrupt leaders, divided amongst ourselves, and mired in co-opted institutions, I believe we need to do four things:

1. unify the concerns and approaches of the different parts of the indigenous peoples movement—there is currently no focus to activism either in terms of goals or strategies;
2. appeal to uncommitted people for their active support—most Onkwehonwe are disillusioned and apathetic and do not participate in public life at all;
3. aggressively attack the hypocrisies and inconsistencies in Settler society to delegitimize it or even win over various segments of the Settler society and the people who administer state authority; and
4. maintain consistency with the teachings and vision of peaceful coexistence that is the heritage of all Onkwehonwe.

We also need to define the "success" of the movement for psychological and strategic reasons as incremental, occurring in various forms and degrees. The state concedes power on a cost-benefit calculation—when the cost of a concession to justice is less than the cost of continued maintenance of injustice, it will make that concession. So how do we know when we are winning, when we are decolonizing? The first sign of victory will occur when we define the moral terrain of politics, creating norms of judgement and expectation by which Settlers will begin to judge and evaluate their own behaviours and choices. This gradual seizing of the moral high ground makes delegitimizing the state possible. Secondly, on a practical level, success is achieved as Onkwehonwe withdraw from and attack the networks of institutional power that make up the state, like free radicals invading the colonial body. By the cumulative effect of many small resurgences and abdications, the state will be rendered useless in its central function of control. Another sign of victory will come when the power of the state is in such disarray that it can no longer interfere with people's existences, enabling them to begin to implement and enliven authentic alternatives to the colonial reality. Lastly, success will be seen in a more forceful sense, when the proud actions of aggressively assertive Onkwehonwe engender violent reactions from the state or groups organized to protect Settler interests. When these violent or legally threatening repressions are repelled by Onkwehonwe, it will become clear that the state is incapable of controlling or eliminating Onkwehonwe freedom of action in either a political, strategic, or tactical sense.

As part of the heritage of struggle in our peoples' political and cultural make-up, we have asserted defiance, tenacity, and an incredible ability to bear suffering; as a result, we have developed moral courage and awesome patience. We have the constitutional heritage to break the unjust rule of the colonial state. But we have been patterned into a destructive acceptance of colonialism.

One of the strongest arguments in favour of this approach to making change is that it is completely outside of the experience of the state in dealing with Onkwehonwe. Simply put, it breaks the stereotype of unthreatening, ineffective, or merely symbolic aboriginal activism and thus levels the political and strategic playing field with state authorities.

We do need a new pattern, and we need a new analysis of our situation. There has been a fundamental change in global politics since the 1960s and 1970s, the era of the formation of our present political institutions. They were formed, and their basic strategic approach set up, in another, long past reality.

Before 1989 and the demise of communism, all of our struggles were defined in anti-colonial or anti-imperial terms. There was a strong basis for cultivating sympathy and support for indigenous causes within the United Nations, as the so-called "non-aligned" states, along with Cuba and other anti-Western states, sought to limit the power of the United States and its allies for their own reasons. For example, veteran indigenous activists know that during those days the more militant Onkwehonwe groups benefited from Libyan leader Moammar Khadafi's financial support and that both the Irish Republican Army and the Palestine Liberation Organization made overtures and sought to link their struggles with Onkwehonwe warrior societies. This explains the rise and support (both cultural and political) for radical action in Anówara. African-American and Onkwehonwe groups emerged in the 1970s at the height of the anti-imperialist struggle on a global scale and in the context of intense ideological, financial, and political support for radical anti-Western movements by states opposed to European and American imperialism. By the mid-point of that decade, the United States had lost the war in Vietnam, for the first time suffering military defeat, significantly to an army of Asian peasants; Cambodia and Laos came under communist control despite hard efforts by the United States to prevent this

233

from happening; indigenous people in Angola won their freedom by waging a successful guerrilla war against colonial occupation, despite European and American support for the colonizers; and Mozambique and Ethiopia were decolonized in communist victories over the Europeans and the United States. To put things in perspective: violence and armed struggle in a context of a global anti-imperial struggle were proving to be the way to win national independence.

Things are different now.

Whereas the first wave of globalization was European colonization and "resistance" was defined in political terms as a contest of sovereignties, struggles in the context of the second wave of globalization are defined instead in terms of culture wars or, as Samuel Huntington has called it, a "clash of civilizations."[33] Now the struggles are thought of as defences of culture or as religious conflicts. They are that, but the struggle for cultural survival has not replaced struggles for land, political authority, and the capacity to exert physical force. The adversary has changed. The state has reformed from the first to the second wave and has been subsumed by the consolidated power of groups of corporations and the capitalists who control them. In this second wave of globalizing Euro-power, it is not so much politicians and people who make decisions based on cultural or religious motivations, but boards of directors of transnational corporations, global financial institutions, and the societal elites who own stocks, all of whom make decisions on the basis of self-interest and greed. In *ethical* terms, nothing has changed. Rich white people still control governments and exploit all of the world's non-white people and the earth for their own selfish benefit, but they have now devised a way to completely insulate themselves from accountability by eliminating the controls that "democratic" institutions used to place on their activities, replacing them with financial and legal rules designed to guarantee that the only logic that matters for decision-making is that of the market.

History, rights, and morality all become even more meaningless to Euroamerican governments than they ever were in the past as global politics is reconfigured as a network serving as a simple arbiter of trade relations between and among corporations. Working white people used to benefit along with the rich from the exploitation of indigenous lands and resources. There was never a complaint from the mainstream public against the injustice of globalization when the only people to suffer from the exploitation were brown and black! Now that white middle- and working-class people are feeling the effects of exploitation, job loss, and cultural dissolution, we find that globalization has been labelled as evil. Every day unprivileged whites wring their hands and whine on the airwaves and in public displays about how they've seen their communities destroyed and how they've felt the loss of control over their future to sell-out politicians and foreign elites with other concerns, priorities, and ways of life that threaten the very existence of their identity.

I have to say, when I see a white fisherman or logger or factory worker complaining about the pain his family is feeling because of the disruptions globalization has caused in their lives, I try to muster sympathy and to stifle my recollection (short-term memory at that) of that same white man blaming Onkwehonwe misfortune and poverty on the "lazy Indians" themselves. I try, but I always find myself thinking something like, "Looks like we're all Indians now, heh?"

After 1990, struggles are defined in terms of resurgence against the inevitable forces of the second wave of globalization, the total United Statesification of cultures and the corporate dominance of political life. There is no longer a basis for any regime to lend state support to Onkwehonwe struggles; there is no longer an oppositional bloc of states in contest with the American-led Western bloc. Any organization's potential support for indigenous armed struggle has evaporated or been destroyed as a result of the ongoing American so-called "war on terror." Bringing armed force to bear against state authorities is neither possible nor viable. The organizational bases of such a strategy are inaccessible due to the severe restrictions on civil freedoms and the security measures recently implemented by all of the allies of the United States. The only potential sympathy and support for indigenous causes exists in some, but not all, of the transnational organizations and movements that oppose globalization. Domestic opponents of globalization in colonial countries like Canada and the United States are in fact adversaries of Onkwehonwe because they are nothing but staunch defenders of the first wave of globalization against the second wave. They are Euroamerican nationalists intent on preserving colonial institutions and relations of power.

All of this points to the fact that the landscape of politics has changed fundamentally since the 1970s, and failing to adapt to the new global geopolitical context renders our entire institutional structure absolutely useless.

So who are our allies then? Who are those non-indigenous people who could become part of the network of indigenous resurgences? A classic question—one I am sure that has been put to every Onkwehonwe leader who has ever given a speech and then entertained questions from the audience afterward—is this: "What can I, as a white person, do to help indigenous people?" Honestly, what does one say to that? "Get the ball rolling on land claims by signing over your backyard to us?" "Quit your job and come be my personal assistant for free?" "Stalk and kill the Minister of Indian Affairs?" It's tempting to be so facetious. I believe the serious answer to that all-too-common question is the same as when Malcolm X answered it for the *Young Socialist* magazine in 1965: "Whites who are sincere should organize among themselves and figure out some strategy to break down the prejudice that exists in white communities. This is where they can function more intelligently and more effectively."[34] Word, Brother!

OLD ROOTS INTO THE EARTH

An important aspect of "commitment" is dedication to the ultimate goal of all politics and action: the achievement of peace. From an Onkwehonwe philosophical perspective, politics and social movements are part of a larger perpetual struggle to generate meaningful relationships that reflect the fundamental indigenous imperative to seek life and harmony over all the forms and faces of death and destruction. In Onkwehonwe cultures, the objectives of human life are defined in the commitment to seek to understand basic spiritual teachings and to shape one's life to embody the values that emerge from respecting those fundamental principles: honour, and the ethic of courage; interdependency, and the need to share; humility, and the necessity of respect; freedom, and the inevitability of struggle. These Onkwehonwe principles and values are the framework for peace, and they are rooted in the natural law worldview shared by all indigenous peoples. The philosophies that are formed out of these elements are the true pathways to the re-achievement of peaceful coexistence. These Onkwehonweneha are the authentic alternatives to the visions of the capitalist, the communist, the aboriginalist, and all the other ways of thinking and behaving that have emerged from within European and Euroamerican cultures.

We have knowledge of the good indigenous way, and we have teachings on how to bring about peaceful coexistence. The spirituality and the culture of our ancestors are preserved by people who have committed themselves to hold on to the old ways, and the knowledge and ceremonies that gave our ancestors such power still exist in our communities. The challenge for us is to commit ourselves to those teachings and to walk those indigenous paths; we each face a challenge in seeking ways to merge our new voices with the ancient teachings. It is a good thing that we still have people who can show us the way.

Oren Lyons is a Faithkeeper of the Onondaga Nation and has been one of the most influential figures in Onkwehonwe politics in the last two generations.[35] He has been a member of the traditional Rotinoshonni Longhouse government since his youth and was active in the reassertion of not only Rotinoshonni but of the larger Onkwehonwe identities in the turbulent era of Red Power activism in the 1960s and 1970s. He has also, in the footsteps of the Cayuga chief Deskaheh, led the resurgence of indigenous peoples' activism on the international stage and at the United Nations; he was among the first in the modern era to bring forward assertions of indigenous nationhood in many international forums as well as to articulate and represent the crucial connection between Onkwehonwe identities, nationhood politics, and global environmental issues. Oren Lyons is one of the few universally respected and admired living Onkwehonwe leaders, and now in his seventies, he is still active politically on the international level and in the affairs of his nation and that of the Rotinoshonni.

It was with great respect and admiration that I approached Oren Lyons to ask if he would talk with me about being Onkwehonwe and about our philosophies and how they express an authentic way of being human in this world. We spoke at Onondaga in a room surrounded by Rotinoshonni from all over our confederacy of nations. For more than two hours, Oren offered thoughtful reflection and guidance, displaying the persuasive force of his passionate belief in the ways of our people.

TA: *Are we fighting the same battle our ancestors did?*
OL: I think the battlefield has changed more than anything; it has become global. Our people always thought in those terms. That's what our Thanksgiving Address is, when you think about it. You start with the grass and you wind up with the heavens and the universe, so obviously you're thinking even more than just global, you're thinking universal. So we have always had that perspective. That's probably what has secured our existence up to this time, that long-term vision, understanding, and that consistency of being. We are still maintaining ourselves as people. But things have started to change. Every generation has to speak for itself, but I see a lot of degrading of leadership today, right across the country. I don't see the kinds of leaders that were there when I was young. We've got a lot of very active young

leaders today, but their goals are different. They've caught the white man's gold fever. That's what's happened with our people, to put it quite simply.

TA: *It's happening everywhere?*
OL: Yes. I've seen the damage that it's done, and it's hard to deal with. I know both roads myself; I thought I had an identity crisis when I was a young man. I wasn't sure where I was going to go, or who I really was. I was caught in the white man's process of education, goals, and values. Literally. So I had a lot of problems. These kinds of problems can be very severe; they can debilitate your ability to be productive. Confusion is really the main problem. I understand what goes through young people's minds when they're trying to find their way. You know, I think it's very difficult now for young people.

TA: *But you found your way.*
OL: It wasn't easy.

TA: *What brought you from the identity crisis to where you are now?*
OL: I guess when I was a very young boy I had the good fortune to know some of the elders here in Onondaga. One of my very best friends was a man by the name of Newton Green, and he used to like to take me fishing. I learned a lot from him, you know, from just going out fishing with him. I must have been pretty young, only seven or six years old, but I used to go with him. He was very patient with me, and we would go a long ways to go fishing. I remember one time as we were walking, it was early in the spring because there were still patches of snow on the mountains. We stopped, and he took his knife out, and he took a piece of grass, or what I thought was a piece of grass, and he dug around it with his knife. He made a circle around it and pulled the whole chunk out of the ground, and there was a big bulb on the end of that grass. It just looked to me like an ordinary piece of grass; there was a bulb on there, and then he cut it in half and it was pure white. He looked at it and said, "It's good for cancer," and he put it aside. You know what? I still have not been able to find that kind of bulb. I've looked for it, and I've looked for it, and I can't find it. But he knew just by looking at it. It was things like that, his kindness as an elderly man to just take the time to take me around, to talk to me, to spend a lot of quiet hours just fishing. I learned a lot. So, I had good friends like that, and I kind of hung out with older people a lot, for one reason or another.

But I grew up in the 1930s, a long time ago, and things were hard, I suppose. I found out later on that this was the Depression time. For Indians, we were always in that position, so we never noticed anything. As a matter of fact, things got better for us! The Depression worked the other way around. And I had a good time growing up. Hard, hard work though, we had to really, really work hard.

TA: *Could you tell me how they passed on our ways and knowledge back then?*
OL: You know we just lived that way. When the ceremonies came, that's where we were, in the Longhouse. We never thought of it as training or learning. That's just what we did. Everybody was there, all your friends and so forth. I was always looking at the chiefs, and they were always meeting and talking about things that were just too big for our heads, but we were always glad they were there. I remember seeing the Longhouse and seeing the smoke coming out, and we knew the chiefs were meeting, and it would make you feel good. That's because we knew that they were meeting for something, and whatever it was, it was important, and it was on our behalf. So that's the way we grew up.

TA: *What do you think it means for kids these days when they don't have that kind of upbringing? There's not much hard work to be done, and ceremony is not a big part of their lives.*
OL: It weakens the people, weakens the people... It weakens their understanding of who they are, because if you don't have that constant reminder, you will fall into the surrounding society, which is a very powerful society that has a lot of influence on everything. If you go into any house that I know these days, there are at least two or three televisions in there. There's one in every room; that seems to be standard. That is probably the most invasive and consistent presence in our lives, and it's totally commercial. So you are just bombarded by commerce, and you don't know anything, you don't know any better. When I went to New York City after graduating from university...

TA: *How did you make it to university if you quit school early to be with the elders?*
OL: I could play lacrosse. The first thing I learned in education was: "it's who you know." I learned that very quickly. I was a good lacrosse player—I wasn't exceptional, everybody here was good. But I was goalkeeper, and goalkeepers are hard to find sometimes. When I came out of the military service, I was recruited by Syracuse University. Then I went to New York City and worked in advertising, so I learned about the manipulation of thought and ideas.

TA: *How did you turn away from that life and become the person we all know?*
OL: I had a grandmother who called me back. I was also bringing up my own children, and I could see very clearly that New York and New Jersey were not places for bringing anybody up. And I was always thinking about this place, "I got to get home, I got to get home." So, I learned a lot in New York. I learned a lot about printing, about production, and I was a good graphic artist. But I never missed a ceremony here in Onondaga. You know, we would just get into the car and come on back.

You were talking about identity, and I remembered that when I graduated from Syracuse University, I felt pretty good. I had the Orange Key Award for scholastic and athletic achievement. I had all kinds of awards; you just name it, I had a whole bunch of them. The old man Herb Powless said to me just a couple days after that, "We'll go fishing." I used to like fishing with him because he knew where they were, and he had a boat. So we went up to this lake, and we got out there on the lake and settled in for some good fishing. He was over there on the other end of the boat, and then he says, "Well, just graduated from college?" And I said, "Yes." And I also said to myself, "Oh oh, this doesn't sound like an opening remark to me." So anyways, he says, "That's good. You know a lot of things then." He says, "You must know who you are then." I said, "Yeah, sure, I know who I am." So we went through the whole thing: the Indian name, everything that I could think of. And he would keep saying, "That's it, huh? That's all?" So I just sat there. He had me cornered. I was in a boat, and he had the motor on the other end. So that was it, I had no other place to go. And he laughed, you know? I toughed it out for awhile, back and forth, back and forth, and every time he would say, "Mmm hmm... That's it? That's all." So finally I had to say, "Alright, I need some help!" Then he said "Good. I'll help you out a little bit."

The way we were sitting in the boat, we could see where a cliff came right down into the water. Up on the topside of the cliff, there was a tree, a nice pine, not a big one. And then he says to me, "You see that tree?" And I said, "Yup." "Well," he says, "you are the same as that tree. You're no different. You see where the roots are, where the roots go, finding the earth? That's how your roots are too." He said, "You got old roots that go back a long way. I know your father, and I know your grandmother, and I know this sister..." And he went on and on. "Old roots, that's who you are," he told me, "The earth, where it goes in, that's your mother. That's all you have to remember. Can you remember that?" I said, "Yeah, yeah. Well, I will never forget it now!" But he was a man who saw that I had something that I had yet to know. He saw that I was pretty full of myself, pretty cocksure about everything, cocksure about my abilities, and so forth. And he took the time and made that point. You see, when I reflect back on that now, he had to think about that before he set that whole thing up. He thought it was important enough for him to take the time to teach me something. So what if I went through university and I had a degree? I learned more in those couple of hours on the lake than that whole four years in college. After that he said, "Well, it's about time we try another place." And I said, "Yeah, good idea." That was it, he never mentioned it again.

TA: *That's a great story. I wanted to ask you: When did you start to get involved in politics anyway?*
OL: I was always interested in it. I got even more interested when I learned that the meetings they had weren't all just meetings, they were ceremonies. I began to put things together, and then my aunt asked me to be the Faithkeeper for the Turtle Clan. I didn't think that was a good idea. But she told me to think about it, "just think about it." About that time, the Confederacy was having a hard time. I didn't realize how hard it was, but the people that lived here were having a hard time finding leaders. People were starting to drift away from the Longhouse and starting to go to church. Even some leaders went to church! I remember some ceremonies when there were maybe only ten people there. And I would come all the way from New York to be in the ceremony. I saw the steady ones, the older people who were there holding it together. And my aunt said, "Just think of what you can do for the people." It took a long time, but I finally said, "Okay, I'll try," because we have to fill those seats in the Longhouse, it's the most important thing. That's our government.

TA: *Some other people might not see it that way. I've heard some of our people say that the main job of a leader is to provide food and jobs and houses for the people. They might hear what your auntie told you and not think about saving the Confederacy and filling seats in the Longhouse but think about making money so the people can be better off in their lives.*
OL: I can tell you that whoever you're talking to, they're not chiefs. Chiefs don't talk like that. Some people might say those things, that's what ordinary people might say. But chiefs won't, clan mothers won't. They see what the importance is. There is something you have to learn, and you will learn in the course of being a leader, and that is about betrayal. Betrayal is one of the worst things that could happen to anybody, but it does happen to every-

body, and we were betrayed by our own people. Some of our people just flat out gave up the concept of what we were fighting for.

TA: *What do you think motivated this "betrayal" for them?*
OL: I think it's because they got money, money, money, money. They couldn't wait to do it. In the prophesies, it talks about the time we are going to see young men walking in front of the leaders, talking in a loud voice, saying what they are going to do.

TA: *I know we've seen so much greed and disunity. What do you think we can do to bring our people back together and start heading in the right direction?*
OL: Never lose track. You see, we never lost sight of what it was all about in terms of protecting the nation, the land, and so forth. Those other people, they got sidetracked. They wanted to become very wealthy, they did it for money, and that's the whole deal. The idea of casinos is, for our nations, probably the most problematic thing right now. Ray Halbritter, he's now running a group of people just like a corporation, not like a government, not like a nation. He even calls himself a "CEO." You can't run a nation like a corporation, because it's not a corporation.

TA: *I've talked with Ray about this, and I know he sees real leadership as standing up for your people and providing them with a good life, as opposed to advancing a theory of nationhood or defending what he sees as abstract principles that don't do any practical good for people.*
OL: That's a short vision. If you really want to provide something for your people, you are going to have to provide a solid base for the next generation and the next seven generations up. The business we have here in Onondaga now could easily have been a casino too. Actually, we have the best location for a casino—we could put Ray Halbritter out of business if we wanted to. But that's not what is going to happen; that's not how to protect your nation. It opens the door to too many things. In order to open up a casino, you have to give up your sovereignty. That's the very first thing they ask for: jurisdiction.

TA: *You mean in the kind of legal agreements you have to sign with the white governments to get a casino approved?*
OL: Yes, in the "compacts," as they are called. You see, Indians have a funny way of thinking. They think any kind of agreement they sign is a treaty. Really, it is a business agreement, and you give up what they say they want in the process. You give up jurisdiction. I can show you right there in the gaming

compact where it says, "Okay, you have it." There is no short way around giving up jurisdiction. And when you give up jurisdiction, the next thing is taxation. Taxation is going to come. It's not going to come this generation, but in the next one after that. It may be even quicker than that, because right now what I see are Indian nations across the country giving up all kinds of things for the privilege to gain money. And their rationale is, "Well, we will make enough money to secure our future…" But money is not your future. Look what is happening now: land and jurisdiction on that land, that's your future.

TA: *Is there any way to reconcile these two visions?*
OL: There is no reconciliation with that kind of enterprise. No. Right next door to this building we're in, we have a smoke shop. That smoke shop generates enough money for us to build this new arena, and we just put in a new water line. Do you know what a water line costs?

TA: *It must be millions of dollars?*
OL: Yeah, it's an enormous amount. And it all comes out of our smoke shop. So you can imagine what one individual is making and not giving back to the people. You see, there is the corruption. We were defending the idea of our sovereignty, and then that's when the betrayal comes. Simple and pure, but a part of life. You have to know what it is, and you have to understand what it is. When you see it, you can't let it detour you from what you have to do.

TA: *So what do we do when it does happen?*
OL: When betrayal happens, you are just going to have to deal with it. It's a part of life. It's hard to talk in terms of reconciliation. I believe strongly that that is exactly what has to happen, but also that reconciliation has to come from over there to here where we are. When a branch goes crooked, the tree doesn't come up and go over to where the crooked branch is, the crooked branch comes over to the tree where it left off. That has to happen, and it probably will. But these things take time. Time has a way of taking the sharp edges off of things. But people don't forget. They especially don't forget a betrayal, because once you get betrayed, you don't trust again, you are always a little wary.

TA: *So I hear you saying that we should stay true to the old ways. Is it always wrong to branch off from the tree?*

OL: No. Because as you move along, all things change. Nothing stays the same, except your principles. Our principles cannot change. Circumstances will change around those principles. Our Confederacy has lasted through a lot. It's still here. The tree and the heart is right here, and that is what I learned you have to have above all. You can't lose it. So that's "sovereignty," and when we use that word, that's what we mean. We have our own way here in Onondaga, we have our own rule. We don't talk to the federal government and ask, "Who are we?" We tell them who we are. If we do things like that consistently, which we have, they accept it as reality. So, they respect the Six Nations. They respect the Six Nations because they have to.

Listening to Oren Lyons speak about his upbringing and the way he absorbed the Onkwehonweneha from his elders, the ceremonies, and just being immersed in a culture and community that was still rooted in the ancient teachings made me think about the importance of language. Specifically, I started to think about how difficult it would be for someone to gain the knowledge and perspective of a person like Oren Lyons without speaking the language of his ancestors and elders. The culture is, we are often told, contained in the language. But I was surprised to learn from Oren, when I asked him about the elders and the importance of speaking our indigenous languages, that he in fact did not speak Onondaga or any of the other Rotinoshonni languages. When I asked him about this aspect of being Onkwehonwe, he told me:

> I was encouraged to see our young people going back to their language. They are struggling to do it and carrying it on. They are doing better than I did. My youngest brother has become fluent, and he is taking care of business there. I have to look up to him, because he can do things that I can't do. But there are other things that I can do that other people can't do. What's more important? What's most important is what is right here in my heart.

This brings us to one of the most lively and interesting debates within Onkwehonwe communities today: Do you need to speak an indigenous language to be truly indigenous?

There is much talk among Onkwehonwe that our languages *are* our culture, and that it is impossible to understand and appreciate the teachings and principles of Onkwehonwe cultures without understanding the languages. But what does this position say about the indigeneity of people like Oren Lyons and myself and most of the people I know, people who may understand the basic concepts but who are not fluent in their language? The vast majority of Onkwehonwe do not speak their ancestral languages, and indigenous language fluency among indigenous peoples in Anówara is in serious decline generally. This is fact. Are all of these people not Onkwehonwe? To put it another way: Is speaking an indigenous language the defining characteristic of being Onkwehonwe? It is a compelling argument to put forward: colonialism sought to destroy us by erasing our languages and in so doing deculture our people and destroy the worldviews and value systems that were the foundations of our distinct ways of life; thus, language is the *prima facie* evidence of indigeneity. It is a compelling argument, until one considers the facts.

First, ways of seeing the world and of constructing value systems are not contained only in verbal languages. Songs, pictures, ceremony, and many varied art and cultural forms contain knowledge and can be *read* for insight, knowledge, and guidance on how to be indigenous. Second, languages are constantly changing. The Onkwehonwe languages held as sacred repositories of culture today are very different from the languages spoken by our ancestors, who were the originators of the ceremonies, clans, and stories that are the substance of the traditional culture we are seeking to preserve and reinvigorate. And thirdly, if language is the essential characteristic of an Onkwehonwe mentality, how do we explain that the men who signed treaties surrendering millions of square miles of our ancestral homeland, who waged war against their Brothers and Sisters, and who worked with the colonizer to decimate the earth for profit, were all mother-tongue, unilingual, indigenous language speakers?

These are tough and emotionally charged questions. And they must be dealt with, because however much credence one gives to a line of logical connection or argument about the relationship between speaking a language and one's culture, everyone instinctively *feels* that what language one speaks is a crucially important feature of one's human existence. So what is the relationship between speaking indigenous languages and living indigenous existences?

The world's leading linguistics scholar, Noam Chomsky, argues that there is one universal language, a largely "predetermined" biological function of human beings. Language is, according to Chomsky:

a biological object with highly intricate and very specific proper-
ties, quite unlike the constructed formal systems called, "language" by metaphoric extension that is harmless if not taken
seriously, but that has in fact been highly misleading. In particular, there is no question of how human languages represent the
world, or the world as it is thought to be. They don't. [36]

Even if we accept Chomsky's notion of a single ancestral language, differences in language are still key to our lived experience as human beings
and as the main factors in political and social relations. Genetic research has
led to the conclusion that differences between people based on "race" are a
fallacy (genetic differences exist between individuals and cannot be linked
to collectives) and that the only true differences between people organized
into groups are "cultural." So, given that languages are the repositories of particular understandings and patterns of knowledge that shape the way people
see the world, believe, and live their lives, language is in fact the only true
source of distinctiveness among human group identities. [37]

The word "source" is, I think, important here. If we are trying to preserve
and reinvigorate a way of being in the world that is distinctive in the values
it promotes as the framework for defining the conduct of a good life and a
notion of justice between peoples, Onkwehonwe languages are essential as
sources of knowledge. Quite apart from the political objective of preserving language differences as markers of boundaries between peoples, or as the signals of national tenacity and survival, there is an inherent value to
Onkwehonwe languages which makes them worth fighting to preserve.

Yet, there is a growing fear about the continuing loss of indigenous languages. Whether they are lost to death, extinction, or suicide (choosing to
let the language die), the fact is that fewer and fewer people are speaking
or are capable of understanding Onkwehonwe languages. But the charting
of loss does not fully or accurately explain what is happening in a political
or cultural sense. There are reasons people are letting their languages go and
why they are embracing colonial languages (English, Spanish, and French).
The language scholars Daniel Nettle and Suzanne Romain have asserted
in their insightful book, *Vanishing Voices*, [38] that there are very clear reasons
indigenous languages get replaced by others. Language "death" is defined as
occurring when a language is replaced by another over its entire functional
range, when it is not transmitted to children. The death of Onkwehonwe
languages, Nettle and Romain explain, happens in a context of duress and

246

social stress, the conditions created by colonial aggression and the dispossession of Onkwehonwe from their lands. The wide-scale abandonment of indigenous languages and the adoption of European languages can be seen, in this context, as a rational survival strategy. Up to the 1960s at least, extreme and hostile racist aggression by white people, social degradation, and forced assimilation, combined with the construction of economic opportunities predicated on speaking European languages, meant that it was a reasonable decision to abandon Onkwehonwe languages and adopt the colonizers' languages. This was true even from the perspective of a Native Nationalist ideology in which the objectives of the movement were defined in terms of physical survival and the protection of land and the political status of the community.

That was then. Today the opposite is true. The battle is for the reclamation of an Onkwehonwe spirit, mentality, and way of being in the world. In this context, our survival as peoples is dependent upon the survival and revitalization of indigenous languages.

Language loss is an indicator of social stress and happens in the context of a particular economic and political matrix. The dominance of one language over another is a single manifestation of the social and economic dominion of one group over another; this explains the growing global dominion of English, which is associated with the United States and the United Kingdom, over myriad other languages across the globe. *Dominion* always has been a state of mind as much as a social and economic relation, though. One group's domination over another is itself a spiral matrix of the loss, defeat or death of population; land; political, economic, spiritual, and cultural independence, and language. Herein lies the main argument for the resurrection of Onkwehonwe languages. It is not their sacredness, essential superiority, or divine or mystical quality that is the reason for wanting to save them, but the combination of their usefulness as philosophical systems and as the gauge of peoples' success at reasserting their authentic existences. Dominance of European thought as reflected in the hegemony of European languages can and must be challenged, and the pattern must be reversed if we are serious in our objective to reassert the existence of Onkwehonwe identities in the face of homogenizing imperial-capitalist culture, its languages, and the political-economic power of the global empire.

It is when we look at solutions that the linkage between language and political power becomes clearest. Nettle and Romain conclude that saving Onkwehonwe languages will require a political process to rectify the imbalances of power that led to the dominion of European languages: "We need

247

to explore other forms of governance as alternatives to the nation-state ... which arose in particular Western historical circumstances and was predicated on the achievement of linguistic unification as part and parcel of political unification."[39] So, imperialism is inherently a process of homogenization, culturally and politically. It follows then that acting against empire by regenerating culture through the revival of indigenous languages is inherently anti-imperial. The act of speaking and using Onkwehonwe languages to reorganize and reframe our existences is perhaps the most radical act we can perform as Onkwehonwe warriors.

Add to this political objective the cultural objective of generating innovation and adaptation of our languages themselves, and we have a powerful vision capable of reorienting our understanding of the relationships we share and of the land we all coexist upon. The social and political agenda of the state is to mediate ethnic and racial conflicts. This is called "multiculturalism" in liberal-democratic states, but it is in reality nothing more than a surface celebration of folkloric traditions from various immigrant cultures combined with the promotion of deeper assimilation to monocultural societal norms (though it is sometimes reflected through more than one of the European colonial languages). Whether multiculturalism communicates itself in English-French or English-Spanish, it is still only an accommodation of the ethnic power of colonial Euroamericans and their more recent immigrant allies. True justice leading to eventual peaceful coexistence between Settlers and Onkwehonwe will require a shift away from the objective of bilingual (to use the colonial terminology) monocultural assimilation to what we might call a multilingual bicultured coexistence. In this way, a just political relation may evolve as nation-to-nation between what has become a culturally and linguistically diverse Settler society and indigenous peoples who will continue to exist as linguistically and culturally distinct communities. Holding the conceptual keys to a non-imperial worldview, Onkwehonwe languages are indispensable to this liberating possibility.

Onkwehonwe languages are unique conceptual frameworks of ideas, insights, and understandings of the world that are vastly different from the frameworks represented by European languages. This alone is cause to invest the time and energy into learning indigenous languages, as it seems impossible to imagine a way out of the European imperial reality using conceptual tools (languages) that represent the very framework being challenged. Only indigenous languages carry the specific insights of non-imperial ways of viewing and organizing our understanding of the world. They are, as Chomsky referred to them, "objects" which are crucial tools in recon-

structing a way of life outside of the imperial frame. Specific understandings and indigenous ways of seeing the world conveyed through story are
likewise fundamental necessities of a decolonized mentality. If indigenous
languages are the tools we will use, then indigenous narratives are the foundations upon which our indigenous identities and resurgent cultures will
be reconstructed.[40]

Beyond the languages used to express cultural perspectives, beliefs, and
values, we must consider the importance of stories, ceremony, and rituals
in the regeneration of authentic indigenous existences. These are also basic
elements of culture, and they are of course tied to language. For humans to
enjoy happiness at all, they must be integrated politically, socially, spiritually and culturally; language, stories, and ceremonies are the building blocks
of an integrated human being. Without the sense of self-awareness and
psychological rootedness that being part of a cohesive culture gives a person,
and lacking basic consistency between one's identity and the legal and experiential reality of the world one lives in outside of the individual mind and
body, human fulfillment, happiness, and peace are simply not possible.

The effects of ritual and ceremony on a person and community are profound. Whether they are "traditional" or part of an innovative regenerated
Onkwehonwe culture, celebrating our heritage and living the rites of our cultures are crucial to being Onkwehonwe and to being human. Participating
in a community and culture gives people psychological wholeness, the satisfaction of basic human needs, and emotional release. It creates and
strengthens the connections between people, fostering relationships of
mutual support and caring. Ceremony keeps people connected to their
past as well; it preserves memory. It reminds us of our responsibilities as
human beings, and, in the face of cynical and sometimes harsh existences
as we confront the political and economic realities of our lives, its rituals reit-
erate that the underlying force of the universe is love. Ceremonies remind
us, too, of the beauty and power of nature and of how we should try to live
in accord with the laws of nature. Ceremony and ritual are not mystical, they
are real needs in human beings. And they serve real purposes in grounding
us and keeping us together as persons and as communities, in spite of the
disintegrating tendencies of the world we live in. Through them, we have
the opportunity to experience life outside of our own material beings, freed
for a time from the needs and wants of our own bodies to experience a higher
truth, a spirituality. Restored to strength through ritual and ceremony or
the healing power of stories, we can then return to the *real* world to continue

the fight and to persevere in the struggle to bring this world into accord with the higher values to which we are exposed in our spiritual lives.

How can anyone confront the depressing, disintegrating reality of this world without the restorative strength provided by spirituality? How can we imagine and work for a better existence in our own lives and for that of the world as a whole without the loving and natural reminders that our Onkwehonwe ceremonies give to us? I don't know that it is possible. Yet many, if not most, of the spiritual ceremonies and practices of Onkwehonwe have been destroyed or lost. If spiritual practice is so crucial to the regeneration of Onkwehonwe identities, and by extension to the achievement of justice and peace in Anówara, some thought must be given to the forms of belief and practice that we are seeking to preserve, restore, or reconnect with.[41]

Is there something of a unified or singular indigenous spirituality, beyond or deeper than the by now obvious point that Onkwehonwe cultures are all about harmony and relationship? Another way to ask the question is to wonder if there is philosophical unity in the stories Onkwehonwe tell each other to root themselves to each other and their homelands and in the multiplicity of ceremonial and ritualistic practices that make up Onkwehonwe cultures? If there is unity, then all Onkwehonwe rituals and ceremonial practices, quite aside from how attracted or repelled people are to them because of histories of religion, division and conflict among Onkwehonwe, have equal validity and value in helping us to understand and practise an indigenous existence. Ceremonies are gifts to be shared, and in this time of loss and disconnection, sharing and learning together and building unity among Onkwehonwe through ceremonial relations is a powerful example of anti-imperial practice.

The wisest among our elders and spiritual teachers tell us that there is a connection between all of our peoples and that each ceremony possesses *part* of the knowledge we need to survive. What are the basics of this Onkwehonwe spiritual and philosophical belief system?[42] They are simple, and I have been referring to them directly and indirectly throughout this book: interdependency, cycles of change, balance, struggle, and rootedness.

There is nothing unique taught in the Lodge, the Longhouse, or Hogan or through the tobacco or sweetgrass. All over the world, all indigenous peoples' dances and songs tell us the same things. Wherever people are still close to the earth and living in harmony with nature, the teachings are the same. The ceremonies do more than connect us to a particular tradition or community, they connect us to the earth and to our true, natural existences as human beings.

There is a story told among my people about how the sapling without roots is easily pulled out of the earth and tossed around on the winds, but the young tree with roots in the ground can bend and sway and yet hold firm when the winds blow. Once, one of my cousins, a hard-working and successful capitalist, cynically told me, when I mentioned the sapling story to him, that he had no use for roots. Ceremony, culture, language, and all that stuff were wastes of time for him because he had a stronger power to protect himself from those winds: he made enough money selling black-market cigarettes that he could afford to bring in a backhoe and pile a whole load of dirt around his little sapling to make sure it stayed where it belonged. Money, culture: same thing; the sapling stayed where it was. I didn't like (or buy!) my cousin's version of the story, but hearing his deft deconstruction of a traditional metaphor, I felt that I needed to talk with someone a lot older and wiser to sharpen my knowledge and my ability to respond to jaded capitalists!

I was fortunate in being introduced soon after to two respected women, both elders and clan mothers from the Six Nations reserve in Ontario, who were willing to tell me what they thought and felt about the importance of indigenous languages and their relationship to being Onkwehonwe.[43]

I spoke first with Kawinéhta, a long-time language teacher in the community.

TA: *How important is it for us to know our Onkwehonwe languages?*
K: I have to answer you truthfully. I am my tradition. I am Longhouse. I actually go to the Longhouse and to those ceremonies. And in the Longhouse, all the ceremonies are in the language. So that tells you what I think about how important our language is.

TA: *But what does it mean then when most of us don't speak our own language?*
K: It's disappointing. My belief is that if we lose the language, we're no longer Onkwehonwe. We're just like everybody else. There's nothing unique about us any more, we're just regular people. The Onkwehonwe name I have comes out of a clan, and nobody else can have it. My grandchildren, their Onkwehonwe names don't belong to anyone else. The English names we have, anyone can have them. One of my grandchildren is named Gail, one is named Merle, and somebody else is named Duncan. That's fine, but that's not important, because it was given to them by the white man. Sometimes I even forget those names, because I always use their real names.

TA: *Some people might say that being Onkwehonwe is not only the language you speak, but a lot of other things too. What do you think about that? Is it that language is the most important thing, or is it the only thing about being Onkwehonwe, where if you don't know Onkwewenna then you are not really Onkwehonwe?*

K: Before anything else, you have to have the language. What good is knowing all those other things if you don't know the language? Like if you know June is strawberry time, what good is it if you can't do the ceremony that goes with that? And when you have a meeting, if you don't have the Thanksgiving Address, everybody's going to be thinking what they want to think, they're not going to think as one. I think language is the whole thing: it's beliefs, it's culture, it's custom, it's what's important. I can't get over how some people don't see this!

When my husband and me, we were living in Rochester, we always talked in our language. This one lady came up to us and said, "What are you two talking, Chinese?" I thought to myself, "Poor thing." We told her that we were talking Onkwehonwe language, and she said that she thought that it was all dead and gone. They asked us where we were from, and we told them we were from Six Nations, and they said, "Six Nations? We are too!" And I said to myself, "I don't know about that…" That's when I was fresh off the Rez going into the city, when my husband and I started teaching urban Indians the language. We started out with just how to say, *Shékon*, "Hello." In the back of their minds, it was important to them too. It's always been there. Everybody wants to learn. If I had enough time, I would record everything I know and maybe it would keep us Onkwehonwe for a long time. Maybe.

TA: *So you think that we will survive as a people if we dedicate ourselves to preserving and passing on our language and our culture to the next generations?*

K: Yes. And it's not just for us, it's for the whole world. If there are no more Onkwehonwe, there is no more world! That's what we were told. But as long as there's smoke coming out of those six fires, we're still Onkwehonwe.

I also was fortunate to be able to sit down for a conversation with Gaihohwakohn, a woman who had been working tirelessly for years using traditional Rotinoshonni teachings as a model for counselling to change self-destructive and violent behaviours and to restore the integrity of family life in the community. She focused on the inherent and powerful wisdom contained in our indigenous languages.

G: The main teaching we give to people is that it's really important to be conscious of what you're doing. Because we're not, we're just going along with the flow. When we identify ourselves, we should say that we're *Kaion'kwenna*, there's more value in that than if I say, "I'm a Cayuga" or "I'm a Seneca." Where's the value in that? Language is very important; it is the core of who we are. Without it, we won't exist no more. That's why I pay so much attention to language and what words mean. When I was learning the language and listening to the Thanksgiving Address, I would ask the older people, "So what are they talking about?" And they would say, "They're talking about the birds, and they're talking about the trees." And then I would ask, "So how come it takes them an hour and a half to talk about that?" Now I understand! As a teacher, I ask the people who are learning to speak our language, "So tell me, what do you see?" They should see pictures, because that's what we should see when we use the languages. We should see the connectedness of everything—how we talk, our relationships, and everything. It's using that Thanksgiving every day, applying it to our lives, and asking, "What does this really teach us." It's teaching us that relationship is everything. From the time we leave *Sonkwaiatison*, the Creator, there are so many places that we can look for *koiataista*, that place of completeness. When we listen to the creation story, when it talks about *koiataista*, it means that the Creator thought that it was time for this person to travel and experience the human existence. So we travel, and we come into the earth through the wombs of the women. Here, in our wombs, is that *koiataista*.

TA: *All of us in Six Nations, Kahnawake, Akwesasne—we all come from pretty much the same kind of family background and life experience growing up, yet some of our people find the good path to being true Onkwehonwe, and some of us wander around for a long time lost or searching.*
G: It's not a matter of being better than anyone else, it's just that you have a kindness and a compassion and a caring for everybody, and you want to help in the hopes that maybe some day all of our people will come to understand the power of our teachings. I heard another thing from my mother: *enkaienkwen*. That means, "there will be a fog," or a mist, that will cover the people and cover the earth so that we won't be able to tell people what is right any more. Even though we know what is right, we won't say anything. We will just let things go.

TA: *Did she say what would happen after this confusion came down on us?*
G: That's when everything will be lost.

253

TA: *Doesn't it scare you to see how many of us are lost in that fog?*
G: I see that, and I say to myself, "What I can do to help people understand."

The theme of reconnection kept reasserting itself in these conversations. Reconnection and recommitment to our intellectual and spiritual heritage is the guidance I was given every time I spoke with an elder about what is right and wrong about the way things are with our people and about the direction we need to be headed. Connection and commitment to land, language, and each other as communities seem to be the struggle we are faced with in trying to transcend colonialism. Yet, it seems impossible to conceive of a path to health, justice, and peace that is simply a restoration of old ways of doing things and living our lives. The *resurrection* of a reality experienced by our ancestors is obviously impossible; thus, a *regeneration* is the way to think about the challenge we face. Beyond speaking of re-establishing connections though, what does it mean to be reconnected and re-rooted, recommitted, and to have our strength restored? What is the new reality that we would create for ourselves and for our people in struggling against the persistence of our colonized existences?

I am searching for an understanding, a way to articulate and then to think about replicating not the surface aspects of the lifestyle and manners of our peoples in past times, but the *quality* of an indigenous existence, the connective material that bound Onkwehonwe together when "interests" and "rights" were not a part of our peoples' vocabularies. Another way of putting this is to ask the question, "What is the force or reason of an indigenous existence?"

I turned again to my friend Thohahoken to help me think through to a balanced understanding of this basic philosophical question from within the Rotinoshonni culture. I thought of the need for re-establishing connection, and at first supposed that the Kanienkeha word, *Konoronkwa* perhaps might lead us somewhere. Konoronkwa is usually translated as "love," but I knew that it conveys much more than that. In its full meaning the word conveys a sense of what one values and reflects the universal connection we feel to other beings and the force of love that binds us together as humans. Rather than giving me a corrected literal translation or providing me with a direct answer to my question, Thohahoken listened to what I had to say, and then offered a teaching:

> In the Rotinoshonni creation story, the very first person on earth was a woman. She came from the sky to the as yet unformed world below, landing on a turtle's back. The first woman then danced the

earth into existence. This much we know. But in coming down from the sky world, did we know if she fell, was pushed, or jumped? Being philosophers, this is an important thing to know! The implicit nihilism in the view that she accidentally fell was antithetical to the Onkwehonwe experience. Her being pushed would mean that another agency, likely her husband, was in fact responsible for her reality, and this was not possible in our culture either. That is why our people believe that Sky Woman jumped to the earth from the sky world. She saw that humanity suffered. We describe Sky Woman's motivation through the act of the jump. Sky Woman had some inner desire to help humanity, and we describe this powerful agency as *konoronkwa*.

The make-up of the Kanienkeha word for Sky Woman's inner desire to help humanity is itself a teaching on the layered philosophical underpinnings of an indigenously rooted notion of the nature of true human power. There are several roots to the concept in our language. The first part of the word, *kono*, comes from the word for "female," *kononkwe*. When someone refers to females, they say *kononha*. The affect on us all is implied in the end part of the word, *onkwa*, which literally means "our." Thus, "our" and "female" are related (just as in the word for "our mother," *sanistonha*). The middle part of the word, *ron*, is another part of this femalized notion of power. *Wakenoronse* means "insurmountable": the *noronse* combined with *kononha* and *onkwa* creates "something that cannot be resisted." So the Rotinoshonni concept konoronkwa links the three notions of "female-insurmountable-ours."

The only way to translate the whole meaning of the concept into an English idiom would be to say the word "passion." Sky Woman *passionately* embraced humanity for good purposes. Our conception of the good life, reflected in Sky Woman's redemptive sacrifice, is based on a passion for all life. Our conception of the good life in our interpersonal relations relies on basic human decency and compassion. In Kanienkeha, if the suffix *sera* is added to the word konoronkwa, it becomes *konoronkwasera*, meaning "compassion." As the foundational principle of our conception of the good life, konoronkwa intrinsically expresses our sovereignty based on Sky Woman's jump.

I really like the idea that the motivating force of an indigenous existence was a femalized insurmountable power shared by all of us! A passionate
commitment to help the people survive and an indomitable compassion for
other human beings best sum up the strength and spirit of the people I know
who have kept the fire of their nations alive.

But even within communities with such powerful conceptual and spiritual tools that should allow all of us to find new and creative paths to achieve
the ancient values of peace, power, and righteousness, the indigenous way is
a struggle. It is worth saying again as a reminder of what we face that we live
in a reality shaped by the forces of destruction and disconnection, and the
regeneration of ourselves as people to be true human beings and of our
communities to be true nations is a spiritual war. Regeneration of power gives
us the strength to continue to fight; restoring connection to each other gives
us the social support that is crucial to human fulfillment; reconnection to our
own memory roots us in a culture; and reconnection to spirit gives us a
strong and whole mind. These are the elements of resurgence.

Life is a struggle. But after listening to Thohahoken, Kawinéhta, and
Gaihohwakohn, and realizing the depth of their understanding of the
Rotinoshonni philosophy, I am more convinced than ever before that gaining an understanding of indigenous languages is *the* way to become rooted
in an indigenous worldview and way of living one's life. I do not take a fundamentalist stance on this; it is without a doubt possible to be Onkwehonwe
without knowing an indigenous language. People are cultured in different
ways and can be more or less rooted, conversant, and knowledgeable about
being Onkwehonwe. But insofar as gaining a deep and profound appreciation for the teachings and wisdom within Onkwehonwe cultures is the path
to transformation and decolonization on a personal level, one can only
begin the journey by committing oneself to understanding the Onkwehonwe
spirit and mentality uniquely contained and conveyed in Onkwewenna,
indigenous languages. In understanding our self-identity, who we are as
people, even in our names and the way we refer to ourselves, our languages
provide the means of confidently re-rooting ourselves in the solid ground
of our heritage.

VIGILANT CONSCIOUSNESS

Whenever I travel to and visit in Onkwehonwe communities, I am always struck by the fact that there are still so many strong, culturally rooted young people who are making their way in the world as indigenous warriors in spite of the challenges they face and despite the fact that as committed, decolonized, action-oriented people, they are in the minority, even among Onkwehonwe. There are people in every indigenous nation who have turned away from colonial identities and ways, recreating themselves in a creative and courageous way. The sad thing about this, though, is that these same people are usually struggling in isolation and face reactions to their self-determination from their own people and even from their own families.

In all of our nations, there are young people who are starting their lives as political activists in a much stronger position than the generations that preceded them. They speak their indigenous language, they know their history, they are educated in both indigenous knowledge systems and in the Euroamerican system, and they are free from dependency on drugs or alcohol. Not only young people but a growing number of educated Onkwehonwe have shed their colonial skins and have dedicated themselves to active anti-colonial struggle. With all of the negative portrayals of our people in the corporate media, and the focus on the negative aspects of indigenous community life, it may be hard for many people to believe it, but there are Onkwehonwe like this! And what may be even more shocking to know is that these same young people are far from complacent or cooperative—that is the posture of the older generations.

As my work on this book came to a close, I knew that to gain a full understanding of what it was to be Onkwehonwe, I needed the perspective of the young people of our nations. I needed to appreciate how they were taking our heritages and translating them into ideas and practices to form frameworks for their own lives which will eventually become the intellectual, social, and political landscapes of our nations as they become the leaders of our peoples. I wanted to end my journey by finding young people who embodied and were living the ideals I had come to know as the essence of being an Onkwehonwe warrior: creative contention, rootedness, and the ethic of courage. And I found them everywhere I travelled. These are people who are reorienting their lives thoughtfully and preparing themselves for what is to come in the ongoing struggle against the injustices of colonialism. They reflect the surging energy and confident spirit that is widespread among the committed young Onkwehonwe warriors in all of our nations; they are the new warriors of Anówara.

What will the next generation make of their heritage? The questions of what do we do with the knowledge that has been passed on to us, and where do we go from here, are important not only for the conclusion of the journey of understanding reflected in this book, but for every one of us who has been passed a gift of knowledge from our Onkwehonwe experiences and cultures, from our elders, and now must decide how to commit herself and himself to making change in their lives and their communities. People will have to figure out for themselves how to make change in their lives and what kind of warrior to become. Yet we are travelling together in solidarity, and we must come together and support each other in the personal and collective struggles we face in our lives as Onkwehonwe.

With this need for sharing and solidarity in mind, I offer you a conversation among a circle of young people from different nations and backgrounds. When I met them, I wondered if the thoughts I was offering in this book resonated, or even made sense at all, to young people living on Indian reserves or in urban centres across the country. But rather than test my ideas by throwing theory at them, I decided to tell them from my heart why I wrote this book and ask them to speak on some basic questions about their lives and struggles as Onkwehonwe. I would listen with sincere respect and trust in their innate wisdom as Onkwehonwe.

With the help of some friends in Saskatoon, Saskatchewan, I met a group of five young high school and college students. We talked about how the spirits of our nations were once strong fires that had now become weak and were close to dying out because all the embers had been taken away by the many forces of destruction and division that have affected our people so harshly. We talked about how people have been trying hard for a long time to snuff out whatever heat remained in the circle of our fires, and how we needed to restoke those fires by bringing all the embers back to where they belonged, inside the circle of our nations, by constantly feeding the fire, and also by protecting the fire from the harsh winds and other forces that would always be there to kill the fire if we did not keep it safe.

All of us were people involved in education and the arts. We agreed that it is our role to be living outside of the fire-ring and work in the space between the fire and the forces that would destroy it. We recognized that there was a place for all Onkwehonwe in the regeneration of the fires no matter whether we were born in the secure centre of the ring or were brought into this world living separate from the core of our cultures, lands, and communities. Some of us were right in the middle of the community and the culture, living it fully and keeping it alive that way. Others worked to bring the embers, the people, back to life and back into the circle from the places where they have been scattered. Still others were outside of that circle altogether, but still connected by the work we do to protect the land, the culture, and the community from the forces of evil and to fight off danger and destruction. Wherever we lived and worked was our warrior zone, a place outside the safety and security of the community and right in the face of the enemy. We all agreed it was a good way to think about our relation to the land, the community, and the struggles that our peoples faced.[44]

CHRIS: Our elders will tell you: "It's good to get your education, but not at the expense of your culture and your language and your traditions." There's four directions, right? And you want to equal all of that: you're physical, say you play sports; you're spiritual, your dancing and your ceremonies; you're mental, your studies; and you're emotional, your relations with other people. So you have to balance that. Sometimes it's hard, like during school when you have to focus on that. But when you get the chance, you go back to your community to do your traditions and your ceremonies and community events.

TA: *What does it mean to you anyway when you hear the word, "warrior"?*
BRANDON: To me, being a warrior is just knowing your culture or getting to know your culture and who you are and what you want to do in life. It's how you want to bring your Native culture into the society now and help out youth on your reserve or wherever you're from, or to try to make change and make things better. Reserves right now, they're home, but it's really hard to live there. I think that being a First Nations warrior, or wherever you're coming from—for me I guess it would be Cree and Mohawk because that's who I am and what I believe in and where I come from—would be just knowing your culture and helping our people who don't know their culture. We need to know our culture so that we're recognized for who we are, so that we can keep our tradition and be proud of who we are.
CHRIS: I think a warrior is someone who breaks down barriers. Sometimes the non-native people, they bring you down, they make you not want to try harder. Like, I play a lot of sports, and that happened to me lots of times: I get benched, whatever... but that could be because of my playing ability too, who knows? (Laughter.) And I think that our language is the most important thing. That's the reason why we're not as strong as we should be, because we don't speak our language as much as we should. Like

259

I don't know my language—I mean, I know some words and stuff, but I think I should learn it to be a stronger person. I agree with you when you said that to make the people stronger is for you to be strong. To not be involved with drugs and alcohol, to be involved with your community and the songs and dances, and even if you're not doing these things, to participate somehow.

TA: *You said a warrior is someone who breaks through barriers. So it's not just a way of thinking, but a way of doing?*
SHANA: It's not just a state of being, it's someone who actually has the courage to stand up and break barriers and to even reject values that they've been socialized to accept that maybe just don't work for them or don't work for their families or their community. I think being a warrior involves a lot of risk, in that you might be standing alone, you might have to lead some people.

TA: *How much of a need do you think there is for warriors today?*
MIKA: Our youth always need people to look up to, because if you don't have people to look up to, you don't have any idea about where you want to go with your life. If you see a strong role model in front of you, it leads you in a good direction. You always need people to make pathways for you to follow.
SHANA: I think it's important to look at who designates himself as a "warrior," or who is designated as a warrior. They serve the people, so they should be chosen by the people. A lot of times, people self-designate themselves, and maybe they're not serving the interests of the main community. People become socialized to want to advance themselves as a person, as an individual, and that means money, that means possessions, and they lose sight of the direction and forget about helping other people. What you need to do is to look back, at your history and your traditions before advancing forward in kind of an unconscious way.

TA: *It's one thing to have the mentality of a warrior and to try to act like one, but you need to have support. Do you find that support is there among our people?*
CHRIS: Well, it is in some ways, but in other ways it's not. There's a lot of corruption and stuff in politics, with our leaders and with the councils. Like a lot of people have good intentions, to get where they are, to be a leader, but sometimes they don't do it in the right way, the way they should be doing it. Our leaders should lead by example. They shouldn't be doing certain things, like embezzling money and getting involved with drugs and alcohol, you know? There's always someone like that, but there's always some-

one who is there only for the people too, they work for the people and that's their whole intention.

TA: *You've been talking about the warrior as a kind of protector. What are some of the dangers and threats or barriers that our young people are facing today?*
CHRIS: Well there's lots of things that people say, and the way they are towards Native people—they don't give you a chance. They expect the stereotype, they think that you have no education, you should be on drugs, you should be selling your body for money, you should be drinking. That's what I face a lot: people write you off. Even our own people, they have their own stereotypes. It just makes it harder, and when you don't do those kinds of thing, you're always kind of having to be proving it to people. But you don't always want to be proving something to people, you just wanted to be treated fairly, heh?
MARILYN: There are some difference in the obstacles younger people face in relation to the ones our parents had to face, especially for the youth who are growing up in urban areas and who are not always in touch with what their homes are like or what's happening at home. Sometimes its easier if you get caught up in the security of just existing in this world out here and kind of forgetting about the things that are happening at home. I find that to be a danger sometimes, because my home community is so remote and so far north that sometimes I feel that I'm just so out of touch with them. I get so caught up in my life here, and we live in such an individual rights-oriented kind of system here where we're all thinking that we should be advancing ourselves, that I find myself looking back and thinking, "What am I going to school for after all?" It's not to advance myself, it's beyond myself and to hope that I can do something to help out my home community. This is a different kind of challenge; poverty is not so much of a problem when you live in the city as opposed to the reserve. There are other challenges, like knowing that you're losing large portions of your culture if you don't have the opportunity to speak your own language and to speak with your elders. Those are the dangers to me.

TA: *How do you deal with this separation between yourselves and your communities?*
SHANA: You can't change the way someone feels or thinks over a short period of time. They feel that, and it's genuine to them. You prove yourself more by what you do with what you've gained from the system. If you gain an education and then someone sees you working hard to help other people, and not just buying a new car and living in a really nice apartment or something

like that, eventually their view of you will shift. If not, there's not much you can do about it, really. You just hope that eventually that resentment or anger will change.

BRANDON: There are some people on my reserve who don't like me for who I am. Because of the way I look, they think that I'm just some white boy who came onto the reserve, or something like that. There's lots of stereotypes that I get too… But I try to look at that and not let it matter because the people that don't like me are going to be helped in the end anyway, even though they don't see it now.

CHRIS: I have a friend who thinks that you're not really an Indian if you don't drink or smoke up or if you're not into that party scene, or whatever. When people say that they'll only be your friend if you go and drink with them—and I'm a person that doesn't drink or smoke up—these people think that you're only Indian if you're out on the street or living in poverty or home-less, or if you're making babies here left and right… It's tough, heh?

TA: *How do you deal with it?*
CHRIS: I don't really know how to deal with it. But I just try not to pay attention to those people. But it does affect you. It makes you mad, and you want to teach them, but sometimes there's just no hope for that person. You want to say something to give them some kind of hope, but they're far too deep into that stereotype to bring them out of it. You'd have to do some-thing real drastic to bring them out of it. They're fighting their culture so hard, they're so tied into the stereotype, it's tough for them.

MIKA: Most of my friends are actually white. My friends don't really judge me; it's other people.

TA: *Do you ever feel that Native people are looking at you like you're not one of them?*
MIKA: Yeah. Because I don't look very "Native," I guess. But sometimes I'll go shopping with my mom, and the sales ladies are such jerks to us. They'll, like, stare at us as if we're going to steal something or whatever. It's kind of stupid, because they just naturally assume that, like Chris said, all Indians are drunks or will steal. I guess some of my friends are like that too, they'll see a homeless Indian man drinking when we're driving, and they'll be like, "Oh, lock your doors!" And I'm like, "He's stumbling, what's he going to do to you? He can't even walk." They're just really narrow-minded sometimes.

TA: *So do you set them straight then?*

MIKA: I'll just talk to them. I'll say, "Just grow up. You have to understand that not all Indian people are like that." And you have to get into the deeper issue of why they are like that? It's because we make them like that.

TA: *Do you have to deal with that all the time from your friends, being half-Native and hanging around with whites mostly?*
MIKA: Yeah, but it's not towards me, it's towards other people. They just don't get it, they'll push for things that will just make the situation worse, like "Don't give that homeless man money, he'll just spend it on booze." They all bitch and complain that all these Indian people are homeless with no money and no job. Well, then, find a way to help them get a job, instead of bitching and sitting on your ass and doing nothing about it!
BRANDON: I was driving in the car with my girlfriend and a young Native hooker came up to the door of the car. My girlfriend was really surprised and she said, "Do you know her?" I said, "No, that's a prostitute, Rosie." And she said, "No way!" And this girl was running up to the truck waving at us. People put down all these Natives who have problems and who are poor and on the street, but for me, they are my strength and my power. I talk to Native people on the street all the time, and they're there because they have problems that they can't deal with. They don't have the power to get up and say, "Hey, I gotta change." The main reason Native people drink is because they have problems they can't deal with. I have so many relatives that just can't get out of that, they can't just get up and walk off the reserve. When I see those people on the street it empowers me to make something of myself.

TA: *How are you going to take up the struggle for survival that has brought our people to this point?*
MIKA: I think that to break free, we have to link up with other indigenous people all over the world, because they're dealing with lots of the same problems that we are, like racism and land issues. We have to look at what they're doing, and work together with them, because you can't do it as one nation, you kind of have to think globally and deal with it all together. It makes you more powerful that way.
CHRIS: Self-government, or anything like that, should not be funded by the federal government, and should not answer to the higher person— which is the non-native person. We need to have something organized by our own people. Our own educated people need to build our own things before we move on to self-government. Right now, we're asking the white govern-

ment to give it to us. That's not really any good, because then we've got to answer to them. That's not what we want, eh? We want to do it ourselves. That's what I think our leaders should be doing; but people can just talk and talk and say, "Yeah, we can do this," but to actually do it is something else, not just to bullshit.

SHANA: There's this massive push for sovereignty or for freedom or liberation from the government which oppresses us. But then, the result will, in my opinion, be the same. We'll be under the same structures, the way we've been educated. Even in institutions like the university, we're educated in the way of the people that dominate us. You're not going to get people who are not whole to gather together and support this cause; they have to be whole and they have to have the same direction. There needs to be people who go back to their communities and try to make a difference and try to build strength again. With that strength, you can then start to build a sovereign nation. But I don't think it can happen just by asking to be separate from the government, because the result will just end up being the same as we have now.

MARILYN: Our people have to learn how to live without the Indian Act. There's so much of a dependence on that. It's like, "That's where our rights derive from..." That kind of thing is really what's perpetuating our dependence on the Canadian government. Really. Our rights are here because we're here. We occupied this land before anybody else was here and that's where our rights come from. If we learn to depend on the Indian Act, and like, "That's the only thing that's given us our aboriginal rights..." We should start with that, just get rid of it altogether and learn how to make alliances across the country so that we stand united instead of being separate units. If you can build strength that way, then you have a base from which you can start turning the tables— *we* can make the demands and not have to follow *their* rules anymore.

This is the spirit of regeneration. The youth are clear-eyed and so, so smart. And they are impatient, not only with white society, but with their own leadership and organizations. They know what the priority is, and they will not take bullshit for an answer. The challenge is to combine the energy and strength of these youth with the collective wisdom of older people who have the cultural knowledge and strategic and tactical experience. Translating Onkwehonwe teachings into a concrete set of goals for a social and political movement is the vital task for the future. Transcending strictly materialist concerns and the fetishism of money means going beyond the constrained thinking that is embodied in the visions of decolonization that would have us accept a share of the status quo in place of real justice for fear of the inevitable

264

reprisals against action. Self-government agreements, land claims settlements, and aboriginal rights doctrines all contain basic concessions to the colonial status quo. And, as the young Onkwehonwe I spoke with in Saskatchewan pointed out, these things are not really what we want anyway, heh?

There is a logic to the injustice contained in the whole analysis of history, economics, and politics we call "colonialism." And there is also a logic to achieving justice as well. It is a logic of defeating imperialism's genocidal intent with the perseverance and the continuing survival of our indigenous nations, overcoming its destruction of culture with our revitalized social and cultural existences, and opposing its imposition of a weakening isolation by re-establishing crucial connections that strengthen and sustain our peoples.

In concrete terms, this means people must come to share a genuine concern for the future of our nations—outside of simply thinking about how the idea of their people's nationhood promotes their own individual interests—and must construct an alternative vision that can offer release from the interminable war that has poisoned relations and psyches on both sides of the divide between Onkwehonwe and Settlers. In spite of the vast amount of money spent by governments and corporations to obscure the truth of the situation, we are at a political and social stalemate in the so-called reconciliation process. The economic injustices, social problems, and inconsistencies of the law are well known, yet the economic impact of the moral and logical means of redress and recompense for Onkwehonwe remain intolerable to the Settlers. Existing paths for reconciliation of colonialism are failing on many different fronts, most importantly as a means of resolving satisfactorily the injustices of colonialism in the hearts and minds of the younger generations of Onkwehonwe leaders.

The present framework and the end-state of the decolonization process has left our societies nose-to-nose and on the verge of a violent future. Think about it. Either Onkwehonwe accept the Settlers' response that justice is unaffordable or simply too onerous a cost for them to pay—an acceptance that would mean Onkwehonwe will continue the suicidal death spiral we are currently embroiled in—or Onkwehonwe will rise to challenge the Settlers' cowardly and selfish unwillingness to redress injustices. Having exhausted all legal and political means to bring justice to the relationship, Onkwehonwe will begin to engage the Settlers in a real struggle for land and the power to determine their own future.

Onkwehonwe may choose to use violence as their means of confrontation. But there is an alternative, one which respects the rights and humanity of both Onkwehonwe and the Settlers. Further, it is one that seeks to

265

create a future in which the original treaty visions of peace and friendship are realized. However, it will take courage to think and act in support of those original visions and to challenge ourselves to go beyond solutions contained within and defined by a greedy, ignorant, and consumption-obsessed culture. This means that Settlers will need to grow beyond their cultural arrogance and learn to be pluralist in their worldviews. And for Onkwehonwe, it will mean generating governing capacity, economic self-sufficiency, and internal social reforms.

Space must be created—intellectually and socially—for peace to be achieved. In the Rotinoshonni Great Law of Peace, the Kaianerekowa, there is reference to "the clearing," the space between the village and the woods, between home, family, safety and the dangerous space of freedom. Before any agreement or reconciliation can happen, there must be a connection made between people, there must be a demonstration of respect, and love must be generated. Then and only then can "issues" and interests be spoken of sincerely and resolved. This is what a commitment to coexist means.

The notion of a universal relation among autonomous elements of Creation is embedded throughout indigenous cultures, for example, in the *Tekani Teioha:te*, known as the Two Row Wampum, or the widely used Four Directions teaching. The idea of recognizing our universal connection and at the same time respecting our differences is the fundamental theme in these teachings; it is the first principle that must be regenerated in our lives and brought to meaning in non-indigenous cultures and society. Understanding and accepting this first principle and Original Instruction is crucial. Without a recognition of the holism of the universe, there can never be peace among peoples here on earth. We must overcome the ethical constraints of the Judeo-Christian heritage of empire, which set us on a path of a self-centred, violent contest between peoples divided over delusions of their own superiority. We need, as a whole race, to recognize and transcend the primitive ethic which has become so destructive as it merged with the technological means of dominance and advanced weaponry of modern empires. We need to move to accept the interdependency of all people and beings. Existing outside of empire, indigenous spiritualities can be the foundations for the cultures of universal responsibility and respect that are needed to achieve peaceful coexistence and ensure our survival on this earth.

From the spiritual to the political, this means committing ourselves to make fundamental shifts in relations of power between peoples. We must move from colonial-imperialist relations to pluralist multinational associations of autonomous peoples and territories that respect the basic imperatives of indigenous cultures as well as preserve the stability and benefits of coopera-tive confederal relations between indigenous nations and other governments.

Recognizing that violence is the foundation of state power and that vio-lence is expressed implicitly in all of its institutions, we must acknowledge that social peace is not a benign situation. Social stability, as it is com-monly conceived, is in fact a relation of force, of acts and threats of violence, of a coercion of Onkwehonwe to silent surrender. Resistance to this injus-tice in either its open or implicit form means escaping the role Onkwehonwe have been assigned: not so much as victims in this post-modern age, but as complicit subjects of violence and threats of destruction. Complicity is the large problem, because in its relation with indigenous peoples, the state has evolved to the point where terror has been embedded into Onkwehonwe societies, ensuring complicity without the common use or explicit threat of punishing force. Yet, we are always reminded, in popular culture and in everyday language, of the past effectiveness and future potentiality of vio-lence being turned against us. Onkwehonwe who reason within the frame-work of the dominant mentality and through the lens of their colonized cultures are made incapable of defending themselves from annihilation. Without breaking the psychologies of imperialism and the mentality of colonization, organizing resistance is futile.

But freed from the culture of complacency and using the technique of applied intelligence, it is possible to generate a new perspective on the state and new potentialities for movement towards resistance and far beyond that to the resurgence of Onkwehonwe power and the reconstruction of soci-ety as a whole. We live in an age when, because of the refinement of state coercion away from a war machine into an integrated belief system oper-ating exclusively within the realm of relations between indigenous com-munities and the state itself, the state has cultivated an image of itself as beneficent and honourable in its dealings with Onkwehonwe—although this is completely against all facts.

If the legal and political power that states and Settler populations have over Onkwehonwe is based on complicity, then the first question for a people seeking freedom should be: "Is the state capable and willing to use violence to enforce existing laws and policies, beyond intimidation of indi-viduals and small isolated groups?" If the state is confronted by a widespread movement and intensive, coordinated, collective action by Onkwehonwe to reoccupy their lands and reassert their rights and freedoms, the answer would be "no." The political objective should be to force a social and polit-ical crisis on two fronts:

1. a disjuncture between the political consciousness of the Settler society and the realities of state power (meaning, in Canada for example, the disconnect between that country's weighty claims and its light armaments); and

2. a moral conflict between contemporary Settler identities and the forced renewal of the need for the use of explicit colonizing violence (the psychological conflict between the self-perception of being a peaceful, safe, stable, and just democratic society and scenes of open violent repression of indigenous peoples).

As a result of these disjunctures and the exposure of illogic and incapacity, the legal regime and the institutions of power in the society would be forced to adjust to the realities of power. And the Settler public as a whole would reject the use of state violence in support of colonial objectives against Onkwehonwe because of the social chaos it would quickly and thoroughly produce.

In this environment, the most basic changes in colonial states required to create a just relationship and to set the foundation for lasting peaceful coexistence will finally become achievable: the return of unceded lands, reforms to state constitutions to reflect the principle of indigenous nationhood and to bring into effect a nation-to-nation relationship between indigenous peoples and Settler society, and restitution.[45]

Our notion of power must evolve to address the political and social reality of the twenty-first century. Onkwehonwe possess neither economic nor political power. Therefore, we have no way to bring about change in the political system in place today. As things stand, we have been set up in a losing contest with the state over "rights"; thus, assimilation or isolated self-destruction are the only choices for Onkwehonwe who refuse to accept and adapt to colonialism. The only hope for indigenous peoples to survive as nations is in the power of movements outside of the established political structures and beyond the paths provided by state law and government policies. These times call for the generation of new power by new means. One of these is to gain economic power and thus the basic means to influence law and policy. The other, short of immediate access to land to generate economic power, is to reorganize ourselves to force change through the power of the demonstration of our collective will to survive. The white man has set the rules: assimilate or self-destruct. It is time to change the rules.

Eddy Benton-Benai, the Anishnaabe spiritual leader, has said, "Personally, I am sovereign. So sovereignty isn't something someone gives you. It's a responsibility you carry inside yourself. In order for my people to achieve sovereignty, each man and woman among us has to be sovereign."[46] The guiding wisdom of this is that we must live fully the lives we have been given and confront the challenges that are in front of us. True heroes take up these challenges with courage, dignity, and integrity. They symbolize and activate the hopes, dreams, and ideals of the young people of their generation. These people are true revolutionaries—some even unconsciously so. They are people who change the world by first gaining an understanding of the dynamics of the world they are living in and then by engaging those forces to generate a new reality.

I often think of the example set by Mahatma Gandhi, who was faced with the challenge of modernity brought to India by British colonialism, which resulted in the overturning of tradition and the political and economic transformation of Indian society and the assumption of British dominance over India in the severe chaos that followed in the wake of this transformation. One way of looking at what Gandhi did for India is to see that he made Indians understand their world and gave them a way to gain control over their lives again. His method was particular to him; he worked out an answer to the question of modernity for Indians by what he called "experiments with truth" in his own life. He decolonized himself through trial and error, then shared the message with his people. Gandhi was a unique person and hero, but the challenges and choices he and other Indians faced are basically the same as the ones young Onkwehonwe face today. It is not by any means a simple choice between an obvious good and evil, nor are the answers that emerge even palatable at first glance: emulation of the colonizer, uncritically accepting either colonialism or resistance and the traditionalist reaction to it. What Gandhi did was challenge *both* colonialism and tradition; he created a new reality for Indians by generating an entirely new form of struggle out of his heritage.[47]

When I reflect on what Gandhi did for India, I am reminded yet again of the power of our own Onkwehonwe teachings. It seems to me that Gandhi's philosophy and practice were no different than what the Anishnaabe elder Jimmy O'Chiese, spiritual leader of the Anishnaabe people in the foothills of the Rocky Mountains, told me when I asked him what it was to be indigenous: "To be born from the land, to follow natural law... relationship... respect... hard work... self-sufficiency."[48]

The last conversation I will share is one I had with two people who have never met Jimmy O'Chiese and who are of a different age and a different nation, separated from Jimmy by thousands of miles and vastly different circumstances of life, but who nonetheless are one with him and all of the other indigenous people who understand implicitly the meaning of the words he shared with me that morning standing outside his sweat lodge.

Teyowisonte and Konwatsi'tsá:wi are two young Kanien'kehaka who embody in their minds and in the practice of their lives all of the truths I have discovered in my quest to understand what it is to be Onkwehonwe and a warrior.[49] Teyowisonte has been involved with the Mohawk Warrior Society since he was a young teenager, which gives him a good perspective on not only the philosophical but operational aspects of asserting an Onkwehonwe identity. I was interested in talking with both of them about their concept of a "warrior" and understanding how they saw our peoples' struggles playing out in their own lives and in public life in Onkwehonwe communities. Where did their ideas come from? Were the ideas that guided them as young people changing now that they were taking on different responsibilities in the community and more mature identities in their own lives? I believe these are crucial questions not only for people living in their home community of Kahnawake, but for all indigenous nations.

I started our conversation by remarking on how interesting it was that Teyowisonte's bookshelf held books by Che Guevara, Mao, the Nation of Islam, and even *The Lord of the Flies*, but didn't have much in the way of "indigenous" or "First Nations" literature.

TA: *Are none of your literary or philosophical influences from Onkwehonwe traditions?*
TEYOWISONTE: Nope. The only thing is, Che Guevara did say that the land should go back to the indigenous people. And what you said about my influences, I'll take that even further. I have to say, I've always seen the Iroquois Confederacy as being just like the movie *Star Wars*! I was weaned on that stuff since it first came out, and since at least 1990, I've seen myself as Luke Skywalker! You know, I'm going to restore freedom to the nation. (Laughter.) I've been in that romantic rut ever since. Anyway, I think we all have an innate thirst for adventure...

TA: *The Great Law of Peace is "The Force"?*
TEYOWISONTE: Yeah, because it binds us. It penetrates and it holds the galaxy together.

TA: *So, Luke, tell me: Who's Darth Vader in this worldview?*
TEYOWISONTE: The sad thing is that "DV" is actually our own older people, the ones who took the traditional knowledge and tried to do things

270

too fast. A lot of the people that I used to look up to were manipulated because they just dove into it too fast, and they thought they knew everything. It was undisciplined. Discipline is one of Che Guevara's biggest teachings. When you rush into something, you let go of that discipline. That's when bad things start to happen.

TA: *Che Guevara's basic message was one of armed resistance. Armed force, violence, used against the United States as the centre of the evil empire—to stick with your Star Wars analogy. This is key to his idea. Is that a good message to be sending to our people?*
TEYOWISONTE: That's something I struggle with: the thirst for adventure. You have to keep it disciplined, that whole adventure part. It's like boxing, in a way. I have my training tips taped to my fridge to remind myself: "Never Get Mad." Because if you take off that discipline, you're leaving yourself subject to something you're not expecting.

TA: *That sounds like something from* The Art of War.[50]
TEYOWISONTE: I think it's more my boxing training, because it's something I figured out on my own. When I read *The Art of War*, it just reinforced what I already knew. It's kind of like our traditional Longhouse teachings, they reinforced what I already knew from *Star Wars*! (Laughter.) I'll tell you, my evolution as a thinker started when I was 14 years old, as a fighting person. From 1990 on, I was just waiting for the next fight. I wouldn't say I wasted my teenage years, but since then, I've dedicated my life to that cause. My weekends were spent at checkpoints, going on recon patrols, patrolling town, patrolling the perimeter, learning how and then timing ourselves on how fast we could dismantle AK-47s. That was our culture at the time. Every day was just waiting for the next war. When is it going to happen? Of course, we were all taught that the ideological basis of what we were doing was the Longhouse, and we were taught the Longhouse way of life. So, from that point on, I studied what I was going to be fighting for. That's what we did.

But over time, we became disillusioned with our leaders, after finding out that what they were fighting for was more about what was going into their own pockets rather than for the good of the Nation. Once I found that out, I left the rhetoric and I started trying to find the true meaning of our teachings: peace, power, and righteousness; the power of the good mind. From that point on, you could say I became more open-minded. I started talking to people whom I would have considered "the enemy" when I was a bit younger. I moved away from thinking that the Warriors were a secret society. I started to believe that we should be more open about what we think, and the things our teachers were talking about. That's when I felt a burden lift off of me. You know? I felt a lot more comfortable with what I was doing and with the things I was talking about.

TA: *What have you learned through all of this about the meaning of the traditional teachings?*
TEYOWISONTE: I think that so much of it is common sense. Traditional teachings are just common sense. They are ideologies of common sense that have been refined over a long period of time. When you adopt Longhouse teachings, you're finding a way to recognize elements that are already out there and using them to better yourself, your life, and the life of the collective. And all of these are great ideas. I really do believe that they are great ideas. But in time, we lost them. We lost it, that greatness. We lost it through colonization, both voluntary and involuntary.

TA: *You have any ideas on how we become, as you say, "great" again?*
TEYOWISONTE: One of the components in my own thinking is this: self-betterment for the collective. I said this in a speech to the graduating class at the high school a couple of years ago. I said to them, "Now you're going to embark on your life journey. The trick is to learn as much as you can and to try to accomplish personal success. Through a number of personal successes, we are going to achieve a collective victory." I believe that whether you're an ironworker, an artist, a writer, or whatever, every one of these occupations has a place in our collective, in our Nation. We need all of these people strategically placed for the collective. So my advice to those students, and this is a significant part of the warrior spirit, is to go about your life in that way. You have a certain thing that you want to accomplish? Go for it.

That, of course, combined with fighting spirit. Fighting spirit is essential. We can't have a passive attitude. I mean, we have to exhibit self-restraint and discipline and these other things, but we have to have an attitude where we can see ourselves victorious. It's like Che used to say, "Until the Victory, Forever!" We have to have that. That's the way we are going to succeed. You can never doubt these things, because the smallest bit of doubt will stop it from happening.

TA: *Lots of people will share your view of history and agree with your principles in theory. But most people react with fear or skepticism when you start talking about armed resistance.*

TEYOWISONTE: A significant number of our people are complacent. They are stuck being too comfortable. They don't want to do anything to jeopardize their standing, you know? They don't want to lose their jobs; they don't want to rock the boat. And unfortunately, in their minds, when you bring up weapons, that is about the most boat-rocking kind of thing that you can do.

TA: *What do you mean by "armed resistance"? Are you talking about pulling some IRA or PLO kind of shit, or what?*
TEYOWISONTE: I don't think you can justify doing things like blowing up buildings or killing innocent people. We can't justify initiating armed activity. Especially in our case, it'll just do damage to the cause. Our weapons are strictly, strictly, for defence. The only time weapons should be used is when all peaceful means have been exhausted.

TA: *What does that mean?*
TEYOWISONTE: That means when the leadership is at a stalemate and the only thing that is going to save us is to pick up our weapons.

TA: *So "armed resistance" is the defence of life, property, and well-being?*
TEYOWISONTE: I always say it like this: "The Warrior Society is in the business of defending people and territory." You're the one who said the word, "property," but I wouldn't even include businesses myself. Us Mohawks, particularly the Warrior Society, got a bad name because we were always associated with cigarette smuggling and super bingos. I'll tell you something, when I was out there, it wasn't for cigarettes and bingo. I was defending the people and the territory. Every nation has the right to defend itself, and we are no different than any other nation.

TA: *I guess what you're saying is that if we have the rhetoric of nationhood, then we have to act like it too.*
TEYOWISONTE: It reflects sacrifice and devotion. You have to have a national defence establishment; it's a symbol of your acquiescence if you don't.

TA: *Have you sacrificed anything, walking this warrior's path?*
TEYOWISONTE: Highly paid jobs, I would say!

TA: *But hey, I look around this place, and it's a nice house, your girlfriend is sitting in her chair smiling at you, there's a couple of fat cats on the couch, and you seem to be happy and healthy. It doesn't seem much like a life of sacrifice.*

273

TEYOWISONTE: Everything you see here, we worked hard for. I never did, and neither did she, take the easy street. We went to school, and we did what we had to do. I think things might have been easier if...
KONWATSI'TSÁ:WI: If you worked for the band council!
TEYOWISONTE: Yeah, if I worked for band council. The other sacrifice is this: total frustration in your life! Every day, you see the people in the community doing whatever they want to do. We even had a drive-by shooting right here in our back yard a couple of weeks ago. I see things like that, and I can't believe they are happening when we have such a great alternative to the troubles and vices we've inherited. We have such a great alternative in our traditional culture, but yet we choose to ignore it. Dealing with that frustration is one of the biggest sacrifices we make. When I see these things going on, there's always the temptation to say, "The hell with it," and to go get drunk, or do whatever. But it all comes back to discipline.

TA: *Listening to you speak, lots of people would hear reasons to not do something, like, excuses for inaction. I could almost hear people saying, "I'd get fired from my job if I did that." Or, "I can't just take off for weeks at a time, my wife would dump me for sure!" Or, "I can't get involved with those radical assholes, my friends won't party with me anymore."*
TEYOWISONTE: I haven't made too many enemies. I think that's because when I put out my vision, if it's criticisms I'm offering, I always have solutions to go along with them. One of our teachings is that we're always supposed to show respect to all living things, no matter who they are. In the interests of peace, you have to maintain a certain attitude of respect for others.

TA: *What about some of the things you've gained by following this path?*
TEYOWISONTE: I get to influence people, and educate people. A lot of people come up to me and say that I'm opening their eyes to things they never knew before, and that feels good. Yeah. Also, I have to say that one of the biggest rewards is just being enlightened to our way of life. Having this knowledge makes it easier to deal with the frustrations of life. Longhouse ways teach you how to have an exterior that repels *kanikonraksa*, "the bad mind." It puts a kind of emotional and mental bullet-proof vest on you. It teaches you to deal with just simple things in life. If you look at the story of the Great Law, it teaches you about yourself and to ask, "Are you doing all you can?" Or, "Is the path you're on the right one for you?" It celebrates renewal and doesn't dwell on the past.

TA: *What makes you different from so many other young people who, it seems to me, don't give a damn about any of this?*
KONWATSI'TSÁ:WI: We don't drink, we don't do drugs, we don't smoke. We try to be as independent as we can be. We were both "only children," with predominantly absent parents, and we were forced to raise ourselves. And in that, we learned to value independence and to not resent the parenting we didn't have. Instead, we learned to value what we could give ourselves.
TEYOWISONTE: I totally agree with her. Another thing is the idea that you should practise what you preach. If I'm going to go around telling everybody that we have to be financially independent and politically autonomous, well, what am I doing on my own to achieve that? It's also practising things like keeping a garden—having our own food is one more part of making our nation independent. And if we build a house that doesn't have to rely on Hydro power so much, or not at all, then that's another step for the Nation.

TA: *That kind of consistency in one's thought and deed is rare these days, anywhere.*
TEYOWISONTE: This is the traditional concept of "autonomous responsibility." This idea is a big part of our traditional culture; it means that you lead your own life consciously aware of how your actions affect the Nation. In my own career, I do artwork. I could be trying to get a job in the city, in a marketing firm, or whatever. I could probably do that, since I have the training and the talent. But instead, I work in a school here in Kahnawake, and I don't get paid nearly as much as if I were working in the city. But the thing is, I'm using my talents and the gifts that I have for the good of the Nation.
KONWATSI'TSÁ:WI: "Autonomous responsibility" is a big-picture form of respect. It's not really so much like a responsibility if you have that respect to begin with.
TEYOWISONTE: It's self-discipline. Like they say in our language, we're *Rotiskenhrakete*, "they're carrying the bones." It means that we are carrying the legacy of our ancestors. That's what autonomous responsibility is: carrying that burden. It comes out in everything that you do. For me, when I do my artwork, I'm fulfilling my autonomous responsibility to the Nation.

TA: *You've put a lot of thought into how to achieve balance between the reality of this colonized world and living an authentic Onkwehonwe life. It means sacrificing something, in this case money. It means you don't get paid what the labour market says you should be getting paid for your talents, but yet you are able to live a comfortable life and one that is not compromised politically. That's the important thing.*

TEYOWISONTE: There's a certain integrity to that; it's a "dignity in poverty" kind of thing. I was just told this by one of our elders recently. He said to me, "I don't think we Indians were meant to be rich. Cigarette money, bingo, all those things did more damage than good." That's important to think about.

TA: *He's right. There are a lot of compromises you have to make if you want to be rich. But let's talk revolution some more. In your mind, how will the revolution unfold, and what will be your role in it?*
TEYOWISONTE: First of all, I hope that my vision will be victorious here in my own community. From there, it will expand and harmonize with the rest of our nation and then with the other Iroquois nations. Once we have that, the ultimate vision is for a union of independent indigenous nations in the whole of the Western Hemisphere. That's my ultimate vision. It's similar to what Che had in mind for South America, but he didn't make it because he jumped the gun and went right away to armed revolution. In my vision, I don't think of revolution in the common contemporary sense of the word. I see "revolution" in the technical sense of the word, meaning our situation will evolve, or revolve.

TA: *That's interesting, because the original meaning of the word, in Latin, and in early European thinking, was, as you say, "technical." It described a cycle or something coming around again.*
TEYOWISONTE: I think that each indigenous society had achieved a nearly perfect utopia-like state in our social and political organization. But because of colonization, we were de-evolved: we lost what made us great. We lost our culture, we lost our freedom.

TA: *I heard my friend Leroy Little Bear say once that we were "de-cultured" by colonization.*
TEYOWISONTE: That's a perfect way of describing it. And now what we're trying to do is re-evolve back to that great state. This effort is reinforced by traditional teachings because through them we learn that everything happens in cycles. Everything begins and ends and turns into the same thing again. This is the way of the world.

TA: *Is your vision of the future a threat to white people?*
TEYOWISONTE: I could see the ultimate stage of the indigenous revolution being so. But as far as our nation goes, we're not a threat to them.

276

As Mohawks, we're bound by the principles of the Two Row Wampum, and we have to respect each other's independence and each other's way of life. Hopefully, an indigenous revolutionary movement would thirst for something similar to the guidelines of the Two Row, so that it wouldn't look to banish white people from the continent or to storm their parliament buildings and bring them down. Although, if you think about it, that would be pretty cool! (Laughter.) Victory to me means everybody having political autonomy, economic independence, and a way of life that they choose, including white people.

KONWATSI'TSÁ:WI: I think that the real threat is fear. Fear of the revolution is scarier than the actual revolution itself. Both sides have fear. That's why our people behave so complacently, because they fear retaliation. Other people fear what we can do, not with a stick, but legally, worldwide, with the rights we have. I think that's the threat they see. But here's where education comes in again: they need to understand that we're not trying to send people back to England or France and that we just want some acknowledgement.

TA: *In this struggle, where is the battlefield?*

TEYOWISONTE: The battlefield is in my garden, and it's everywhere, the whole of North America. It may not be a battlefield filled with soldiers and tanks—although we've seen that it comes to that sometimes. It's accepting our teachings and following through with our teachings, wherever that takes us.

KONWATSI'TSÁ:WI: I think the real battlefield is the arena of educated opinion. Like when we talk about having a garden and all of that, people will say, "Why do you keep a garden anyway?" And then when we talk to them about it, the reasons come out, those people say, "Hey, that's a good idea." Your battlefield is the process of getting people to believe in your ideas. If you truly believe that you're right, you won't have to stuff it down anyone's throat. They will end up saying, "That's really smart, you're right." Then, right there, you have support for your cause. In our contemporary society, where news travels so fast, you have to have support, and you have to have most of the people behind you. The best way to make this happen is to educate them as much as possible about your goals and your means. That way their support isn't fickle, and they're not going to sway with whoever else comes along talking.

A long time ago, our people didn't need to be educated about these things. They knew it from being raised in the culture. They trusted their leaders because they knew who they were and that they would be good for the community. We didn't need education; we had trust. But now there's too much mistrust, and there's too much potential for being led astray. Today, we can't afford to be sheep following anyone around. We need to be the wolves.

The indigenous intelligence and clear-minded commitment to remaking their lives which are so evident in these two Kanien'kehaka result from raising young people in an indigenized culture of resurgence, disentangled from the colonial mentalities that are still oppressing the vast majority of Onkwehonwe. Key to this mentality is the release from dependency on the colonial state and regaining our independence in every form possible: financial, political, physical, and psychological.

Yet for so many of our people, even forms of freedom that imply a severance of one's reliance upon the comfortable yet corrupting state welfare and other governmental programs are unthinkable. These people do not have the benefit of the kind of leaders and teachers and the cultural rootedness that produces people like Teyowisonte and Konwatsi'tsá:wi and the other young warriors that live in our communities. The distinction between the warriors and the still-colonized reminds us that decolonization happens at a different pace and in different ways for everyone and in every community.

Withdrawal from our dependency on the state is like breaking an addiction. Communities and individuals are all at different stages of this separation from their harmful dependency on colonial government moneys and ideas; they exhibit on a personal and collective level the very same symptoms of an addict who is drug dependent and trying to break free. The effects of this withdrawal syndrome are usually attributed by health professionals and psychologists to biological causes (poor health) or to cultural factors (social suffering). These are certainly realities and factor into people's problems. But, overall, the root cause of the whole spectrum of health and psycho-social affect is the political and economic situation of Onkwehonwe as colonized peoples: the law and the government of the colonial state have dispossessed Onkwehonwe from the lands that are the source of their health and well-being in psychological, physical, and cultural terms.

As it stands, the psycho-social syndrome caused by dispossession and colonization manifests as a whole set of attitudes and behaviours that are all too common among our people and consistent among all peoples enduring a colonial relation. At the risk of sounding insulting or insensitive (I do not mean to be either one), I argue that we need to acknowledge how our contemporary cultures have been shaped by colonialism. If we are to transcend our present reality and transform our situations, many more of us need to start walking the warrior's path by looking honestly at how our contemporary community cultures have been shaped to service and validate the image of the "Indian" created by white society in its drive to divide, disempower, and ultimately dehumanize our peoples. Do I need to spell out the basic flaws in our contemporary colonial character? Again, I do not intend insult or further injury, but acknowledged truths, though sometimes painful to administer, are powerful medicine.

Rather than taking the fight to the white man, the true source of the injustice in our lives, indigenous men are aggressive against their own people. This is a form of self-hatred that is not open, but hidden and coded, especially in the behaviour of our supposed community leaders towards young women and the open disrespect shown by many of our people for their own languages, traditions, and elders. Plain facts are denied, and people willingly participate in the delusion of normalcy as a cover for the loneliness and emptiness that is inside Onkwehonwe who are disconnected from their lands, their communities, and their cultures (which is to say, all of us). We all know people who are aloof or who act as if they think they are too good for everyone else in their community and turn their back on their own people. It hardly needs to be pointed out again how self-destruction—most commonly by obesity, drugs, and alcohol—affects our families and nations. But we don't often associate the excessive emotionalism of many of our people as a symptom of colonization, nor do we attribute the recent rise of Christian religiosity or other mystical forms of traditionalism as substituting religion for action. These too are part of the syndrome of colonial behaviours.

And these behaviours are all inauthentic to being Onkwehonwe. They are directly attributable to the psychological and social damage that has been suffered by our people. None of what I am calling the characteristics of contemporary indigenous community life are acceptable if we hope to survive as peoples. But how do we change these behaviour patterns once they are recognized for what they truly are?

The cure for the colonizer's disease that has affected us all at the core of our existence and that lives inside us is not a public, political exercise and not a method of mass movement. People must be made whole and strong and real again before they can embark on a larger struggle. The antidote for this painful affliction consists of self-transformation encouraged through one-to-one mentoring, face-to-face interaction, and small-group dialogue to effect the regeneration of our minds, bodies, and spirits. This is the ancient way of the warrior. All cultures and ancient traditions contain essentially the same teaching on transcendence, which is that regeneration starts with a thorough and proper investigation of one's own life. It is a form of self-challenge, a contest really, between the lies and the truth of the self, where the task is to convince us to take care of ourselves and to change our lives—to internalize the warrior's journey, the self-challenge, and the struggle to remake reality on a different and more truthful footing.[51]

In ancient Greek society, people formed healing circles to work out the truth among trusted friends, a form of mutual confession where each member in turn would disclose their thoughts, faults, misbehaviours, etc., a process that was described by them as "the salvation by one another." Our Onkwehonwe rituals and ceremonies serve the same purpose of taking our weak, or our weaknesses, and forging them into strength through shared struggle. This process of group consolation is crucial to true healing.

The ancient Greeks also had a concept called *parrhesia*, which referred to a kind of philosophical gaming and self-challenge. Directed towards those who were unashamed in their abuse of power, parrhesia involved challenging the powerful to verbal battles, forms of mind games, so as to expose their ignorance and their ignorance of their state of ignorance. This relates to another important aspect of the character of the decolonized, not in relation to our weakness but to those who have power and have been made overly prideful as opposed to hurt and humbled by their colonization. It may be thought that Onkwehonwe are less culturally adept or equipped to deal with confronting the colonized individual in such a public and direct way, but public debate and oratory were in fact ancient and venerated traditions among all of our peoples before we were silenced by white power. These ancient Onkwehonwe traditions can provide what the Greeks recognized as the necessary process of humiliating the ignorant and arrogant into seeing the lie of their wrong existence.

Decolonization, to make the point again, is a process of discovering the truth in a world created out of lies. It is thinking through what we think we *know* to what is actually true but is obscured by knowledge derived from our experiences as colonized peoples. The truth is the main struggle, and the struggle is manifest mainly inside our own heads. From there, it goes to our families and our communities and reverberates outward into the larger society, beginning to shape our relationship with it. In a colonized reality, our struggle is with all existing forms of political power, and to this fight, we bring our only real weapon: the power of truth.

Freedom is deliverance from the imperialism of the lies that keep us tied to realities that we despise and rebel against in self-destructive ways. It takes an absolute commitment and unwavering dedication to follow the struggle on this principle. Failure to do so has always led to failure to achieve any meaningful change in the relations between Onkwehonwe existences and the lie of empire.

The Zapatistas, whom I have been holding out as the most exemplary of Onkwehonwe movements, are illustrative of my vision of transformation and regeneration. The Zapatista movement started in the mid-1980s, when six people were involved in a strategic mission to protect the indigenous population of the Chiapas region of southern Mexico. They organized to protect the Mayan population from the mixed-blood retribution squads that served white landowners. The Zapatistas tried to accomplish their mission based first on revolutionary Marxist doctrines, but failed. It was not until they brought those foreign ideas together with a Catholic movement called Liberation Theology and the ideas of the indigenous culture that a new kind of movement capable of attracting support from the Mayan population was formed. This new movement was rooted and pragmatic; it recognized the absolute need to base indigenous struggles on indigenous truths articulated in indigenous ways in indigenous languages.[52] It was also a significant factor that the Mayans in Chiapas were "awakened" by a charismatic leader. Like with so many movements before it, stretching back to time immemorial all over the world, outsiders crossing boundaries brought a cross-fertilization of ideas as well as the important notion of deliverance to the Mayan people.

The interplay of these two factors—indigenous cultural roots and re-energizing via an awakening brought on by an outsider—led to what has come to be the only successful Onkwehonwe movement in recent generations of struggle. Taking a lesson from the Zapatistas, it is clear that movements for freedom and for social and political change in our time must develop new strategies and an action plan to seize free space, defining "liberation" as the achievement of autonomy in social, political, cultural, and economic spheres. And rather than setting out to destroy or replace the state or eject the colonizer, the end goal should be formulated as the achievement in positive terms of the creation of a new society. This is liberation as transformation. Anówara has felt this kind of movement in the past. It is akin to what we might call militant messianism, reminiscent of the great movement led by the Shawnee war chief Tecumseh and his brother, the prophet Tenskwatewa, in the early 1800s.[53]

Tecumseh's goal was to clear space on the ground for the free and unfettered existence of Onkwehonwe. His goal was not to live without white government, culture, and society, but to live *against them*. To do this today, Onkwehonwe warriors will need to engage the colonizer in a rebellion of truth, redefine the meaning of our renewed world in a mythic vision of struggle and justice, and force a reckoning with our regenerated and unified Onkwehonwe power through rites of resurgence. This is the warrior's path of spiritual self-determination that has been laid before us by the ancestors and the Brothers and Sisters who share our values and vision.

To close this book, I will state simply and concisely what I have learned so far on this journey to find the living heart and spirit of the Onkwehonwe. The overall challenge for all of us is to cause a mental awakening, beginning inside ourselves, to give people knowledge of themselves and of the world, thereby restoring the memory of who we truly are as Onkwehonwe. We need to make our people and our movement courageous again, by reinstilling the emotional fortitude that comes from being rooted in a strong community and supported by strong families. We need to heal and strengthen our bodies through discipline, hard work, and rejection of the junk food and trash culture of the mainstream society. And we need to reconnect with our indigenous spirituality, the foundations of our cultures and guarantors of psychological health. If we can work together toward accomplishing these things—liberation from domination, freedom from fear, a decolonized diet, a warrior ethic, and reconnection to indigenous cultures—then we will be freed from the cage of colonialism and know once again what it is to be Onkwehonwe on this land. We will be independent, self-reliant, respectful, sharing, spiritual, and adaptable. And we will be powerful in peaceful coexistence with those who live among and next to us as neighbours and friends. This is all that human beings have a right to ask for.

We have a long way to go. But I believe that Onkwehonwe will continue to live if we follow the path of struggle. As people taking up the challenge of confronting imperialism, we should take heart from what Gandhi said at his death fast, when he told people that, for him, after all he had been through, fulfillment lay "in the effort, not the attainment." This is the mark of the true spiritual warrior, and it is the spirit we must carry as we fight to regenerate our people. For all time and in all nations, being a warrior is living a life formed in the struggle for freedom and dignity.

So it is time to sing our war songs and continue on the journey.

Taneh Toh.

Watkwanoneraton tsi ionwentsateh, tanon ne rononkwe
rohnatahskwaronnion, tsi kanientarehnion, watnehkokwanionkwa,
ne onensteh tanon kahihsonha, onhnonkwasonha tanon tsi iokwiroton,
tanon ne iokwirowanens ientiniaheshas, tanon ne kario onkwatennatsera
ihken nahoten tehwaniaheshas, tanon nihtehwetha nahoten
iontionniosta tanon tsi tsionneh.

Onen enska neiokwanikonra.

NOTES

1 Subcomandante Marcos, *Our Word is Our Weapon* (New York, NY: Seven Stories Press, 2001) 86.

2 I met with Joan and Stewart Phillip at the offices of the UBCIC in Vancouver in May 2002.

3 See Peter McFarlane, *Brotherhood to Nationhood: George Manuel and the Making of the Modern Indian Movement* (Toronto: Between the Lines Press, 1993).

4 On the Canadian province of Ontario's 1995 armed assault on Stoney Point Anishnaabe people occupying land that had been seized by the Canadian government during World War II, see Peter Edwards, *One Dead Indian: The Premier, the Police, and the Ipperwash Crisis* (Toronto: McClelland and Stewart, 2003) as well as the extensive database of information and research collected for the official Government of Ontario inquiry into the incident: <http://www.ipperwashinquiry.ca/index.html>.

5 Felipe de Leon's research on this question was discussed in "An Anthropology of Happiness," *The Economist* 361 (20 December 2001): 42–43.

6 I spoke with Sximina in the House of Smayusta at the Nuxalk Nation in October 2001.

7 Gandhi, *An Autobiography*.

8 See Arthur C. Parker, *The Code of Handsome Lake, The Seneca Prophet* (Albany, NY: University of the State of New York, 1913); Annemarie Anrod Shimony, *Conservatism among the Iroquois at the Six Nations Reserve* (Syracuse, NY: Syracuse University Press, 1994); and Anthony F.C. Wallace, *The Death of Rebirth of the Seneca* (New York, NY: Random House, 1969).

9 See Michael George Doxtater, *Indigenology: A Decolonizing Learning Method for Emancipating Iroquois and World Indigenous Knowledge* (PhD dissertation, Cornell University, 2001). The conclusions referred to here are found on page 10, and the quotation is taken from pages 265–66.

10 See Jiddu Krishnamurti, *Total Freedom* (New York, NY: HarperCollins, 1996) 88.

11 Chaliand, *Revolution in the Third World* 194.

12 Kyi, *Freedom From Fear* 183.

13 Fanon, *The Wretched of the Earth* 223.

14 Arendt, *On Revolution* 9, 44–56.

15 Fanon, *The Wretched of the Earth* 43, 222–225.

16 See Shridharani, *War Without Violence* 5-42, and Gandhi, *Non-Violent Resistance*.

17 Gandhi, *Non-Violent Resistance* 86–99.

18 See Doug Boyd, *Mad Bear: Spirit, Healing, and the Sacred in the Life of a Native American Medicine Man* (New York, NY: Simon and Schuster, 1994).

19 In this section, I draw on Tarrow, *Power in Movement* 111–40.

20 Extensive resources on the Mi'kmaq people and background information on the Burnt Church conflict can be found on the Internet at Mi'kmaq Resource Centre <http://mrc.uccb.ns.ca/>.

21 Internet resources regarding the administrative structure, operations, and budgets of the Mohawk Council of Kahnawake and the council's ancillary structures include the council's own Website <http://www.kahnawake.com> and the anti-band council watchdog Website <http://www.kahonwes.com>.

22 Marcos, *Our Word is Our Weapon* 161.

23 See W. Dale Mason, *Indian Gaming: Tribal Sovereignty and American Politics* (Norman, OK: University of Oklahoma Press, 2000); Angela Mullis and David Kamper, eds., *Indian Gaming: Who Wins?* (Los Angeles, CA: University of California Indian Studies Center, 2000); and David E. Wilkins's excellent section on tribal political economy in his textbook, *American Indian Politics and the American Political System* (Lanham, MD: Rowman and Littlefield, 2002) 157–84.

24 Ray Halbritter was interviewed in the Executive Offices of the Turning Stone Casino on the Oneida Nation of New York in September 2001.

25 Alfred, *Heeding the Voices of Our Ancestors.*

26 Alfred, *Peace, Power, Righteousness.*

27 Raronhianonha was interviewed at a Dunkin Donuts shop in Dorval, Québec, in September 2001.

28 See Alfred, *Heeding the Voices of Our Ancestors* 149–82.

29 Tarrow, *Power in Movement* 23.

30 Ted Robert Gurr, *Why Men Rebel* (Princeton, NJ: Princeton University Press, 1970) 317.

31 Havel, *Disturbing the Peace* 109.

32 For more on the question of why movements go wrong, see Brecher, Costello, and Smith, *Globalization from Below* 30–66 and 115–17.

33 Samuel P. Huntington, *The Clash of Civilizations and the Remaking of World Order* (New York, NY: Simon and Schuster, 1997).

34 Malcolm X, *Malcolm X Speaks*, ed. George Breitman (Berkeley, CA: Grove Press, 1965) 221.

35 Oren Lyons was interviewed in the new arena on the Onondaga Nation in November 2001. See also Steve Wall and Harvey Arden, *Wisdomkeepers: Meetings with Native American Spiritual Elders* (Hillsboro, OR: Beyond Words Publishing, 1990) 64-71, and *Oren Lyons the Faithkeeper with Bill Moyers*, a Public Broadcasting Corporation documentary broadcast on PBS television on 3 July 1991.

36 See Chomsky, *Perspectives on Power* (Montréal, QC: Black Rose Books, 1997) 52–53; and also, Noam Chomsky, *New Horizons in the Study of Language and Mind* (Cambridge, UK: Cambridge University Press, 2000).

37 Luigi Luca Caveli-Sforza, *Genes, Peoples, and Languages* (New York, NY: Farrar, Strauss and Giroux, 2000).

38 Daniel Nettle and Suzanne Romain, *Vanishing Voices: The Extinction of the World's Languages* (New York, NY: Oxford University Press, 2000).

39 Nettle and Romain, *Vanishing Voices* 197. See also John McWhorter, *The Power of Babel* (New York, NY: HarperCollins, 2001).

40 For a discussion of the importance of storytelling to cultural rootedness in the context of colonial relations, see J. Edward Chamberlain, *If This Is Your Land, Where Are Your Stories? Finding Common Ground* (Toronto, ON: Alfred A. Knopf, 2003).

41 Here I am not referring to, and won't dignify with analyses, the New Age wannabes, patently phony plastic shamans, and other self-indulgent, capitalist, or corrupt so-called spiritual practices that unfortunately have become so widespread.

42 Here I am drawing on the *12 Principles of Indian Philosophy*, Four Worlds Development Project (Lethbridge, AB: University of Lethbridge, 1982).

43 I spoke with Kawinéhta and Gaihohwakohn at Oshweken on the Six Nations of the Grand reserve in September 2001.

44 Thanks to Patricia Monture-Angus and Darlene Okamaysim, in July 2002 at the University of Saskatchewan, I was introduced to and spoke with the group of young people, including Mika Settee, a 17-year-old Métis from Prince Albert; Chris Standing, a 17-year-old Dakota from Saskatoon; J. Brandon Monture, an 18-year-old Cree/Mohawk from the Thunderchild First Nation; Shana Laframbroise, a 24-year-old Métis nursing student from Saskatoon; and Marilyn Atsis, a 30-year-old Taku River Tlingit from northern British Columbia (who was at the time studying law at the university).

45 On restitution generally see Elazar Barkan, *The Guilt of Nations* (New York, NY: W.W. Norton, 2000); see the same source for arguments for and against restitution (xxxii) and the idea of decolonization as a "transaction" (168).

46 Harvey Arden and Steve Wall, *Travels in a Stone Canoe* (Richmond Hill, ON: Simon and Schuster, 1998) 95.

47 Here I draw on Sunil Khilnani's insights into Gandhi and his effect on Indian society, from the Introduction to Gandhi, *An Autobiography*.

48 I visited Jimmy O'Chiese's home and lodge on a hunting trip in the Rocky Mountain foothills near Hinton, AB in the fall of 2003.

49 I spoke with Teyowisonte and Konwatsi'tsá:wi in their home at Kahnawake in September 2001.

50 *The Art of War* is a classic text of war strategy and political counsel by the ancient Chinese philosopher Sun Tzu.

51 On this point and for the discussion of the ancient Greek idea of *parrhesia* I draw on Michel Foucault's analysis of Socrates and Greek traditions in Foucault, *Fearless Speech*, ed. Joseph Pearson (New York, NY: Semiotext[e], 2001) 103–33.

52 See Marcos, *Our Word is Our Weapon*.

53 See Sugden, *Tecumseh*.

glossary

ANÓWARAKOWA KAWENNOTE: "Great Turtle Island" (Kanienkeha: ah-NO-wara-go-wah ga-way-NOH-day), referring to the northern land mass of the continent of North America. I use it herein as *Anówara* in place of annoyingly persistent colonial terminology.

HATSKWI: (Kanienkeha: HUT-skwee) an expression of encouragement, akin to the English "Let's Go!"

KAHNAWAKE: "beside the rapids" (Kanienkeha: ga-na-WAH-gay), a Kanien'kehaka community. Also, *Kahnawakero:non* (ga-na-wa-gay-row-noon), the people of Kahnawake.

KAHWATSIRE: "all of our fires are connected" (Kanienkeha: ga-WAH-tzee-ray).

KAIENEREKOWA: "the great good way" (Kanienkeha: ga-yon-eh-ray-go-wa), referring to the Rotinoshonni Great Law of Peace.

KANIEN'KEHAKA: "people of the flint" (Kanienkeha: gun-ya-geh-haw-ga), the proper name for the Mohawk people. Also *Kanienkeha* (gun-ya-GEH-ha), the Mohawk language.

KANIKONRAKSA: "the bad mind" (Kanienkeha: ga-nee-goon-RUK-sa), unreasonableness.

KANIKONRIIO: "the good mind" (Kanienkeha: ga-nee-goon-REE-yo), reasonableness.

KANONSEHSNEHA: "the long-house way" (Kanienkeha: ga-noon-ses-nay-ha).

KARIHONNI: "the reason for…" (Kanienkeha: ga-ree-HO-nee).

KARIWEHS: "a long time" (Kanienkeha: ga-REE-wes).

KARIWIIO: (Kanienkeha: ga-ree-whee-yo), the Code of Handsome Lake.

KASHASTENSERA: (Kanienkeha: ga-saas-dun-say-ra) strength, power.

KONONKWE: (Kanienkeha: go-noon-gway), woman.

KONORONKWA: (Kanienkeha: go-no-roon-kwa), universal connection, or love.

KONORONKWASERA: (Kanienkeha: go-no-roon-GWAH-sir-raw), compassion.

OHENTEN KARIWATEHKWEN: "words that come before all else" (Kanienkeha: oh-honda ga-ree-wa-day-gwah), referring to the Thanksgiving Address of the Rotinoshonni.

ONKWEHONWE: "the original people" (Kanienkeha: oon-gway-hoon-way), referring to the First Peoples of North America.

ONKWEHONWENEHA: "the way of the original people" (Kanienkeha: oon-gway-hoon-way-NAY-ha).

ONKWEWENNA: "indigenous language" (Kanienkeha: oon-gway-waa-na).

OYENKO:OHNTOH: "hanging tobacco" (Kanienkeha: oh-yoh-CONE-doh), spiritual protectors, warriors.

ROTINOSHONNI: "the people of the longhouse" (Kanienkeha: ro-di-no-show-nee), referring to the people of what is commonly known as the Six Nations, or Iroquois Confederacy.

ROTISKENHRAKETE: "they carry the burden of peace" (Kanienkeha: row-dis-gun-ra-geh-tay), warriors.

SANISTONHA: "our mother" (Kanienkeha: sa-nee-stoon-ha).

SKENNEN: (Kanienkeha: ska-na) peace.

TEKANI TEIOHA:TE: "two roads" (Kanienkeha: day-ga-nee-day-yo-HAW-day), used to refer to the Two Row Wampum.

TÓ:SKE: (Kanienkeha: DOS-gay), a commonly used expression meaning, "It's True!"

WAKENÓRONSE: "insurmountable" (Kanienkeha: wah-gay-NO-roon-say).

WASÁSE: (Kanienkeha: wa-sáwz-say), a word in Rotinoshonni languages referring to the Thunder Dance, or the war dance.

bibliography

Ackerman, Peter, and Jack DuVall. *A Force More Powerful: A Century of Nonviolent Conflict*. New York, NY: Palgrave, 2000.

Alfred, Taiaiake (Gerald). *Heeding the Voices of Our Ancestors: Kahnawake Mohawk Politics and the Rise of Native Nationalism*. Don Mills, ON: Oxford University Press, 1995.

——. "From Sovereignty to Freedom: Towards an Indigenous Political Discourse." *Indigenous Affairs* 3/01 (2001): 22–34.

——. *Peace, Power, Righteousness: An Indigenous Manifesto*. Don Mills, ON: Oxford University Press, 1999.

—— (Gerald). "From Bad to Worse: Internal Politics in the 1990 Crisis at Kahnawake." *Northeast Indian Quarterly* 8,1 (Spring 1991): 23–32.

Alfred, Taiaiake, and Jeff Corntassel. "A Decade of Rhetoric for Indigenous Peoples." *Indian Country Today* (11 May 2004).

Alinsky, Saul. *Reveille for Radicals*. 1946; New York, NY: Vintage, 1969.

——. *Rules for Radicals: A Pragmatic Primer for Realistic Radicals*. New York, NY: Vintage, 1971.

"An Anthropology of Happiness," *The Economist* 361 (20 December 2001): 42–43.

Anaya, James. *Indigenous Peoples in International Law*. Oxford, UK: Oxford University Press, 1996.

Arden, Harvey, and Steve Wall. *Travels in a Stone Canoe*. Richmond Hill, ON: Simon and Schuster, 1998.

Arendt, Hannah. *On Revolution*. New York, NY: Penguin, 1963.

——. *On Violence*. Belmont, CA: Harcourt Brace, 1969.

Barkan, Elazar. *The Guilt of Nations: Restitution and Negotiating Historical Injustices*. New York, NY: W.W. Norton and Company, 2000.

Barsh, Russel, and Sakej Henderson. *The Road: Indian Tribes and Political Liberty*. Berkeley, CA: University of California Press, 1980.

Basic Call to Consciousness. Rev. ed. Hogansburg, NY: Akwesasne Notes, 1981.

Basso, Keith H. *Wisdom Sits in Places: Landscape and Language Among the Western Apache*. Albuquerque, NM: University of New Mexico Press, 1996.

Battiste, Marie, ed. *Reclaiming Indigenous Voice and Vision*. Vancouver, BC: University of British Columbia Press, 2000.

Bauerle, Phenocia, ed. *The Way of the Warrior: Stories of the Crow People*. Lincoln, NB: University of Nebraska Press, 2003.

Benn, Carl. *The Iroquois in the War of 1812*. Toronto, ON: University of Toronto Press, 1998.

Berman, Morris. *The Twilight of American Culture*. New York, NY: W.W. Norton and Company, 2000.

Besteman, Catherine. *Violence: A Reader*. New York, NY: New York University Press, 2002.

Bey, Hakim. *Immediatism*. San Francisco, CA: AK Press, 1994.

———. *T.A.Z.* San Francisco, CA: AK Press, 1985.

Bighorse, Tiana. *Bighorse the Warrior*. Ed. Noel Bennett. Tucson, AZ: University of Arizona Press, 1990.

Borrows, John. *Recovering Canada: The Resurgence of Indigenous Law*. Toronto, ON: University of Toronto Press, 2002.

Boyd, Doug. *Mad Bear: Spirit, Healing, and the Sacred in the Life of a Native American Medicine Man*. New York, NY: Simon and Schuster, 1994.

Branch, Taylor. *Pillar of Fire: American in the King Years, 1963-65*. New York, NY: Simon and Schuster, 1998.

Brecher, Jeremy, Tim Costello, and Brendan Smith. *Globalization from Below: The Power of Solidarity*. Cambridge, MA: South End Press, 2000.

Brody, Hugh. *The Other Side of Eden: Hunters, Farmers and the Shaping of the World*. Vancouver, BC: Douglas and McIntyre, 2000.

Brotherston, Gordon. *Book of the Fourth World: Reading the Native Americas Through Their Literature*. Cambridge, UK: Cambridge University Press, 1992.

Brysk, Allison. *From Tribal Village to Global Village: Indian Rights and International Relations in Latin America*. Stanford, CA: Stanford University Press, 2000.

Cairns, Alan. *Citizens Plus: Aboriginal Peoples and the Canadian State*. Vancouver, BC: University of British Columbia Press, 2000.

Campbell, Joseph. *Reflections on the Art of Living: A Joseph Campbell Companion*. Ed. Diane K. Osbon. New York, NY: HarperCollins, 1991.

Cardinal, Harold. *The Unjust Society*. 1969; Vancouver. BC: Douglas and MacIntyre, 1999.

Castaneda, Carlos. *The Teachings of Don Juan: A Yaqui Way of Knowledge*. New York, NY: Washington Square Press, 1998.

Casteñeda, Jorge. *Compañero: The Life and Death of Che Guevara*. New York, NY: Random House, 1997.

Caveli-Sforza, Luigi Luca. *Genes, Peoples, and Languages*. New York, NY: Farrar, Strauss and Giroux, 2000.

Césaire, Aimé. *Discourse on Colonialism*. New York, NY: Monthly Review Press, 1972.

Chaliand, Gérard. *Revolution in the Third World: Currents and Conflicts in Asia, Africa, and Latin America*. Rev. ed. New York, NY: Penguin, 1989.

Chamberlain, J. Edward. *If This Is Your Land, Where Are Your Stories? Finding Common Ground*. Toronto, ON: Alfred A. Knopf, 2003.

Chandler, Michael J., and Christopher Lalonde. "Cultural Continuity as a Hedge against Suicide in Canada's First Nations." *Transcultural Psychiatry* 35 (1998): 191-219.

Childs, John Brown. *Transcommunality: From the Politics of Conversion to the Ethics of Respect*. Philadelphia, PA: Temple University Press, 2003.

Chomsky, Noam. *New Horizons in the Study of Language and Mind*. Cambridge, UK: Cambridge University Press, 2000.

———. *Perspectives on Power: Reflections on Human Nature and the Social Order*. Montréal, QC: Black Rose Books, 1997.

———. *Understanding Power: The Indispensable Chomsky*. Ed. Peter Mitchell and John Schoeffel. New York, NY: The New Press, 2002.

Chrisjohn, Roland, and Sherri Young. *The Circle Game: Shadows and Substance in the Indian Residential School Experience in Canada*. Penticton, BC: Theytus Books, 1997.

Churchill, Ward, and Mike Ryan. *Pacifism as Pathology: Reflections on the Role of Armed Struggle in North America*. Winnipeg, MB: Arbeiter Ring Publishing, 1998.

Clark, Bruce. *Native Liberty, Crown Sovereignty: The Existing Aboriginal Right of Self-Government in Canada*. Montréal, QC: McGill-Queen's University Press, 1990.

Cleary, Thomas. *Classics of Strategy and Counsel. Vol I: The Collected Translations of Thomas Cleary*. Boston, MA: Shambhala, 2000.

———. *The Way of the Sumurai*. Boston, MA: Tuttle Publishing, 1999.

Coates, Ken. *The Marshall Decision and Native Rights*. Montréal, QC: McGill-Queen's University Press, 2001.

Colaiaco, James A. *Martin Luther King, Jr.: Apostle of Militant Nonviolence*. New York, NY: St. Martin's Press, 1998.

Day, Richard. "Who is This We That Gives the Gift? Native American Political Theory and *The Western Tradition*." *Critical Horizons* 2:2 (2001): 173–201.

Day, Richard, and Tonio Sadik. "The BC Land Questions, Liberal Multiculturalism, and the Spectre of Aboriginal Nationhood." *BC Studies* 143 (Summer 2002): 5–34.

Deloria, Vine, Jr. *For This Land: Writings on Religion in America*. New York, NY: Routledge, 1999.

Denis, Claude. *We Are Not You: First Nations and Canadian Modernity*. Peterborough ON: Broadview Press, 1997.

Díaz Polanco, Héctor. *Indigenous Peoples in Latin America: The Quest for Self-Determination*. Boulder, CO: Westview Press, 1997.

Dowd, Gregory Evans. *A Spirited Resistance: The North American Indian Struggle for Unity, 1745-1815*. Baltimore, MD: Johns Hopkins University Press, 1992.

Doxtater, Michael George. *Indigenology: A Decolonizing Learning Method for Emancipating Iroquois and World Indigenous Knowledge*. PhD dissertation, Cornell University, 2001.

291

Duiker, William J. *Ho Chi Minh: A Life.* London, UK: Allen and Unwin, 2000.

Duran, B., and E. Duran. *Native American Post-Colonial Psychology.* Albany, NY: State University of New York Press, 1995.

Edwards, Peter. *One Dead Indian: The Premier, the Police, and the Ipperwash Crisis.* Toronto: McClelland and Stewart, 2003.

Elgin, Duane. *Voluntary Simplicity.* Rev. ed. New York, NY: William Morrow, 1993.

Fanon, Frantz. *The Wretched of the Earth.* New York, NY: Grove Press, 1963.

Flanagan, Thomas. *First Nations, Second Thoughts.* Montréal, QC: McGill-Queen's University Press, 2000.

Forbes, Jack. "Nature and Culture: Problematic Concepts for Native Americans," *Ayaangwaamizin* 2,2 (1997): 203–29.

——. "Intellectual Self-Determination and Sovereignty: Implications for Native Studies and for Native Intellectuals." *Wicazo Sa Review* 13/1 (Spring 1998).

Foucault, Michel. *Fearless Speech.* Ed. Joseph Pearson. New York, NY: Semiotext(e), 2001.

——. *The Politics of Truth.* Ed. Sylvère Lotringer and Lysa Hochroth. New York, NY: Semiotext(e), 1997.

Four Worlds Development Project. *12 Principles of Indian Philosophy.* Lethbridge, AB: University of Lethbridge, 1982.

Furniss, Elizabeth. *The Burden of History: Colonialism and the Frontier Myth in a Rural Community.* Vancouver, BC: University of British Columbia Press, 1999.

Galeano, Eduardo. *Days and Nights of Love and War.* New York, NY: Monthly Review Press, 1983.

——. *Memory of Fire.* 3 vol. New York, NY: W.W. Norton and Company, 1985–88.

——. *Open Veins of Latin America: Five Centuries of the Pillage of a Continent.* New York, NY: Monthly Review Press, 1973.

——. *We Say No: Chronicles, 1963-1991.* New York, NY: W.W. Norton and Company, 1992.

Gandhi, Mahatma K. *An Autobiography, or The Story of My Experiments With Truth.* Trans. M. Desai. 1927, 1929; New York, NY: Penguin 2001.

——. *Non-Violent Resistance, Satyagraha.* New York, NY: Schocken Books, 1961.

Gibson, Nigel C. *Fanon: The Postcolonial Imagination.* Cambridge, UK: Polity, 2003.

Grossman, Dave. *On Killing: The Psychological Cost of Learning to Kill in War and Society.* Toronto, ON: Little, Brown and Company, 1995.

Gruzinski, Serge. *The Mestizo Mind: The Intellectual Dynamics of Colonization and Globalization.* New York, NY: Routledge, 2002.

Guérin, Daniel, ed. *No Gods No Masters: Book One.* Trans. Paul Sharkey. San Francisco, CA: AK Press, 1998.

Guevara, Che. *Guerrilla Warfare.* New York, NY: Monthly Review Press, 1961.

Gurr, Ted Robert. *Why Men Rebel.* Princeton, NJ: Princeton University Press, 1970.

Hale, Charles R. *Resistance and Contradiction: Miskitu Indians and the Nicaraguan State, 1894-1987.* Stanford, CA: Stanford University Press, 1994.

Hall, Anthony J. *The American Empire and the Fourth World*. Montréal, QC: McGill-Queen's University Press, 2003.

Harbury, Jennifer. *Bridge of Courage: Life Stories of the Guatemalan Compañeros and Compañeras*. Montréal, QC: Véhicle Press, 1994.

Hardt, Michael, and Antonio Negri. *Empire*. Cambridge, MA: Harvard University Press, 2000.

Harpur, Tom. *The Pagan Christ: Recovering the Lost Light*. Toronto, ON: Thomas Allen Publishers, 2004.

Hassam, Nasra. "An Arsenal of Believers." *The New Yorker* 19 November 2001.

Hassrick, Royal B. *The Sioux: Life and Customs of a Warrior Society, 1830-1870*. Norman, OK: University of Oklahoma Press, 1964.

Havel, Václav. *Disturbing the Peace*. Trans. Paul Wilson. New York, NY: Vintage, 1991.

Havemann, Paul, ed. *Indigenous Peoples' Rights in Australia, Canada and New Zealand*. Aukland, NZ: Oxford University Press, 1999.

Hayden, Tom, ed. *The Zapatista Reader*. New York, NY: Avalon, 2002.

Henrikson, John B. "Implementation of the Right of Self-Determination of Indigenous Peoples," *Indigenous Affairs* 3/01 (2001): 6–21.

Hobsbawm, Eric. *Revolutionaries*. 1973; New York, NY: The New Press, 2001.

Holloway, John, and Eloina Peláez. *Zapatista!* London, UK: Pluto Press, 1998.

Holmes, Richard. *Acts of War: The Behaviour of Men in Battle*. New York, NY: The Free Press, 1985.

Huntington, Samuel P. *The Clash of Civilizations and the Remaking of World Order*. New York, NY: Simon and Schuster, 1997.

Johnson, Troy, Joane Nagel, and Duane Champagne, eds. *American Indian Activism: Alcatraz to the Longest Walk*. Chicago, IL: University of Illinois Press, 1997.

Josephy, Alvin M. *Red Power: The American Indians' Fight for Freedom*. Lincoln, NB: University of Nebraska Press, 1973.

Kaplan, Robert D. "Looking the World in the Eye." *The Atlantic* (December 2001: 68-82.

Kaufman, Edy. "Limited Violence and the Palestinian Struggle." *Unarmed Forces: Non-violent Action in Central America and the Middle East*, ed. Graeme MacQueen. Canadian Papers in Peace Studies 1. Toronto, ON: Science for Peace, 1992.

Krishnamurti, Jiddu. *Total Freedom: The Essential Krishnamurti*. New York, NY: HarperCollins, 1996.

Kyi, Aung San Suu. *Freedom From Fear*. Rev. ed. New York, NY: Penguin, 1995.

LaDuke, Winona. *All Our Relations: Native Struggles for Land and Life*. Cambridge, MA: South End Press, 1999.

Lambertus, Sandra. *Wartime Images, Peacetime Wounds: The Media and the Gustafsen Lake Stand-off*. Toronto, ON: University of Toronto Press, 2004.

Lao Tzu. *Tao Te Ching*. Trans. Victor H. Mair. New York, NY: Bantam, 1990.

Lapham, Lewis. "Res Publica." *Harper's Magazine* (December 2001): 8–10.

Littlebird, Larry. *Hunting Sacred Everything Listens: A Pueblo Indian Man's*

Oral Tradition Legacy. Santa Fe, NM: Western Edge Press, 2001.

Lorde, Audre. "The Uses of Anger." *Sister Outsider*. Freedom, CA: Crossing Press, 1984.

Malcom X. *Malcom X Speaks*. Ed. George Breitman. Berkeley, CA: Grove Press, 1965.

Maloney, Sean M. "Domestic Operations: The Canadian Approach." *Parameters*, US Army War College Quarterly (Autumn 1997).

Mander, Jerry. *Four Arguments for the Elimination of Television*. New York, NY: Quill, 1978.

——. *In the Absence of the Sacred: The Failure of Technology and the Survival of the Indian Nations*. San Francisco, CA: Sierra Club Books, 1991.

Manuel, George, and Michael Posluns. *The Fourth World: An Indian Reality*. Toronto, ON: Collier-Macmillan, 1974.

Marcos, Subcomandante. *Our Word is Our Weapon*. New York, NY: Seven Stories Press, 2001.

Marshall, Peter. *Demanding the Impossible: A History of Anarchism*. San Francisco, CA: HarperCollins, 1993.

Mason, W. Dale. *Indian Gaming: Tribal Sovereignty and American Politics*. Norman, OK: University of Oklahoma Press, 2000.

Matthiessen, Peter. *In the Spirit of Crazy Horse*. New York, NY: Penguin Books, 1983.

McFarlane, Peter. *Brotherhood to Nationhood: George Manuel and the Making of the Modern Indian Movement*. Toronto, ON: Between The Lines, 1993.

McManus, Philip, and Gerald Schlabach, eds. *Relentless Persistence: Nonviolent Action in Latin America*. Santa Cruz, CA: New Society Publishers, 1991.

McWhorter, John. *The Power of Babel*. New York, NY: HarperCollins, 2001.

Memmi, Albert. *The Colonizer and the Colonized*. Boston, MA: Beacon Press, 1991.

Mills, C. Wright. *White Collar: The American Middle Classes* (New York, NY: Oxford University Press, 1956) 110.

Mohawk, John. *Utopian Legacies: A History of Conquest and Oppression in the Western World*. Santa Fe, NM: Clear Light Publishers, 2000.

Momaday, N. Scott. *The Way to Rainy Mountain*. Albuquerque, NM: University of New Mexico Press, 1969.

Moore, Barrington, Jr. *Moral Purity and Persecution in History*. Princeton, NJ: Princeton University Press, 2000.

Morris, Glen T. "Vine Deloria, Jr. and the Development of a Decolonizing Critique of Indigenous Peoples and International Relations." *Native Voices: American Indian identity and Resistance*. Ed. Richard Grounds, George Tinker, and David Wilkins. Lawrence, KS: University of Kansas Press, 2003.

Mullis, Angela, and David Kamper, eds. *Indian Gaming: Who Wins?* Los Angeles, CA: University of California Indian Studies Center, 2000.

Nagel, Joane. *American Indian Ethnic Renewal: Red Power and the Resurgence of Identity and Culture*. New York, NY: Oxford University Press, 1996.

Nettle, Daniel, and Suzanne Romain. *Vanishing Voices: The Extinction of the World's Languages*. New York, NY: Oxford University Press, 2000.

Niezen, Ronald. *The Origins of Indigenism: Human Rights and the Politics of Identity.* Berkeley, CA: University of California Press, 2003.

Ochiai, Hidy. *A Way to Victory: The Annotated Book of Five Rings.* Woodstock, NY: The Overlook Press, 2001.

Ortiz, Simon J. *Out There Somewhere.* Tucson, AZ: University of Arizona Press, 2002.

Osho. *Freedom: The Courage to Be Yourself.* New York, NY: St. Martin's Griffin, 2004.

Parekh, Bhikhu. "Liberalism and Colonialism." *The Decolonization of the Imagination.* Ed. J.N. Pieterse and B. Parekh. London, UK: Zed Books, 1995.

Parker, Arthur C. *The Code of Handsome Lake, The Seneca Prophet.* Albany, NY: University of the State of New York, 1913.

Parmenter, Jon W. "Dragging Canoe: Chickamauga Cherokee Patriot." *The Human Tradition in the American Revolution.* Ed. Nancy Rhoden and Ian Steele. Lanham, MD: SR Books, 2000.

Peltier, Leonard. *Prison Writings: My Life is my Sundance.* Ed. Harvey Arden. New York, NY: St. Martin's Press, 1993.

Pieterse, Jan Nederveen, and Bhikhu Parekh, eds. *The Decolonization of Imagination: Culture, Knowledge and Power.* London, UK: Zed Books, 1995.

Redekop, Vern. *From Violence to Blessing: How an Understanding of Deep-Rooted Conflicts Can Open Paths to Reconciliation.* Montréal, QC: Novalis, 2003.

Rinpoche, Sogyal. *The Tibetan Book of Living and Dying.* Ed. P. Gaffney and A. Harvey. San Francisco, CA: HarperCollins, 1993.

Rosen, Michael, and David Widgery. *The Vintage Book of Dissent.* New York, NY: Vintage, 1996.

Roussopoulos, Dimitrios I. *The Anarchist Papers.* Montréal, QC: Black Rose Books, 1986.

Rowland, Christopher, ed. *The Cambridge Companion to Liberation Theology.* Cambridge, UK: Cambridge University Press, 1999.

Royal Commission on Aboriginal Peoples. *Gathering Strength.* Ottawa, ON: Government of Canada, 1996.

Said, Edward. *Culture and Imperialism.* New York, NY: Vintage, 1993.

——. "Impossible Histories: Why the Many Islams Cannot be Simplified," *Harper's Magazine* (July 2002): 69–74.

Schell, Jonathan. *The Unconquerable World: Power, Nonviolence, and the Will of the People.* New York, NY: Metropolitan Books, 2003.

Scott, James. *Domination and the Arts of Resistance: Hidden Transcripts.* New Haven, CT: Yale University Press, 1998.

Seed, Patricia. *Ceremonies of Possession in Europe's Conquest of the New World.* Cambridge, UK: Cambridge University Press, 1995.

Selverston-Scher, Melina. *Ethnopolitics in Ecuador: Indigenous Rights and the Strengthening of Democracy.* Miami, FL: North-South Center Press, 2001.

Sharp, Gene. "Non-violent Struggle Today." *Unarmed Forces: Non-violent Action in Central America and the Middle East,* ed. Graeme MacQueen. Canadian Papers in Peace Studies 1. Toronto, ON: Science for Peace, 1992.

Shimony, Annemarie Anrod. *Conservatism among the Iroquois at the Six Nations Reserve.* Syracuse, NY: Syracuse University Press, 1994.

Shridharani, Krishnalal. *War Without Violence*. Belmont, CA: Harcourt Brace, 1939.

Stokes, Geoffrey. "Australian Democracy and Indigenous Self-Determination, 1901-2001." *Australia Reshaped: Essays on Two Hundred Years of Institutional Transformation*. Ed. G. Brennan and F. Castles. Cambridge, UK: Cambridge University Press, 2002. 181–219.

Sugden, John. *Tecumseh: A Life*. New York, NY: Henry Holt, 1997.

Sun Tzu. *The Art of War*. Trans. Thomas Cleary. Boston, MA: Shambhala, 1991.

Tarrow, Sidney. *Power in Movement: Social Movements and Contentious Politics*. 2nd ed. Cambridge, UK: Cambridge University Press, 1998.

Tenzin Gyatso, the Fourteenth Dalai Lama of Tibet. *Ancient Wisdom, Modern World: Ethics for the New Millennium*. Toronto, ON: Little, Brown and Company, 1999.

Trungpa, Chögyam. *Shambhala: The Sacred Path of the Warrior*. Boston, MA: Shambhala, 1988.

Tsunetomo, Yamamoto. *Hagakure: The Book of the Samarai*. New York, NY: Kodansha American, 1979.

Tully, James. "The Unfreedom of the Moderns in Comparison to their Ideals of Constitutional Democracy." *The Modern Law Review* 65,2 (2002): 204-28.

———. *Strange Multiplicity: Constitutionalism in an Age of Diversity*. Cambridge, UK: Cambridge University Press, 1995.

Ueshiba, Morihei. *The Art of Peace: Teachings of the Founder of Aikido*. Trans. John Stevens. Boston, MA: Shambhala, 1992.

Vizenor, Gerald. *Fugitive Poses: Native American Scenes of Absence and Presence*.

Lincoln, NB: University of Nebraska Press, 1998.

———. *Manifest Manners: Narratives on Postindian Survivance*. Lincoln, NB: University of Nebraska Press, 1994.

Voices from Wounded Knee. Hogansburg, NY: Akwesasne Notes, 1974.

Wall, Steve, and Harvey Arden. *Wisdomkeepers: Meetings with Native American Spiritual Elders*. Hillsboro, OR: Beyond Words Publishing, 1990.

Wallace, Anthony F.C. *The Death of Rebirth of the Seneca*. New York, NY: Random House, 1969.

Wallace, Paul. *White Roots of Peace: The Iroquois Book of Life*. Philadelphia, PA: University of Pennsylvania Press, 1946.

Waters, Frank. *Brave are My People: Indian Heroes Not Forgotten*. Athens, OH: Ohio University Press, 1993.

Weinberg, Bill. *Homage to Chiapas: The New Indigenous Struggles in Mexico*. London, UK: Verso, 2000.

Wilkins, David E. *American Indian Politics and the American Political System*. Lanham, MD: Rowman and Littlefield, 2002.

Yashar, Deborah. "Democracy, Indigenous Movements and the Postliberal Challenge in Latin America." *World Politics* 52,1 (The Johns Hopkins University Press, 1999): 76-104.

York, Geoffrey, and Loreen Pindera. *People of the Pines: The Warriors and the Legacy of Oka*. Toronto, ON: Little, Brown and Company, 1991.

Young, Robert. *Postcolonialism: A Very Short Introduction*. Oxford, UK: Oxford University Press, 2003.

Young, T. Kue. *The Health of Native Americans: Toward a Biocultural Epidemiology*. New York, NY: Oxford University Press, 1994.

index

death of, 246–47
disrespect for, 279
European, 32, 247
and group identities, 246
importance of, 244–45, 259
indigenous languages, 198, 244–45,
    247–48, 251–52, 256
Noam Chomsky on, 245–46
Onkwehonwe *vs.* European, 32
as *prima facie* evidence of indigeneity,
    245
relationship to culture, 244
Laos, 233
Latin America, 111, 134
    armed revolutionary struggles, 103
    indigenous rights movement, 133
    violent repression, 158
Latin American concepts of "indi-
    genism" and "ethnicism," 132
leaders, 52, 63, 66, 119, 181–82, 208. See
    also chiefs
    age of, 123–25
    charismatic, 281
    corruption, 260, 271
    movement, 210
    Oren Lyons on, 241
    warrior-leaders, 186
leadership, 123, 125, 183, 205–6, 214,
    242
    degradation of, 237
    need for a cause, 228
    Onkwehonwe model of, 56
learning (models of), 199
"least resistance" mentality, 41, 43–45
left-wing intellectuals, 105
legalist approach, 23–24, 30. See *also*
    court cases
    dependence on non-indigenous
        values, 104
legitimacy (state), 55–56, 138, 203, 230
    attacking, 228
liberal democracy, 149, 155–56
liberal political theory, 103, 109
liberated zones, 69–70, 74
Liberation Theology, 281
"libratory praxis," 57
listening. See aural tradition

Little Bear, Leroy, 32, 276
Lodge, 250
loggers, 123, 166, 192
    Nuxalk, 195
logging, 117, 167, 194, 196
Longhouse, 239, 250–51
Longhouse teachings, 197, 271–72, 274.
    See *also* traditional teachings
Lorde, Audre, 105
Louise (elder), 186
Lyons, Oren, 237–44

Mad Bear, 206
Malcolm X, 236
Mander, Jerry, 110–11
Manuel, George, 181
Marxism/Leninism, 50
Marxist doctrine, 281
materialism, 84, 93, 188
McLachlin, Beverley, 136
media, 64, 112, 148–49, 152, 207–8, 230
    corporate, 162
    on corruption in Indian Affairs, 44
    indigenous media capacities, 208
    negative portrayals of indigenous
        people, 257
Memmi, Albert, 24–26, 28, 105, 113
memory, 169, 282
    collective memory of myths, 243
    and history, 115
    preservation through ceremony, 249
    sacred, 131
men's roles, 84. See *also* warriors
mentorship, 175, 279
Mexico, 59, 62, 69, 133, 141–43, 210,
    281
    land legislation, 184
Mi'kmaq, 66–67, 209
Mi'kmaq Warrior Society, 209
militancy, 92
militant messianism, 281
militant non-violence, 56
Mills, C. Wright, 58
"mimetic euroself," 128
Miskito Nation, 63
mobilization of people, 63, 201, 208, 210
    necessary conditions for, 64

305

in creation stories, 254–56
disrespect for, 279
grandmothers, 119, 167–71, 173–74,
240
roles, 84
strength, 58

Yashar, Deborah, 134–35
young males, 58, 78
young people, 37, 67, 74–75, 90–91,
123–24, 163, 258, 270
alienation, 44
militancy, 92
Native Youth Movement, 90, 94

occupation of band council offices,
184
political activism, 257
spirit of regeneration, 264
suicide rate, 70
in urban centres, 261
views on being a warrior, 259–60
Young Socialist, 236

Zapatistas, 59, 62, 69, 82, 133, 141, 210,
229, 281
poverty, 211
Zapoteca. *See* Altamirano, Isabel